WRITER
with a
DAY JOB

Inspiration & Exercises to Help You
Craft a Writing Life Alongside Your Career

ÁINE GREANEY

WD

WRITER'S DIGEST
BOOKS

WritersDigest.com
Cincinnati, Ohio

For more resources for writers, visit www.writersdigest.com/books.

To receive a free weekly e-mail newsletter delivering tips and updates about writing and about Writer's Digest products, register directly at www.writersdigest.com/enews.

15 14 13 12 11   5 4 3 2 1

Distributed in Canada by Fraser Direct
100 Armstrong Avenue
Georgetown, Ontario, Canada L7G 5S4
Tel: (905) 877-4411

Distributed in the U.K and Europe by F&W Media International
Brunel House, Newton Abbot, Devon, TQ12 4PU, England
Tel: (+44) 1626-323200, Fax: (+44) 1626-323319
E-mail: postmaster@davidandcharles.co.uk

Distributed in Australia by Capricorn Link
P.O. Box 704, Windsor, NSW 2756 Australia
Tel: (02) 4577-3555

Editor:
MELISSA WUSKE

Designer:
TERRI WOESNER

Cover illustration:
© GETTY IMAGES/
JUNICHI KISHI

Production coordinator:
DEBBIE THOMAS

fw
media

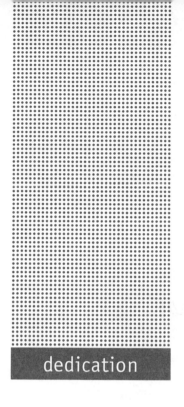

dedication

For all my wonderful students.
Your stories and your writing always inspire me.

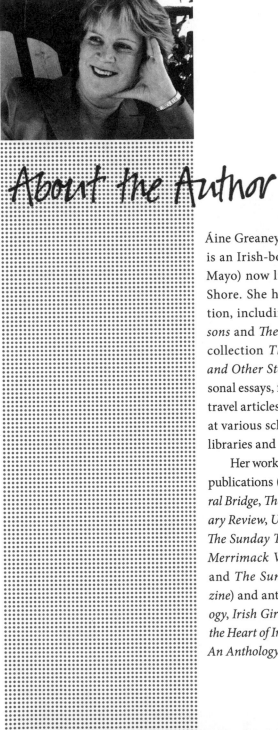

About the Author

Áine Greaney (www.ainegreaney.com) is an Irish-born writer (from County Mayo) now living on Boston's North Shore. She has published mostly fiction, including the novels *Dance Lessons* and *The Big House* and the story collection *The Sheepbreaders Dance and Other Stories*. She also writes personal essays, features, and wellness and travel articles. She teaches and lectures at various schools, wellness programs, libraries and arts locations.

Her work has appeared in numerous publications (*Creative Nonfiction, Natural Bridge, The Larcom Review, The Literary Review, Under the Sun, Stone Canoe, The Sunday Tribune New Irish Writing, Merrimack Valley Magazine, Cyphers,* and *The Sunday Boston Globe Magazine*) and anthologies (*The Fish Anthology, Irish Girls are Back in Town, From the Heart of Ireland,* and *Lost and Found: An Anthology of Teachers' Writing*).

Table of Contents

INTRODUCTION

If you're reading this on the morning commuter train, you know all about the push and pull between writing and earning a living. Ditto if you're standing there taking a quick, lunch-hour browse in the bookstore (and you found this book—lucky you!). You're a writer, a dreamer, a scribbler. People tell you you're a great storyteller. You keep a journal. Ever since childhood, you've kept a book on your nightstand.

From the corner office to the crummy cubicle, there are lots of us out there: creative writers who hold down a day job. It's not that writing *isn't* our job. It's just that the day job and the writing feed separate, but equally important, parts of us.

We often draw inspiration from our longtime favorite authors. One of my favorite contemporary novelists, Olaf Olafsson who wrote *Absolution* (Pantheon, 1994), *The Journey Home* (Pantheon, 2000), *Walking Into the Night* (Pantheon, 2003), and *Valentines* (Pantheon, 2007), is executive vice president of Time Warner.

In his author biography at Bookbrowse.com, Olafsson describes his dual life as an executive vice president and as a writer:

> It still amazes me sometimes that I actually stumbled into the world of business. I don't think I ever intended to. Growing up, I envisioned businessmen as being rather dull, manipulative old blokes, smoking a cigar and making pronouncements, usually not very smart. So much for that. I enjoy working with people in building businesses, putting ideas into motion—it's a bit like starting with a blank piece of paper. Writing on the other hand is a basic need. If I don't write, I'm not content. It's pretty simple.

Writing really is about being content. In his book *On Writing*, Stephen King said that writing is all about getting happy. Writing is never a hobby. Neither is it a dilettante activity for which we salvage some leftover time from our otherwise busy days. Writing *feeds* those days. On the days when I don't write, I underperform as an employee and as a human being.

In fact, I think my boss or the U.S. government should pay me for the time I spend at home with my morning coffee and my journal.

That—not the conference-room pep talks—makes me a happier, more focused employee.

I write. Therefore I work. Simple as that.

MAKING IT HAPPEN

Last winter, this man—let's call him John—arrived at one of my Saturday-morning creative writing classes with a completed first draft of a novel.

John had a wife, a child, and a mortgage. He also had a high-pressure job in a U.S. corporation.

Every day during his office lunch hour, John took his laptop and his iPod and sat in his car eating a sandwich and writing the next few pages of his book. Five days a week. Chapter by chapter. After a year, he had his first draft.

John got two things right. First, he set himself a writing schedule and stuck with it. Second, sitting there in his car in his suit and tie, he ignored that myth of what a creative writer "should be."

In America, we hold this ridiculous vision of the writer as a woman dressed in thrift-store black or as a man in the crumpled shirt with an unshaven visage. There they sit, clacking away on their typewriters inside their garret windows, too deep and distracted to tie their own shoes. It's a grand image. It's grand for Hollywood's central casting. But it's not grand when you let this vision perch on your shoulders as you sit in your neighborhood bagel shop doing your writing—often on your office lunch hour.

DO WHAT YOU LOVE. THE MORTGAGE WILL FOLLOW.

Except for a few best-selling or celebrity authors, most writers work a day (or night) job—either part or full time as nannies, bartenders, copy editors, or CEOs.

Every spring, big-ticket commencement speakers stand on podiums across America advising our high-school and college graduates to "follow your hearts" or to "do what you love."

In today's economy, how many young graduates will walk off that stage and into a gig that really, truly feeds heart and soul? Better to advise these kids on how to ply their passions *while also* paying their landlords.

WE WRITE. THEREFORE WE WORK.

This book will help you to integrate creative writing into your daily life. Each chapter gives you from-the-trenches tips and advice to get and keep you writing—even when work is busy or impossible. Throughout the book, I include numbered tutorials on a different aspect of the craft of writing narrative, including lots of writing exercises which can be completed in fifteen to thirty minutes—on your lunch hour, on the morning train, or even while sitting in gridlock traffic (some are aural activities, not written).

And finally, the book will direct you to the support and resources you need to sustain a writer's life—a real one, not the Hollywood version—and to respect and protect your writing talents.

This is not an employment advice book. However, as someone who has always written and always worked a day job, I offer advice and list some resources to help you navigate both aspects of your life.

LET THE MUSE IN. LET'S WRITE!

"I want to write when I retire." Have you said this? Are you thinking this now? Or are you planning to buy this book as a retirement or summer-vacation gift to yourself? Between now and your retirement or vacation date—even if that's next week—you will have squandered precious writing time.

Turn this page. Before the morning train gets there and before it's time to go upstairs and change into your work clothes. You have ten minutes. So write.

Section 1

GETTING STARTED

I once had an idea to create a glossy coffee table book that showcased office cubicles. Oh, yes, office cubes—in all their nondescript bland-eur. Of course, I don't care about the cubes themselves, nor, indeed, about these corporate architects who keep us workers separate but eavesdropping. Instead, I'm intrigued by how people decorate their work cubicles, lockers, or offices. In my workplaces, past and present, I've seen everything from Dilbert cartoons to pet photos to sports memorabilia to rock bands. Maybe I'm just plain nosy, but I'm always looking for that telltale clue to my colleagues' real or secret selves.

What's on your office or workplace locker wall? What does it reveal about you and your life's passions? Or what would you put there if you could get away with it and the human resources department didn't come knocking?

I'm betting that there's a strong link between this version of you and your writer-self. It's that whimsical, imaginative, creative, subversive side of you that loves to put words on a page or a screen.

This "Getting Started" section will help you (1) explore and (2) define that writer-self and to set your writing goals and objectives.

1
SETTING GOALS
AND OBJECTIVES

As an artist, your goals are broad, visionary statements which will give your daily work direction and a larger context. *Goals, schmoals. Shouldn't I just get writing*, you may be thinking. But setting goals will align your writing work with your own personal values. Nonprofit organizations, large and small, generally publish a formal mission statement. Corporations, large and small, also have a mission statement or some public manifesto about why the company exists and what it seeks to do.

Ask any writer: It's easy for us to procrastinate or muddle along. And, if you're a writer with a day job, it can seem even harder to stick to your goals and manage the competing demands on your time. Speaking of time, the "I'll get to it when I have time" approach doesn't work. To keep your writing on track and moving ahead and to keep yourself in the habit, take the time to set some personal, visionary goals or a vision statement—and you won't need the expensive consultants or the hours of subcommittee meetings to come up with one.

Objectives are more short-term, defined, and measurable. Wherever you work, whether you're at the top, the middle, or the bottom of the organization, I'm sure you've either set or followed a set of monthly or quarterly objectives. Put simply, these are stated, measurable benchmarks which say what you will achieve and when you will achieve it.

Think of this two-phased process as planning a cross-country trip. The goals represent your overall travel plan or dreams. The objectives are like writing the daily or weekly itinerary—planning where you'll be on what day and how many miles you'll drive per day. In other words, it's setting yourself some deadlines.

Did someone say ... d-d-d-deadlines? I've known some creative writers who can't say that word without stumbling. But this book will help you turn deadlines into darlings.

SETTING GOALS OR YOUR CRAZY DREAMS

There's this song *Crazy Dreams* from my teenage years growing up in Ireland. It was written and released by Irish singer-songwriter Paul Brady (check him out on YouTube). Back then, when *Crazy Dreams* came warbling from our raspy kitchen transistor radio, I always thought he was singing just for sixteen-year-old me. Now, all these years later, a line from that song often plays in my head: "Someone else's dreams don't get you nowhere."

When it comes to setting your writing goals, you've got to do a little soul-searching, and you've got to get really honest with yourself. "Someone else's dreams" will not sustain your writing life. And, unlike your company's mission statement, the dream and the goals are in your hands—nobody else's. You're the one-person focus group, holding solitary meetings with yourself, asking all the questions and supplying all the answers. All of which boil down to: What do *you* really *want* out of a writer's life?

Your goals will give you direction. They become your reality check. And, like that line from the song, they become a refuge, a place to return to when publishers, writer-friends, work schedules, or your own self-doubts lead you astray.

To P or not to P? That's Not the (Only) Question

P is for publishing. Whether that's a big *P* (for example, the large advance with a well-known publisher) or a little *P* (your essays published in your local newspaper) is up to you. What's important is that you don't define your writing goals solely in terms of the big *P*. Too many writers do this. Too many writers base their value assessments, their own sense of themselves on their projected, imagined, or actual book sales.

Writing is all about process—the art and craft of putting your words on a page. Publishing is all about product—the skill of getting those words out there in the world, hopefully for a fee or retail price tag. Both writing and publishing are valid pursuits. But when it comes to you setting your overall writing goals, think beyond publishing only.

> ***Writer Beware!*** Getting into the publishing game too early, too exclusively, and too naively can leave you with a write-to-the-market mentality. You're not writing for the market. The publishing market changes from year to year, from economy to economy,

publisher to publisher, and from genre to genre. Especially in the beginning, in those early drafts, you're writing for you. Just you.

I once had an adult student who threw down his pen (literally!), then assured me that our workshop had been a "complete waste" of his time. I was teaching an evening workshop on how to polish and submit creative works to literary and consumer magazines. After I and my eleven other students stopped gawking and after some diplomatic probing, I learned that this man had signed up for my workshop expecting a how-to on snagging one of the big New York publishers.

"Anything else," he said, jabbing a disgusted finger at my handouts and lists, "is just bogus. I want a big New York publisher or nothing."

Kudos to this man for his clarity and forthrightness about his goals, but no kudos for having set those goals so narrowly. Since that night, I've never seen his name in a bookstore or on writers lists. So guess what? He ended up getting the second part—the "nothing" part of his wish list.

At best, an all-or-nothing writing goal sets you on a long—but not unreachable—path to writing happiness. At worst, it may just leave you with, well, nothing.

If, after some self-examination and reflection, you find that a big-name publishing contract is indeed your ultimate and heartfelt goal—your "crazy dream"—then go for it. But before you write it down, stop and do one last check in the honesty mirror: Do I believe this to be the only acceptable payout for my creative writing? Is it "someone else's dream?" Or is this really, truly mine?"

CRAZY DREAMS: LIGHTS! CAMERA! WRITING!

What are you working on now? What writing idea is percolating through your mind and heart—enough to have made you buy or borrow this book? Now, step on the dream machine and fast-forward to a place where that book, poem, essay, or story is polished and final, at perfect pitch, in a perfect place. What is that place? Where is it? Besides you, the writer, who else is there to congratulate you?

For some writers, writing is a way to document their life experiences, their family's past, to chronicle an era quite different from this twenty-first century. I know a memoir writer who dreams about a family reunion when she presents a copy of her completed and bound memoir to each of her adult children and grandchildren. "I want them to know who I really was," she says.

I believe her. And I believe that she'll get her lights-camera-action moment.

For others, writing is just good fun. It's an expression of their creative and whimsical selves. It's as thrilling as eating a huge ice cream sundae or sledding down a hill. Their words and ideas delight and amuse them, and they want to delight and amuse their readers. They imagine their readers turning that page. They can hear those readers giggling.

I don't know about my previously mentioned disgruntled student, but let's imagine that his shining writer moment is his splashy book-launch party or his Pulitzer Prize ceremony.

Other writers want to teach, inspire, or heal. In their personal writer fantasy, they envision a reader who, after that last page, sets about living a better life.

You get the point. Dream your own writer dream. Dream it big. Dream it real. Keep that vision as your holy grail, your guiding light.

DON'T LET THE "BUT" BUGS BITE

Too often, *but* can be the writer's favorite word. "I think this piece is good, **but** ..." "I'd like to get some writing done ... **but** ..." "Yeah, I love writing, **but** ..."

Okay, 'fess up: Have you let this dirty little *but* word sneak into your writing goals? Have you whispered, "I'd love to write a trilogy, **but** with my work schedule/**but** I'm only a novice/**but** nobody is interested in what I have to say/**but** I don't have a college degree/**but** nobody in my family is a writer." Here's an editing exercise: Do a mental "search and replace" right now. Get that *but* word out of there. It's self-limiting. It lets you off the hook way too easily. *Buts* have no place in your creative belief system or overall goals. Search. Find. Delete. No *buts*.

This may be easier said than done for you, and trust me, I've certainly let the *but* word punctuate my own procrastination dialogs. However, *but* usually signals what we cannot do. For example, "I'd love to write but my work schedule is crazy" really says, "I cannot fit in a decent amount of writing." Now turn this "cannot" statement into a challenge to yourself. "Okay, what *can* you do? Can you write for ten minutes every morning?" "Can you write while watching your son or daughter at soccer practice?" If we really, truly cannot change the realities of our lives, then we can nudge ourselves toward small, feasible changes *within the parameters of* those fixed realities.

For the next few days or even for several weeks, spend time thinking about your personal writing mission, your own crazy dream. Then write your goal below.

Write it in pencil first, so that you can edit and refine your goal as often as you need to.

Use this short worksheet to get you started:

As a writer, I want to:

I want to be the kind of writer who:

You may have to think about that one for a while. It's all about who you become as a writer—your writer identity and significance. By all means, take some time to think about it and distill it down to a few short words. When you come back to this exercise, be ready to keep it short and relevant.

When my readers read my work, I want them to:
cry/laugh/think/improve their lives/enjoy a good story
(circle more than one, if needed).

When my readers write to me, I want them to compliment my:

When you're ready, write your goal in the space below.

My writing goal or dream:

SETTING OBJECTIVES

Now that you've set your writing goals, you'll find that listing your objectives is a snap. Or at least, all that soul-searching and know-yourself stuff is behind you. Setting your weekly or monthly objectives means breaking down your writing goal into its tangible and component parts. Your writing objectives should have three attributes:

1. They should be achievable.
2. They should be measurable.
3. They should be clearly stated.

Achievable: Set realistic weekly or daily objectives. But also be ready to stretch yourself. Make sure that your weekly word or page budget challenges you, while also setting you up to feel a regular sense of accomplishment and success. If you're just starting out as a creative writer, don't sabotage your own self-confidence by setting objectives ("I'll write an entire essay collection in a month") that are just plain undoable and are bound to make you feel overwhelmed. Nothing succeeds like success. Take the time to assess your weekly work and family schedules. Then assess your own writing style or speed. And finally, set a reasonable daily or weekly word count.

Measurable: Anyone paying attention here? Yes, I did say "word count." Set yourself a target word or page count, not an amount of time that you will spend writing. It's all too easy to say, "I spent an hour at my writing desk this morning." But what good is that hour if you spent half of it online with the morning headlines or checking your e-mail? Some writers effortlessly bang out one thousand words in an hour or two. Others are lucky to produce three hundred words at a sitting. Find your own comfort zone. Then stretch it just a bit. Whatever word or page count you target, hold yourself to it.

For nine-to-fivers, it also works to set a weekly (not daily) word budget. That way, on those days when you're traveling or honestly have no time, you can pay yourself back by writing extra on the days you're at home or have a lighter work schedule. In chapters eight and ten, I offer tips on how to "visit" your writing on those super-extra busy days, and how to turn your travel or commute time into writing time.

Clearly Stated: *(1) Write it down:* Borrow some goal-setting strategies from your day job. Write down your writing objectives. Plug them into your electronic or wall calendar. Use a whiteboard, project management software, or to-do list. This will keep you focused and honest. And, there's nothing more satisfying than ticking off a completed list.

At the end of this section, see page 12 for a list of online to-do lists and calendars. Or you can, of course, use a simple and inexpensive hard-copy day planner. Whatever you use, finding a user-friendly and portable way of logging your work, deadlines, and daily writing output can keep your writing moving and on track.

(2) D-d-d-deadlines: They're not deadly. They're your friend. There's nothing more motivating, even inspiring, than someone else waiting for your submission or draft. Here are some ways to create some deadlines:

(a) Join a local writers group where each person has an agreed presentation or submission date (see chapter 15 for more on choosing a writers group).

(b) Subscribe to a writers magazine that lists calls for submissions. Pick out and research the publications that seem like a good fit for your work. List the required submission dates or reading periods. Then plug those dates into your day planner or work plan, including electronic reminders.

(c) Join an online writers group where the focus is on fair, knowledgeable, and detailed peer critique (see chapter 15).

(d) Hire a literary midwife or life coach. There are lots of them out there. If you feel you need someone else to keep you deadline, by all means research some coaches or ask around for referrals. From setting goals to meeting your daily objectives, a professional coach can help you stay on track. Or you can find a writing buddy or peer who will support your goals and deadlines.

> *Writer Beware!* If you use magazine submission dates or writing competition deadlines as a way to keep your writing on track, set your own target completion date to several days ahead of that published date. Otherwise, you'll end up pulling all-nighters. And if it's a hard-copy submission, leave enough time for the U.S. mail to get your manuscript there.

GOALS AND OBJECTIVES: KEEP A REMINDER

Okay, let's get back to those cubicle or office walls and your personal knick-knacks or mementos. It's time to create or buy a memento that will keep you reminded of your writing goals.

We have work meetings and family commitments. We have commutes and car pools. Most of us are bombarded by digital, broadcast, and print messages—many of which have nothing to do with or detract from our inner or creative lives. Amidst all of this, it's easy to take your eyes off the prize and to temporarily lose sight of your goals or your vision of yourself as a writer. So find or create a reminder for yourself. I keep a postcard of Walden Pond and Thoreau's cabin on my office wall. What would work for you? Perhaps it's your favorite line from a favorite poet. Is it a song that speaks to you? A photo of an exotic overseas writers retreat where you plan to go someday? Write and post your own book jacket copy. Whatever you choose, keep it within eye view. Or, if there are no workplace rules prohibiting it, make it your laptop or PC computer's screen saver or your secret office log-in word.

Whatever it is, it will remind you that, outside of this day job, you have a whole other life—a writing life.

> Here are some free online task lists and calendars to help you keep track of your writing deadlines. Most allow you to set yourself some electronic reminders.
>
> Google Calendar, www.google.com
> Yahoo Calendar, www.yahoo.com
> Hotmail Calendar, www.hotmail.com
> Ta-da Lists, http://tadalist.com
> Remember the Milk, www.rememberthemilk.com
> Toodledo, www.toodledo.com/
> Voo2do, http://voo2do.com
> Bla-bla List, http://blablalist.com
> ReQall, www.reqall.com

Writing Tutorial 1:
WRITING SCENES

Quick! Don't stop to think about this one. Take a sheet of paper or a sticky note and write down your favorite movie scene of all times. Can you list three movie scenes that have stayed with you? That you frequently quote? That you wish you'd written or created? Once you've selected your top three, brainstorm about what it is that makes each of your selected scenes so memorable.

Psst! If you need a refresher on those favorite flicks or the old black-and-white classics, check out http://movieclips.com/

Favorite movie scenes	Why I remember or love this scene
1. *Christmas Carol The ghost of Christ prints open a note*	*Poinunt - Dramic - This girl is hungr thing by is 16 anmer - gar haus of this*
2. *Foul Play The deary scen*	
3.	

Have any of these terms or phrases made it into your Column 2 lists? Tension. Excitement. Feelings. Funny. Beautiful. Good lines. Touching. Made me laugh. Made me cry. Stunning cinematography. Enigmatic. Complete. I was right there. Exciting.

Whatever our personal movie tastes, whatever makes us love and remember a certain scene from a book, movie, or TV show, all good scenes share one common trait: They let the reader in. Put simply, a good, memorable scene doesn't tell us what's happening, it shows us—right there, on the page, before our eyes.

SHOW, DON'T TELL

Yeah, yeah, I know you've heard this one a thousand times before. But even for experienced writers, it's still good advice. Journalists report ("Shortly after dawn on March 3, a robber broke into Wagging Tales, a popular downtown pet store"). Cops tell ("From my vehicle, I observed the suspect, male, Dalmatian, about three foot, two inches, with a spotty complexion"). But writers *show*.

For example, don't tell about your bad-tempered neighbor, Tom. Show me his thunderous facial expressions. Let me hear that raging, bullying voice screaming at you over the back garden fence. Or let me see and hear that fist crashing through your kitchen window—complete with blood and shattering glass.

Similarly, you could tell me that, at twelve years old, you once traveled halfway across the country on a Greyhound bus. Wow! Tell me, tell me please: What went on in your family? Were you a child of divorce? Bicoastal parents? A runaway? But once you've satisfied my initial nosiness, I begin to lose interest. And, five years from now, I probably won't remember or care about what ultimately happened to you. But bring me onto that bus, let me smell the upholstery. Let me watch the passing landscape out your bus window. Bring me into your twelve-year-old mind, your fears, your trepidations, your regrets. Now, I'm not just nosy and curious. I also care. I fear for you and your safety. Or I'll laugh at your escapades along the way. And, most important, five, ten, or fifteen years from now, I'll still remember your Greyhound Bus scene and how it made me, as the reader, feel.

Bottom line: Whether you're writing a nonfiction essay, a fictional short story, or a blockbuster novel, live-action scenes are the building blocks of your story.

TEN TIPS FOR WRITING LIVELY SCENES

(1) Writing the opening scene: Notice how, just as you're settling in with your movie popcorn or just as the theater stage lights go up, you are suddenly looking at a Technicolor landscape (movies) or a well-crafted stage set (theater)? Generally, dramatic writers set the scene *before* they set their characters loose upon that scene.

As narrative writers, we don't have to be so panoramic or stagy. Instead, we can lead our readers into the story via a creaky back doorway, a tiny attic room, a rickety desk, or a cramped airplane or bus seat. Wherever it is, whoever is in it, your opening scene will set and carry your story—and make the reader want to read on.

(2) What your opening scene needs to do: Your opening scene needs to accomplish four crucial functions:

1. Establish your main character (even if that's you!) in situ; that is, in the story's central or prevailing milieu.

2. Establish the mood, tone, and pace of the story.

3. Tell us some basic (but important) facts: Is the narrator male or female? How old? Are we in a town? In the country? North or south of the Mason-Dixon Line? In the twenty-first century or the 1930s?

4. Raise the story's central question, conflict, or issue. At least in a general way, the opening scene should answer: What is this story going to be about?

(3) Rewriting the opening scene: Once you've written your opening scene, turn the page and write it again—preferably after you've left it for a while. You will rewrite your first scene over and over. As you rework the scene, ask yourself these three questions:

1. Is this really where my story opens?

2. How can I make this scene more immediate, sensuous, vivid?

3. How can I make the reader keep on reading?

(4) Characters in your scene: In the favorite movie exercise on page 13, did you list the departure scene from *Casablanca?* Or did you select that famous diner scene from *When Harry Met Sally?* In either case, there would be no scene, and there would be no big-screen successes without those multidimensional, well-drawn characters. Chapter 8 provides a complete tutorial on creating characters. But for now, let's just move the camera in closer to see how your characters— their actions, speech, and reactions—heighten your scene's impact.

(5) Action: Your characters don't have to jump from bridges or obliterate each other in a shoot-out. But in each scene, make your characters *do or decide* something, even if it's something very subtle and small. Don't leave them sitting there as passive observers of the world and the story around them.

(6) Dialogue in your scene: If you're going to have them speak, have your characters say something that matters. Have their dialogue tell us more about them and move the plot along.

(7) Close-up details: Let me see your characters scratch their noses, pull up their stockings, caress their bald spots.

(8) Specificity: To bring me, the reader, into your scene, you need to give me specifics. For example, if you're writing about your family's annual car trip to the beach, give me the make and model (a turquoise blue Buick Skylark with white hubcaps). Make them specific.

(9) Well-chosen details: As you create your scenes, you will walk a delicate balance between telling enough and not telling too much. Using the example above, if you tell me every single detail from your annual family trip to the beach, I will get overwhelmed and your finest details will be lost in the large, kaleidoscopic muddle of details. Choose the interesting details.

(10) Writing the closing scene: I often compare the closing scene of a short story, essay, or novel to that light, delicious dessert at the end of a satisfying and sumptuous meal. The best desserts are never too heavy, too sweet, or too large. They satisfy the palate. They complement, without overwhelming the dinner courses. Unless you're writing a whodunit, your closing scene does not have to produce any grand philosophical conclusions. If there's one thing your readers will hate, it's being preached at or having the story interpreted for them. In a short story or personal essay, the closing can be as short as a few lines. And it shouldn't come as a big surprise or a huge disappointment. It should match the rest of the story in terms of its voice, language, and genre. Avoid those surprise endings. Just slow down the pace a little and leave us thinking, "Well, yeah, that's how it *should* end."

2
ATTITUDINAL SHIFTS

There's a line from the 1998 movie, *There's Something about Mary* that makes me want to jump out of my chair and pound on the TV screen.

In this scene, the main character's friend Dom (Chris Elliott) tells the lovelorn Ted (Ben Stiller): "You know, Ted, you gotta finish that novel so you can quit that stupid magazine."

"No!" I want to scream. "You've got it wrong! Wrong, wrong, wrong!"

The real-world truth is this: Except for a very, very lucky few, writing and publishing a book—even two books—will not allow you to quit your day job, at least not completely. If it did, half of the employed population of America would be staying up all night trying to pen their way to the Exit door.

So work is what keeps food on the table and pays for your laptop and clothes and the electricity to make that laptop run. These are the facts, ma'am.

Working a day job and maintaining a writing schedule is tricky. On my worst days, it's a giddy and guilty tightrope walk. I feel trapped in a perpetual tug o' war between competing duties, and dueling lives, identities, and deadlines. But here's the good news: Usually, after a slight tweak to my writing schedule, things work out. And often, it's not about time management or a schedule, but a good hard look in the mirror and a few no-nonsense attitude adjustments toward both work *and* writing.

If you're a task-oriented person, the type of person who likes doing, as opposed to thinking or looking in the mirror, this may sound strange orr silly to you. But setting up and maintaining a writing schedule is much easier if you're in the right mind-set to begin with.

TAKE THIS JOB AND LOVE IT! DOES YOUR WORK ATTITUDE NEED ADJUSTMENT?

Sit at any after-work bar in America, and what do you hear? After-work customers sitting there ranting about their jobs: the demanding boss, the lazy coworker, the passive-aggressive lifer who makes this martini

drinker's life hell. Yikes! Often these happy hours have a way of turning, well, unhappy.

The disgruntled employee syndrome is so much a part of modern life that we've produced successful transatlantic TV comedies (*The Office*) and nationally syndicated cartoon strips (*Dilbert*) from it. Often comedy is all about holding up the mirror to make us laugh at ourselves and who we are—individually and collectively.

Every job has stressful days. Bosses change deadlines. Machines break down. The new software doesn't do what it's supposed to do. Your supervisor does a complete one-eighty on that project that you've just slaved over for months.

I'm not going to tell you how to fix your job or career. There are lots of books, websites, and career advice columns that do just that. But I'm going to offer some guidelines on how to adjust your attitude toward work—to make the work-write balance a little happier.

So don't be that guy at the bar whining into his martini and ranting about his job. In fact, you shouldn't even be in that bar. You have much better things to do—like … ahem … write.

FIVE WAYS TO MAKE WORK BETTER— SO YOU CAN WRITE MORE

(1) Just do it. Especially in the wake of an economic downturn, most CEOs or operations managers have sat around boardroom tables and shared their spreadsheets to tabulate how many people they really, *really* need to produce those widgets. So if you still have a job or if you've just started a new job, you're actually lucky. And you're going to have to earn your keep. Sometimes getting the job done is easier and less stressful than whining about the job.

(2) It really *is* only a job: Because it takes up such a large portion of our lives, because today's workplaces are downsized and downright busy, it's easy to allow your job to assume this huge, all-consuming significance in your own life. But here's a little mental exercise for you: Mentally erase your nameplate from outside your office or on your desk or in the company list. In your imagination game, write someone else's name on there. Cindy Smith. José Martinez.

Now imagine Cindy (or José) sitting in your chair, logging into your computer. Walk down to the boardroom. Look! There's Cindy in her perfect little outfit with her little brownnoser's smile. Grrr. You could just … but wait! There's your boss smiling back at her, assigning her the projects that used to be (gulp!) yours. Or there's José, sitting there in the lunchroom, nibbling on his lunchtime salad and laughing with the colleagues that used to be your office friends.

You get the point. Very, very few of us are irreplaceable. Once the ink is dry on your "Goodbye from all of us" card, your boss is already rushing back to her desk to approve final copy on that job-placement ad. To replace you.

Take a step back. Drop the career-ego game. Look at the bigger picture. Yes, you value your job and your work. But, except for those rare organizations who are actually saving lives or rescuing starving children, there's no employer anywhere who's worthy of giving your life to. And even among the world's hero organizations, there's none that needs you to give up your writing.

> *Here's a Tip!* Set an electronic reminder that goes off ten minutes before the end of your workday. When you hear that "Ding!" close out your current project and use those ten minutes to create tomorrow's to-do list. Make your list. Check it twice. Now, you're all done. Until tomorrow.

(3) Envy is deadly: Do you envy those "real" writers sitting in their artsy, bohemian writing rooms, churning pages and pages, only stopping writing to take the next call from their agent or publisher who's offering an even bigger advance. This image is not entirely accurate. In fact, I've met writers who have taken long sabbaticals to write—only to be shocked by how little they actually produce during those long, unpunctuated days. There's an old expression, "If you want something done, give it to a busy person." All that uncharted time can result in less, not more. Your day job can give you the structure you need to get things done.

(4) Avoid the complainers: Remember that TV sitcom *Just Shoot Me?* Remember that smarmy, sarcastic character named Dennis Quimby Finch (played by David Spade) who self-appointed himself as the office cynic?

Many workplaces or departments evolve in this way. Snickering subversion or constant complaints become the lexicon of the workplace.

Instead of running with the pack of moaners, think about ways to make it all work better. Or start to hang with the more upbeat crowd.

(5) Develop a transition ritual: Develop a ritual that will help you separate work and personal time. Take a walk. Go to the gym. Stop at a café for a relaxing herbal tea. Write in your journal. Find something that will help you to let go of your day, feel good about your job, and get geared up to write.

FIVE WAYS TO NURTURE AND PROTECT YOUR WRITING

1. **Who are you now?** So you're chatting to this stranger, your seat neighbor on a train or a plane. Here comes the inevitable, "What do you do?" As a nine-to-five employee, you may be inclined to define yourself by your day job. "I'm an accountant." "I'm in advertising." "I'm an executive assistant." There's nothing wrong with this. It's what you do. Just make sure that you *also define yourself* as a writer. Go on. Take a deep breath and make yourself say it, "I'm a writer."

2. **Think beyond the paycheck:** This self-identification goes much deeper than cocktail party introductions. It's not just about tagging yourself or your profession. And it's not about which career earns you the most money. When you give your writing an equal—if not a higher—priority, the people around you will also respect your dual identities and commitments.

3. **Value time:** We want to be popular. We want to be known as being a team player, a community volunteer, a go-to person. But trust me, as you navigate the competing demands of your day job and your writing life, you must weigh just what all this nice-guy stuff means. If you can work and volunteer and write, that's great. But each time you say "yes," make it a conscious decision and know that each hour you give to others is an hour that you've taken from yourself and your writing.

4. **Love, honor, and protect:** As you set about setting and building your daily writing schedule, regard your writing as a true gift from the universe. And, like all valuable gifts, you will need to cop an attitude. In her blog on writing, Elizabeth Gilbert (www.elizabethgilbert.com) (*Eat, Pray, Love*) writes: "If you are serious about a life of writing, or indeed about any creative form of expression, you should take on this work like a holy calling." Play mother bear and resolve to fiercely protect and fight off those forces that could and would detract you from your gift.

5. **You deserve to write:** Even in our twenty-first century global market-place, we still hold onto that Puritanical streak that values industry and duty over creativity and fun. Often we inherit this duty-booty from our parents or grandparents who regale us with their "in my day" stories. As you balance your checkbook with your checklist of household or family duties, you must believe—*really* believe—that you deserve to write.

> *Writer Beware!* Have you been unemployed for a few months or even a few years? Don't feel like you must abandon your writing to make up for lost work time or to double pay your fiscal dues. You can do all of that. But you also deserve to write.

DUAL LIVES: MAKE YOUR JOB SERVE YOUR WRITING

Writers are famous procrastinators. But if you're successfully holding down a full- or part-time job, you've already developed a key skill that other writers wish like heck they had: time management.

Writers are also notorious for starting but never finishing projects. But in most of today's workplaces, an unfinished project is an unpaid worker—or, at the very least, a reprimanded worker. So our jobs can teach us how to start, sustain, track, and complete a project, nuts to bolts.

If you work in editing, communications, PR, marketing, or publishing (many creative writers do), you've got yourself some valuable copywriting and editing skills that will serve you well as a creative writer. From project management to editing to strategic planning and job completion, there are many ways in which you can cross-pollinate between your two careers.

Write the Job You Know

Before and during a writing project, many authors meticulously research their topics or territories while others look no further than their real-life experiences—including their current or past job. These writers bring an insider's eye and an expert's authenticity to their work.

For example, look at this extract from the creative nonfiction essay, "Girl, Fighting" (published in *Creative Nonfiction*) by fiction author and nonfiction essayist, Laurie Lynn Drummond (*Anything You Say Can and Will Be Used Against You*, HarperCollins, 2004).

> I pulled up in front of a rickety, brown shotgun house squashed up against other rickety shotgun houses. I grabbed my six-cell flashlight and slid the portable radio into its holder. I debated only a minute about my hat, then put it on, even though I despised that hat with a passion. It gave me headaches, created an ugly red band on my forehead and messed up my hair, but the brass loved hats, and my lieutenant had a propensity for writing up officers who neglected to wear them.

No prizes for guessing that Drummond worked as a cop. In fact, she worked for nine years in law enforcement, including working as a uniformed police officer for the Baton Rouge Police Department—an experience on which she bases this essay and *Anything You Say Can and Will be Used Against You.*

Notice how she uses specific details (the brown shotgun house). And see how she makes us privy to the internal doubts and dialogue of a young officer on duty (did *you* know that cops' hats muss up their hair?). As readers, we relish and trust this kind of insider's information. And finally, see how Drummond's voice, language, and tempo match her story? As Officer Drummond strides from her car, you trust her to tell us what happens inside that brown shotgun house.

Here's an example from a work of fiction. It's a scene from a hospital operating room from Tess Gerritsen's 1997 novel, *Life Support:*

> He made the incision, a smooth, clean slice. The scrub nurse assisted, sponging up blood, handing him hemostats. He cut deeper, through the yellow subcutaneous fat, pausing every so often to cauterize a bleeder. *No problem. Everything's going to be fine.* He would get in, remove the appendix and get out again ...
>
> "Retract," he said.
>
> The scrub nurse took hold of the stainless steel retractors and gently tugged open the wound. Mackie reached into the gap and felt the intestines, warm and slippery, squirm around his gloved hand.

Before becoming a *New York Times* best-selling novelist, Gerritsen had a successful practice as a physician. As a doctor-turned-writer, notice her intimacy and her use of pertinent details. Who else would know how the intestines feel in your hand? Who else would have such a command of the tense, staccato language of the operating room?

Your day job and your writing don't have to be at loggerheads. In fact, for many writers there are real advantages to having a full-time day job:

1. **Food and a roof over your head:** I'm sure it's possible to live and write in a no-fee homeless shelter. And perhaps you can write while scavenging restaurant Dumpsters for leftover food and cold, abandoned coffees. But wouldn't you rather have the money for a quiet writing place and three square meals per day?

2. **Professional development:** Classes, writers conferences, magazine contributions, writers retreats. These all cost money.

3. **Less stress:** A steady paycheck frees us from the stress of worrying about paying bills. Collection agencies make very, very poor writing mentors. They will never become the cheerleaders of your writing life.

4. **Professionalism and panache:** Your mother was right. First appearances really do count. Publishers favor a clean professionally printed manuscript in a professional business-standard envelope or manuscript box mailed first-class. If you're meeting with an agent or reading from your work, a crisp, manicured appearance goes a long way toward building your credibility. And all of these cost ... yes, you guessed it. Money.

5. **Time management:** A day job gives you valuable experience in planning and managing your time for maximum efficiency.

6. **Tenacity:** In today's workplace, there really are no free lunches. The tenacity and the problem-solving skills you learn at work are invaluable for when your writing stalls or takes you in an unintended direction.

7. **Marketing:** If you work in a marketing or public relations department, you can use these abilities to market your writing.

8. **Critical mass:** While a patchwork of funky cash 'n' carry jobs may buy you more free slots for writing, they carry their own stresses—including the constant scheduling logistics and the energy switch between tasks and skills. Thankfully most full-time jobs reach a point where things get easier, where tasks become automatic.

9. **Expertise and credibility:** Whether it's explicit or implicit in their actual writing, many authors are inspired by their nonwriting expertise. As readers, we feel privileged to enter their unique world. See the excerpts on page 22 from Tess Gerritsen and Laurie Lynn Drummond.

10. **Staunch in your beliefs:** Because you're not dependent on your writing as a way to pay your household bills, you can write what you really want to write. You may not be as susceptible to the fads and fashions of the publishing industry.

Have you ever arrived at a house party and wondered why the heck you didn't politely decline the invitation? You barely have your coat off when you felt blitzed by the thumping music. Someone passes you a glass of wine that tastes like battery acid. And, though you haven't eaten dinner yet, there seem to be no party snacks except these random baskets of cheese doodles. After a half hour of being elbow jabbed by dancing drunks, you decide to call it a night and call a cab home where you eat a bowl of cereal in front of the late-night TV shows.

Three days later you're lamenting your wasted Saturday night when an acquaintance, another party attendee, waxes on about the best Saturday night she's had in ages. And that music! Wow! And she's never met so many fun people and had such fascinating conversations. Oh yeah, and what about the host's fabulous art collection? And the buffet. Wow! That party really rocked!

Wait! You think. Were we actually *at* the same party? So you double-check with her. Then you interrogate her about her arrival and departure time—just in case things kicked up a notch either before your arrival or after your hasty departure. Nope. She was there at the same soiree for the entire time you were.

There's a simple reason for your different experiences, your antithetical impressions of the exact same party. She has different tastes, different preferences, and different sensibilities from you. Her rockin' party is your cacophonous nightmare. She somehow found a cornucopia of a buffet that you somehow missed. And artwork? What artwork? All you remember from that mosh pit party was the blinking Budweiser beer light.

It all depends on your point of view and who's doing the telling.

POINT OF VIEW: WHO TELLS THE STORY?

Equally, when it comes to writing a narrative story, much will depend on the teller, the eyes through which you, the writer, allow us, the reader, to experience that story. From the *once upon a time* to the *happily ever after*, the reader experiences the story's setting, characters, conflict, crisis, and voice via the story's point of view.

For example, on page 22, in the excerpt from Laurie Lynn Drummond's nonfiction essay, "Girl, Fighting," we are experiencing the streets of Baton Rouge through Drummond's point of view. Another cop would tell it differently. If the inhabitants of that brown bungalow were to relate the night the lady cop came knocking, they would tell another version.

Part 1: Choosing First, Second, or Third Person

Once you've selected your teller—your main point of view—you must decide if your story should be told in first, third, changing, omniscient, or second person. For example, Gerritsen allows us to experience the operating room through Dr. Stanley Mackie's point of view. And she tells the story in third person. ("He made the incision, a smooth, clean slice.")

> *Here's a Tip!* To help me with this process, I imagine that the narrator is carrying an old-fashioned, heavyweight camcorder camera on his or her shoulder. Squinting through the camcorder lens, what will this point-of-view character of mine actually see?

Below are some brief scenes (I made them up!) from a story about a family reunion told from different points of view. As you read each mini scene, ask yourself three questions:

1. Who's holding the imaginary camera here?
2. What's the overall effect of using each point of view?
3. If this were my story, which point of view would I use?

Example 1: First-person point of view

"I woke to some strange voice outside my motel door. "Miss Sally Noble?" a woman yelled. "Visitor downstairs. Visitor downstairs to see you!"

"Yeah, OK," I shouted back, my brain sludgy with sleep. Then, awake at last, I remembered what day it was: the damn family reunion.

In first person, we are going to see, hear, and experience everything through a single narrator's eyes and voice (Sally Noble). We will also be privy to Sally's inner dialogue, her speech patterns, her thoughts, and memories. When we actually go to the Noble family's annual reunion, we will see, hear, and feel the entire event—and the other members of the family—through Sally. Sally only.

A note for nonfiction writers: Laurie Lynn Drummond's essay is told in first person ("I grabbed my six-cell flashlight and slid the portable radio into its holder.") because it must be. First person is the *only* narrator to use for personal essays, memoir essays or books, or creative nonfiction books.

In the first example from the Noble family reunion story, we would follow Sally to the event. We would meet other members of her family. In fact, the story could be all about the entire family, not just Sally. But ultimately, we would see and know them only through Sally's sensibility.

Example 2: Third-person limited point of view

> *Damn. Why am I waking up in this dump,* thought Sally Noble, as she opened her eyes to that white hotel room. Then she remembered why she was here, in this mold-stinking room just off Highway 82 and in the middle of Nowhere, USA. *Oh, no,* she thought. *The family reunion.*

Third-person limited point of view is very similar to first person, except that we use *he* or *she*. Again, we are going to experience this entire hotel room and family reunion—plus Sally's internal thoughts and biases—via Sally Noble, our narrator.

Example 3: Multiple or changing points of view

> Sally Noble woke to the sound of the radio alarm clock chirping and to someone pounding on her motel room door. "Visitor!" said the woman's voice. "Miss Noble? Visitor downstairs for you!"
>
> *Oh, no!* Sally thought. *Dad's here already. And I've overslept for the family reunion. There's going to be hell to pay.*
>
> Joe Noble paced the carpeted hotel lobby of the Whistlestop Motel. He wished the receptionist would stop peering over her computer monitor at him. *Typical Sally,* he thought. *How did he, a third-generation soybean farmer, raise such a god-awful sleepyhead?* He checked the electric wall clock behind the receptionist's head. Twelve-thirty five. Okay, it's time to send that nosy receptionist to Sally's room. Time to get his daughter up and out.

To master the art of changing or multiple points of view, read lots of books and stories that do it well—or at least read all of the transition lines; that is, the parts where the viewpoint switches. In the example above, each point of view is in third-person limited. But some books are also in alternating or multiple first-person points of view. Read some examples of each technique.

> ***Writer Beware!*** Too many changing points of view can set up a dizzying roller-coaster effect for the reader. It can confuse the reader (wait, I thought it was Sally who was the sister with the sleeping problem) or jolt us out of the story's fictional world. In the wrong hands, multiple points of view can also make the reader disinterested in any one character. And ... that's trouble.

Example 4: Omniscient point of view

> The alarm went off in a hotel room on a two-lane thoroughfare just outside Columbus, Ohio. Sally Noble, a forty-five-year-old woman with curly blond hair, woke and groped for the snooze device. It was March 3, 1984, the day of the Noble family's annual reunion.

In omniscient point of view, the imaginary camera is actually in the sky, in the ceiling, or somewhere on an orbiting satellite. In contemporary works, we don't use or see omniscient point of view much anymore. As you can see, it's a formal, distanced way of telling a story. Avoid it.

Example 5: Second-person point of view

> At first you think it's the hotel fire drill. No, it's the damn alarm, you think. Then there's someone pounding on your door. And there's a woman's screeching voice. So you're awake. Again. And then it hits you: It's reunion day.

In second-person point of view, the *you* is, of course, really the teller or the *I*. In fiction, the *you* voice is used pretty rarely. When it is, it has a very specific effect.

To learn more about it, read works in which it is used well (Jay McInerney's *Bright Lights, Big City* (Vintage Books, 1984).

> ***Writer Beware!*** Very, very few books, essays, or stories will lend themselves to using the second person in this way. It has a very particular effect on the reader. It can call attention to itself as a device. But, as in McInerney's book, when it's used appropriately and well, it makes a narrative even more memorable.

Part 2: What the Teller Knows: Maintaining Point of View

Once you decide on the point of view, you must remain within that point of view.

Let's look at our Noble family reunion story again. In Example 1, Sally doesn't know that it's a woman pounding on her motel room door until she actually hears the receptionist's voice. Equally, when Joe Noble is pacing the hotel lobby, he cannot possibly know that his daughter Sally is hitting the snooze alarm. He can surmise it. He can remember other past occasions when he saw her do it. Based on this past memory, he can even picture his daughter Sally in his mind's eye. But he cannot *know* it. Neither can he know how much Sally is dreading the reunion.

In Example 3, Scene 1 (multiple points of view), Joe is holding the camera. And the camera doesn't have an x-ray lens into his daughter's hotel room or her interior dialogue.

In Example 3, sleepy Sally cannot know that her father is out there pacing and waiting. She may or may not know (based on past family quarrels) that he's frustrated with her lack of punctuality. But she cannot *know* how he looked when he left his house this morning to drive to the hotel and the reunion. Under those hotel sheets, while we're in Sally's point of view, she's holding the camera.

Part 3: Which Is Best for My Story?

If you're writing a personal essay or longer personal narrative, there is no choice. It's always *I* or first person. However, there are other issues of choosing the voice and the narrative distance.

But listen up, you fiction scribes! Choosing who tells the story and whether you use first, third, or second person to do the telling is one of your bigger decisions you will make as you start your first draft. I use three approaches, to help me make this decision.

(1) **I mull it over:** Before I write the first line, I spent a lot of time with the story in my head. I walk around with it. I mull it over in my car, while I'm taking a walk, when I shower. I let the story's voice percolate through my mind and heart.

(2) **I trust the story itself to tell me:** Some stories arrive via a fully birthed, fully formed first line. The story comes in the voice it's supposed to be in. There's no changing it.

(3) **I allow myself to experiment and change tack:** I try a few pages in first person. Then I open a new file and try it in limited third person. Which piece has more energy? Which piece was a faster, easier write? Which voice is likely to sustain this story over the long term?

The answers to my self-posed questions will usually steer me toward the right decision and the right voice for my story.

POINT OF VIEW: WRITING EXERCISES

Exercise 1:

Think of someone with whom you're in conflict. Perhaps it's that malcontented office worker who sits in the cube behind you. Is it that difficult, passive-aggressive employee who makes your life miserable? Is it that woman who lives next door and whose dog keeps you awake half the night? Unless you've lived inside a bubble, I'm guessing that you won't have to think too far or too hard to come up with someone who needs a good telling off.

    Now step inside your nemesis's point-of-view voice. Write five hundred words (or longer if you can), from his or her point of view, about you. Try it in first person. Have fun! Oh, and keep it honest, real, and use the kind of pertinent, sensual details we see in the examples from Drummond's and Gerritsen's writings (page 21 and 22).

Exercise 2:

Log onto Monster.com or Craigslist (www.craigslist.org) jobs section. Browse the résumés there. Choose one. Now, write a third-person limited point-of-view sketch of this fictional character and his or her adventures in job hunting. Let your imagination roam free. If possible, get five hundred words on the page or computer screen. Then read back through your piece. Where did the writing gain energy? Where was the voice strongest? The strongest are probably worth revisiting or replicating the voice.

Exercise 3:

This time, let's look at your résumé—not just your employment and its day-to-day tasks, but also your soft skills or your personal attributes—the things that make you ... you! Include the attributes that people value most about you.

Now imagine that your company or organization likes you so much that they want an exact clone of you. In the space below, write your job advertisement. Assume your Monster.com advertisement voice. And make sure you include your personal attributes and strengths.

> **WANTED!**
>
>

Exercise 4:

Anita Shreve's 2005 novel, *A Wedding in December,* uses third-person limited, multiple points of view to tell the story of a group of former schoolmates who gather in a historic inn for a classmate's wedding. Here's an excerpt from the novel told from the point of view of Harrison, a middle-aged wedding guests. Harrison just checked into the inn and went to the main lobby to meet Nora, another classmate and the innkeeper:

> Nora left the window and moved to the chair opposite. He watched her cross her legs, a cuff riding just above the edge of a black leather boot and making a slim bracelet of smooth white skin. Harrison superimposed the woman he saw now over the memory of the seventeen-year-old girl he'd once known, a girl with a soft face and large almond-shaped eyes, a girl who had been graceful in her movements. The woman before him was forty-four, and some of the softness had left her face. Her hair was different, too. She wore it short, swept behind her ears, a cut that looked more European than American.

In this excerpt, we experience Sally and their middle-aged reunion *from Harrison's point of view only.* Now, rewrite this scene from Sally's point of view. Make it up. What's her voice? What does she notice and think about Harrison?

EXERCISES ON WRITING SCENES

Exercise 1:

How do you usually introduce yourself to strangers? For example, if a new neighbor moves in next door or across the hall, how do you typically identify yourself? After exchanging names and your apartment number and how long you've lived in the building, what are the self-labels you apply? ("I'm a nurse." "I'm a single mom." "I'm originally from Iowa." "I'm just finishing night school.")

Write your top three self-labels here.

I am:
1.
2.
3.

Good. Now, circle the identifier that feels *least* comfortable for you. Go on, be honest. Which one has never really fit? Or which one fails to fully describe you—the real you.

Exercise 2:

Now write a scene in which you let the reader see, hear, and experience your discomfort with this one aspect of your life. Is your current job ("I'm a nurse") no longer you? Are you ashamed of or bitter about your Iowa childhood or roots? Whatever it is, move the camera in and let us see you in that setting, being uncomfortable. Write in third person (he, she) if you like. But remember, you must show us. You must let the reader in.

Exercise 3:

Lights! Camera! Write Your Moment of Writing Glory

The big night has finally arrived. Your work is polished, perfect, and ready to present to the world—whether that's your family, your Pulitzer presenter, or the audience at your book launch party.

Write a scene in which you've finally completed your project and it's your moment in the limelight.

This will give you practice writing a scene and will help you clarify your writing goals.

You can do this in two ways:

(a) Just jump right in and write the scene from scratch. Make it come alive with sensual details, vivid characters, and crackling dialogue. Go wild. Make the night pop!

(b) To get that party going, use the work sheet below. Complete the table. It will help you to brainstorm and do some free association to draft your scenes. Then, turn the page and write your scene. Don't stop or censor yourself.

Setting (where are you?)

Who else is there?

What writing project have you completed?

What are they saying about you? Write some lines of dialogue.

Now, go back and read your scene. From your guest list to your outfit, you will find clues to the aspects of writing that you really want and that can and will bring you joy.

Section 2

LET'S GO! START THE HABIT OF DAILY WRITING

For writers with a day job (or two!), the first challenge is finding a time slot to devote to writing. The second challenge: Every time we enter that alloted time, we must switch hats. We must find a way to leave our busy, workaday selves aside and become our creative writer selves.

But both of these can be mastered. Honest.

By the way, the time issue is not necessarily any easier for best-selling or "successful" (read: full-time, published and financed by hefty publisher advances) authors. For those writers, there's the problem of balancing book tours and public appearances and press interviews about the just-published book while also trying to keep up with the current book in progress.

And, even without the day job or the book tour, there is still the issue of balancing writing with family or other responsibilities.

In this section, I offer some savvy guidelines on setting and keeping a daily writing schedule—a schedule that works for you.

3

BUILD YOUR
DAILY WRITING STAMINA

"I really want to write, but I just don't have the time!" I hear this often. And when I do, I believe that what the person is really saying me is this: "I have a vague, undefined notion about being a writer, but I don't desire to be a writer. Or at least, I don't desire it enough to make some lifestyle changes and give up other things so that I can produce some writing."

In my opinion, there are two attributes which distinguish real writers from the wannabes: desire and discipline.

DESIRE

For a writer, desire means you want to write *as much as you want anything else in your life*. In your life's bucket list, writing is listed among the top three.

I've met some writers who have chosen to live alone, who have eschewed romantic relationships in order to have a writer's solitude.

For you, this may sound a little drastic—and certainly a high price to pay to be a writer. But overall, what I'm talking about here is the act of getting tough on yourself. If you really want to be a writer, you must do what it takes. If you want it badly enough, you will have to make real sacrifices and give up other things, other activities, wealth, or ego trips.

All life changes require behavior modification—a process by which you are going to stop one habit or activity (whining, pining, procrastinating) and start and maintain another habit (regular, sustained writing).

Remember that picture or cube memento from chapter 1? The trinket that you keep as a reminder? Make one for your briefcase or your purse or your jacket pocket, too. Do whatever it takes to remind yourself that writing is very, very precious to you.

DISCIPLINE

It's such a grim old word, isn't it? It conjures Dickensian punishments and town-square floggings. But self-discipline is key to writing. The simple fact is this: If you leave writing until "I feel like it," or "I feel inspired," or "I feel I've something significant to say," then you will be doing just that—leaving writing.

In the cliché department, it's an oldie but goodie: Writing is half inspiration and half perspiration. It's true. And it's especially true for writers who are also holding down another career.

From making excuses about going to the gym to stealing that last chocolate-chip cookie, we are all capable of acting like five-year-olds. We'll all push the envelope and spin our own excuses. Worse, we'll even believe these excuses. Wag your finger at yourself. Become your own procrastination police.

DEVELOP A DAILY WRITING HABIT

Some working nine-to-five writers will tell you that the workweek is simply too packed and exhausting to get any writing done. "I'll just do it on the weekend," they say. "I'll devote the entire weekend to writing." Sounds good, right? After all, you have two full, paid days to devote to your craft.

Hmmm … I'm going to wag a finger here and act like your mother and say, "Do you *really* think that's a good idea?"

First, I don't believe those so-called weekend writers. Fine, they may not be actually sitting at their writing desks from Monday to Friday. But I'm going to bet that they are, in some measure, visiting or revisiting their writing projects. As they drive to work or munch on their lunchtime sandwiches, they are imaging or reimagining that last scene they just wrote. Or they are taking time out to jot down lists of ideas, edits, and plot solutions. Then, come Saturday morning and their designated writing time, a portion of the work has already been done.

If you're a beginner or even a beginner-to-intermediate writer, you need to write something—preferably a set, targeted amount—every day. By spending time—even if it's just ten minutes—with your writing every day, you will (a) give creative writing a higher ranking in your weekly and life priorities (b) develop and hone your skills with written language and (c) built up your writing stamina, confidence, and voice.

A Note for Those Starting a New Job
or Rejoining the Workplace

If you're a writer who's starting her first job or rejoining the workforce after a long hiatus or unemployment, do yourself a favor and accept the fact that you may not be able to write in the same way as you did before. You may not have the luxury of long, uninterrupted writing stints, in which you pace the floor of your writing room and then go back to your piece to write ten more pages. Depending on your day job schedule, you may have to retrain yourself to write in short, concentrated spurts. Or you may have to maintain your writing via short writing exercises, lists, and notes, which you expand on during the weekend or on a working vacation. Be ready to problem-solve and think outside the box so that you readjust your writing schedule. The important thing is that you keep writing.

WHY IT'S BEST TO WRITE (EVEN A LITTLE!) EVERY DAY

Let's use the analogy of signing up for a new gym membership. You need to trim up and work out, so you plan a big marathon workout for Saturday and Sunday mornings. But any personal trainer will tell you that the weekend warrior circuit doesn't really work. That Saturday morning marathon will leave your muscles sore and aching. In some cases, it can even create injury. Each Saturday morning, you will probably feel as creaky and sore as you did the previous Saturday. The wellness and fitness gurus advise us to manage a little exercise every day. These regular short spurts build the habit, build your fitness, and build muscle.

It's the same for your writing muscle. This is why I advise new writers to find a way to write every single day.

Speaking of fitness and health, notice how many of our health experts—including our national public health advocacy organizations—have adapted a really commonsense approach and recognize that most of us live busy lives full of car pools and work and other duties? Browse a selection of today's fitness articles and you'll find lots of commonsense tips for daily fitness that … crr … actually *fits into* our busy, daily lives?

In developing a daily writing habit, in building up your writing fitness, you can do the same thing. In fact, if you work a day job, you have no other choice. You're going to have to fit brief writing stints into the rest of your day's tasks. And to do that, you have to find a way to make it happen—especially if you're just starting to write.

Find ten minutes. You'd be surprised how much you get written in ten minutes. Forget that Hollywood image of the writer locked up in her room for long, tortured writing sessions, in which he (the writer) doesn't shower and only leaves his desk to visit the bathroom. As a writer with a day job, this is not going to be your daily reality.

In the beginning, it's all about make a daily commitment to your writing, to building up your writing comfort level and muscle. Think about other changes that you've made in your life. Have you quit smoking? Have you started eating a healthier diet? Developed a better filing system for your household papers and valuables? Started to keep a cleaner car? Developed a more efficient, less stressful morning routine? Whatever past self-improvements you've made in your life, try to remember how you did it. What worked? Recapture and list the steps you took to make that transition and then sustain it as a daily habit. This process worked for you in the past. Now, as you build your daily writing habit, this process can be replicated to work for you again.

For example, almost twenty years ago, I finally quit smoking after many previously botched attempts. This time, on my final and successful quit-smoking campaign, I really analyzed what had gone wrong on the previous occasions. After giving it lots of thought and writing in my daily journal (more on journal writing later), I realized that, on those previous attempts, I had quit because friends, the daily newspaper, relatives, and my mother were all citing health risks and cancer rates at me. These only worked for a while. Then, I would find a way to ignore the health warnings to walk to the corner store to buy a new pack.

This time, I realized that, if I picked up another cigarette, I would be really, really disappointing myself. I would be reneging on my own promise to myself. I would have to look at myself in the mirror and say, "Great. So you've gone back on your word." So I found out that I'm an internally motivated person. In fact, the more everyone out there tells me to do something, the less likely I am to do it.

Once quitting smoking became personal, once it made sense for me on an internal level, I finally quit.

I've often duplicated this process in disciplining myself to write. On procrastination days, it gets me off the chair and up the stairs to my writing desk. *Don't disappoint yourself.* This mantra and process work for me.

So think of a successful habit change that you've made. Can this step-by-step process be duplicated to build a sustained writing habit?

Find a spot in your daily calendar that works for you. Hold that promise. Get into the habit. As day job writers, it can start with a shift in thinking. Instead of beating yourself up because you don't write for two hours a day, learn to value those short, timed—aka available—writing slots. Perhaps it's that half hour between leaving work and picking up your daughter from soccer practice.

Or is it that twenty-five minutes under the hair dryer at your hairstylist's? As a busy writer, these available time slots assume a new meaning.

Boston-based author Karl Iagnemma (www.karliagnemma.com) has written and published a collection of short stories and a novel (*On the Nature of Human Romantic Interaction, The Expeditions*). As well as being an award-winning writer, Iagnemma is also a full-time robotics researcher. With a demanding job and a family, Karl estimates that he has ten hours—at the most—to write every week. Says Iagnemma, "Since I have so little time to write, I try to take advantage of every minute. Even though I have days where I don't feel inspired, or fully engaged with the piece I'm working on, I try to write a few lines or revise a few paragraphs every time I sit down to work."

TEN TIPS FOR DAILY WRITING

1. Make a date with yourself: Yes, I know your schedule is jam-packed. But remember what we said in chapter 2 about believing that you deserve to be a writer? You deserve a writing rendezvous with yourself. We owe ourselves some creative, meaningful time in our lives. So make a date and keep it. Oh, and show up on time.

2. Right brain. Right time. Is there a time of day when you're naturally more whimsical, more in tune with your inner or imaginative self? First thing in the morning? Last thing at night? Right after your morning yoga? Immediately after your lunchtime jog? Sitting at your son's hockey practice? If there's a time when you believe that writing will come more easily, make this your daily writing time.

3. A clean, well-lit place: It doesn't have to be a custom-designed artist studio with an ocean view. But your daily writing spot needs to make you feel comfortable and happy, and it needs to match your personality. Even if it's just a table in the corner of your shared bedroom, this spot should make you feel free to be yourself. It should fit the creative you. At a minimum, make sure that your writing spot is free of any negative associations or memories.

4. Tell your family or friends: You may want to be a mystery writer, but you don't have to be a mysterious writer. Because it's a new or surprising side of you, because it's a new persona that your family may not have encountered before, you may be shy about saying to your family, "I've started writing." Quite simply, it may make you feel vulnerable. Or you may feel that it sets some kind of expectation for blockbusters or huge advances, or that you'll start to walk around talking to yourself. Or you may fear that your friends and family will see this as time away from them or a set of shirked household duties. Actually, it will. Beginning a writing life means sacrificing or cutting back on other things, including your social life. But I encourage you to share your writing dream with your family, friends, or room-mates. A real friend will support you. A fake friend will laugh, tease, condescend, or try to discourage you. Or worse, these friends or family will make it all about them ("but what about our Thursday night movie?"). Believe me, every writer needs a cheerleader or two or three. Also, rearranging your schedule to find some writing time will require the support and cooperation of the other people in your household.

5. Same time. Same place: Set up a place where the writing is going to happen. By going to that same spot with the same view and smells and general feel, you give yourself some sen-sual and spatial prompts to start writing. Yes, we're Pavlovian creatures, and this is especially true in writing. "Oh right," you think, as you sit in that plastic seat inside your usual window in McDonald's. "I'm here. So it must be time to write."

6. Switch off all electronic communication: Take this as fact: E-mail, iPhones, Blackberries, text messaging, and any other electronic-messaging system are the enemies of writing. First, all that time spent reading and responding to messages eats into your precious writing time. And second, those bleeps and pings and newsy e-mails distract you into completely different mental space—a place far away from your writing mind. However hard it is, even if you're chained to your work or personal electronic device, switch it off. All those messages will be there when your writing time is over and complete.

7. Write naked: I have a writer friend who, in the wake of Hurricane Katrina, joined a volunteer crew to help displaced and distressed people in New Orleans. During this devastating time, a local hardware store donated some work shirts for the volunteers. Now my friend wears her old volunteer's shirt when she sits at her writing desk. She cannot get started until she's wearing that shirt. Another writer I know likes to do yoga before penning her first sentence. I once read an article about a writer who plays one game of solitaire before getting started. Say a prayer to the writing gods. Develop a prewriting ritual that works for you—even if it means wearing a Stetson hat or writing naked (not in McDonald's, please!).

8. Set a daily quota or word count: As you look at that calendar or day planner, you may automatically allot a time to writing—a half hour or fifteen minutes or an hour. This works in terms of finding and assigning a regular writing time. But when I'm starting a new project or a first draft, this never works for me. Quite simply, it's just too easy to say, "I spent a half hour at my writing desk today." But that half hour doesn't count if half of it was spent checking the online headlines or just gazing at the computer screen. Make your writing slot work. Set a word quota.

9. Praise! Alleluia! Keep a little calendar above your desk or, at the end of your writing session, open up your online calendar or online to-do lists (see the list on page 12) to record today's completed word count. It will serve as a time sheet—and a rewards system to praise yourself for your excellent discipline.

10. Allow yourself to write badly: At least for the early drafts, you need to just write. If you stop to judge, edit, delete, and rewrite, you will be spending all your time playing reader or critic, not writer. Trust me, you and your work will have enough critics later when you finish your final draft and put it out there for public consumption. But for now, for these early drafts, be gentle with yourself. Love your writing. And above all, trust where it's going.

On her writer's blog, "Thoughts on Writing," best-selling author Elizabeth Gilbert (www.elizabethgilbert.com) offers this advice on shushing that inner critic to allow yourself to just write:

> When I was writing *Eat, Pray, Love,* I had just as a strong a mantra of THIS SUCKS ringing through my head as anyone does when they write anything … But the point I realized was this: I never promised the universe that I would write brilliantly; I only promised the universe that I would write.

By the way, there's a catchy little feature about this "let myself write badly" rule. Personally, when I push my way through that "this-sucks" barrier, when I force myself to keep writing into and past what I think or tell myself is a lousy draft, I have a surprising but familiar outcome. When I return the next day to my so-called "this-sucks" writing piece, it's *never as bad* as I first assumed. In fact, as I reread yesterday's drafts, I often surprise myself. Which all just proves one thing: As writers, we are horribly, horribly hard on ourselves. We stop too often to censure, edit, and worry what the readers, the publishers, or the critics might think. Love yourself. Give yourself a break. Keep writing.

THREE WEEKS TO THAT DAILY WRITING HABIT: TWENTY-ONE SHORT WRITING EXERCISES TO GET YOU STARTED

Note: Each of these exercises should take you no more than ten minutes. Set a timer. Do not stop to think, to self-edit, or to wonder if you're a good writer. Just write until the timer goes off. Some of these might feel silly at first, but the goal is to release your inhibitions and get writing.

1. What's out your window? Your kitchen window, the train window, your bedroom window. Write about the weather, the sky, the buildings, the treetops. Let the writing take you where it will—even if it meanders to the past. Keep writing until the ten minutes is up.

2. Fun with addresses: What are the three roads or streets that neighbor your house or apartment? List the three names of these thoroughfares.

For example:

Myrtle Avenue
Route 54
Harrison Street

Now, take the three *names only* (Myrtle, Harrison, 54) and write something really silly. ("Myrtle met Harrison at the weight watcher's party. He had just dropped 54 pounds.") Keep writing from there.

3. How does it taste? Select one object in your room, office, or wherever you are—a table, chair, an antique vase, the grass growing outside your window. Imagine how your selected object tastes. Describe eating it.

4. Keeping time: Check your wall clock or computer or cell phone. Write down the time. Now start a piece of dialog using that time ("It's eleven minutes after four," said Mary). Keep writing. Let the dialogue take you into a ten-minute story.

5. Daily headlines: Read the first word of the first headline on the front page of today's newspaper. Now open a writing file or a page of your notebook. Write that word at the top of your writing page. Let that word take you into ten minutes of writing.

6. Write a color: Describe the color red, but do not use the actual color name. Instead, finish this sentence and follow it with lots of other sentences: *This color is ...*

7. Remembered smells: What's your earliest memory? During this incident, were you three, four, or five years old? Now try to remember what your first-memory surroundings smelled like. Describe that smell, and why you can still remember it.

8: My friend Frosty: Use this sentence as a starting point—and keep writing. (Hint: Feel free to get silly here.)

Snowmen make warm and reliable friends ...

9. Lottery shopping list. You've hit the jackpot. Write your shopping list. Now write about the most important item on the list.

10. Match.com: Whether you're happily single, married, dating, widowed, or living with your lover, write your own Match.com advertising copy. Remember, this is an advertisement that will make someone want to get in touch and get to know you. So don't hold back. Write your best version of yourself.

11. Banned goods: If you could have one product (just one!) permanently banned from the marketplace and the universe, what would that be? Why?

12. What a character! Write a ten-minute biography on this person (it could be a man or a woman):

Hannaford Cottonfeldt, Junior

13. Imagine this place: Write the travel-book blurb on this tourist attraction:

The White Cloud Fantasy Resort

14. Write this creature: Write a scientific definition for this creature or animal. Then give a layperson's description of this creature. Describe when and where the public can come and view it—and why they should.

Libelius Fallonipus

15. What's your favorite item in your closet? Why is this your favorite? Write about it and describe it in vivid detail until we, the readers, can see and feel it.

16. Real estate blurbs: Write a real estate advertisement for this house:

Your astronaut's dream home! Lots of off-street parking!

17. Precious objects: Look around your bedroom. Or, if you're writing at work or in a café, picture your bedroom back home. If your bedroom was burning down and you could salvage just one thing from it, what would that be? Why that object?

18. Food writer: Pick up a cookbook—any cookbook. Or log onto www.allrecipes .com. Pick out a recipe. Read the ingredients. Now write a scene in which you are cooking that dish. Bring us there, to your kitchen. Let us smell, see, and hear all those culinary delights.

19. Fairy tale: Write the first few scenes of this fairy tale:

Once upon a time, in a faraway kingdom, there lived a boy named Watson Rupus.

20. Write a letter: Who would you name as a personal hero? It can be a public figure, a famous person, or someone from your own life. Write this person a letter, telling her why you admire her so much.

21. Shakespearian speeches: In his plays, William Shakespeare often had his tragic characters deliver a soliloquy. A soliloquy is a dramatic device in which a character relates his thoughts and feelings to himself and to the audience without addressing any of the other characters on stage. Choose a topic from the list below. Circle your topic and then write a soliloquy on it.

Honesty
Trust
Racial equality
The Internet
The role of media
Lying
People and their pets
You should just forget your past
Immigrants
Being happy: It's a duty

4

RISE 'N' WRITE:
WRITING IN THE MORNING

There are two times of the day when my writing seems fresher or flows best: first thing when I wake up and last thing before I go to sleep. But note that I say, "flows best," which, for me, means those creative, let-it-all-out fresh drafts or new material. Equally, there are lots of other times during the day when I can fit in other parts of the writing process, such as reading previous drafts or making edits or scribbling down ideas, making to-do lists or playing around with names for a fictional character or town. All of these processes and time slots matter. Part of being a day-job writer means grabbing time when you have it and making the best use of it, whether it's sitting in the airport waiting for your flight or on your job's lunch break.

But for this part of the book, let's talk about those free-flow morning writing stints.

Creative writing draws on the same subconscious side of our brains as our night dreams. So it's a smart idea to capitalize on these just-awake or almost-asleep versions of yourself. It's also smart (at least for my process) to do this new, fresh-draft stuff before the rest of the day and its duties start crowding in.

I've never been an early riser, so my version of "first thing" may be different from yours. But I find it's much easier to write while I'm still in that fuzzy, just-wakening-up state or when I'm winding down from my day.

If you work the regular, nine-to-five day shift, "first thing" will be in the morning. If you work the swing or night shift, your just-awake or just-before-bed hours will be different.

Ever meet an acquaintance and just blank out on his or her name? As you smile and shake hands, the possibilities ratchet through your head: John? Joe? Jeremiah? You smile and fake it, hoping like heck that nobody else comes along so you don't have to make third-person introductions. Then, eight hours later … bingo! You're wide-awake at 3 A.M. and there's his name—suddenly right there in your head. James. Yes, *James.* Now, why couldn't you have thought of that during daylight hours?

Psychologists tell us that there's a good reason for this 3 A.M. hyper-intelligence. By letting the subconscious brain take over, we suddenly recall facts. We even come up with brilliant and creative life solutions that stumped our awake, conscious minds.

This phenomenon really comes into play for writers. I've woken up in the dark with a plot solution—an issue I've been wrangling with for days—just right there, clear as day. Or I've woken up in the morning with the certain knowledge that my current piece of writing should start three scenes in—not where it starts now. I've also woken up to that allusive first opening line of an essay or story.

Now, wouldn't it be a shame to just lose these dreamy, creative moments?

Whether it's for morning or evening writing, try to harness these lightbulb moments. It can be as simple as making sure you keep lots of bedside pens and notebooks to jot down nocturnal or morning inspirations—even if it has to be in the dark. Sure, it will disqualify your bedroom for a *Better Homes and Gardens Magazine* spread, but it's better than risking losing all those bright, wonderful ideas.

10 TIPS FOR MORNING WRITING

(1) Become a morning grouch: Avoid morning conversations with your spouse, partner, kids, or roommates. "Is there any milk for cereal?' They ask. "Wow! Have you seen this headline today?" "Have you seen my car keys?" All of these will distract you from your creative, dream-writer state. Unless there's been a nighttime emergency, these morning questions and their answers can wait. In the previous chapter of this section, I encouraged you to share your writing goals with your family, roommates, or friends. If you're going to set up a regular morning writing routine, you need to get the other people in your life onboard with your morning plans. For example, if your spouse is going to do breakfast duty with the kids while you sit upstairs or hike off to a café to write, she will need to know how many days per week, how long her breakfast-relief shift will last, and just how "undisturbed" you need to be. By sharing your goals and coming up with a shared set of agreed expectations, your morning writing session will be more peaceful, guiltfree. It will also have a distinct time-slot for you, which can be really motivating for you as a writer.

(2) Get up an hour earlier: During her son's teenage years, a single mother I know (she's not a writer) tells me that she used to get up at 5:00 A.M. every morning, simply to have some silent alone time for herself. As a writer, sharing your life and household with a family, spouse, partner, or roommate can be wonderfully supportive and rewarding. It can also have its moments of … ahem … challenges. You may feel like your inner writing voice and your creative time gets just crowded out. Get up an hour before everyone else. This has the dual advantage of buying you extra writing time and giving you that sense of solitude and time that's exclusively, creatively yours. Memphis-based author, Mark Greaney (www .markgreaneybooks.com), has published a successful international thriller series (*The Gray Man, On Target, Ballistic*). For his first two books, he was still working full-time in the international custom relations department of a multinational medical device company. Greaney wrote before work in the mornings. "Almost all of my writing was done between 5:30 A.M. and 7:30 A.M. I still find that the earlier I get up and start, the more productive my day is. I can't explain it, but four hours writing that starts at 6 A.M. is better than four hours that starts at 10 A.M." (see Greaney's full interview on page 217).

(3) Java! Install an electric kettle next to your writing desk. Or bring up a Thermos of coffee or tea the night before (I use an electric kettle). Trust me, that trip downstairs to the kitchen and the family coffeemaker can take you right out of your writer's dream state or sidetrack you from your morning writing plans altogether.

(4) Use your shower time well: Who cares if your hair is messy or your armpits smell? Shower later or, better yet, shower the night before to buy yourself some extra time in the morning. If you must shower first thing, train yourself to use your shower as creative thinking time, in which you gear up for that morning's writing session. Visit your writing, ask yourself, "Now, where did I leave off?" Project yourself into the scene you were working on last night or yesterday morning. Brainstorm about what you might do next with your draft. Where does your piece need to go next? Then, when you dry off and dress up, you'll already be in full writer mode.

(5) No news really *is* good news: For now, let the local traffic and weather reports wait. Your commute may depend on them, but for now, these have little or nothing to do with your writing life. Resist the urge to log on and read your local or national news feeds or weather reports.

(6) Tune in after the commercial break: A fan of morning T.V. news shows? Now *there's* a certain distracter! Nowadays there's lots of research on the negative brain effects of T.V.-watching on adults and children (see the section on writing in the evening). But as well as dulling our minds, T.V. news delivers those grim and scary headlines. Also, the morning news programs are segmented (that's why they call them news segments) in a way to keep us tuned in and hanging around for more. "This up, after the hour!" Announces the smiley presenter. As a day-job writer, this is your cue to switch it off and go write. Or better yet, write before you hit that "On" button or get your news later in the day.

(7) **Repeat after me:** No early-morning or late night teleconferences with colleagues, bosses, or virtual work teams. The downside of our hyperconnected workplaces is the fact that we're always available, across the time zones and continents. Schedule teleconferences from your home or executive hotel room for late morning or early afternoon or just after dinner—if you must. Or schedule them for a morning when you're unlikely to get to your writing anyway—for example, the morning you will be traveling from your hotel back to the airport.

(8) **Writing in hotel rooms:** I love to write in a hotel room—perhaps because the major hotel chains provide a well-equipped executive desk right there, right between your bed and the en suite bathroom. I also love the rooms' hushed anonymity. Traveling for work or bringing your writing along on vacation? Use this überprivate space well. The night before, make sure to hang out your "Do Not Disturb sign," order breakfast room service, and request a later checkout time. Or avail of that freebie in-room coffee service before you venture out to the T.V.-noisy hotel dining room.

(9) **Homework is for grown-ups:** Before you turn out the lights the night before, jot down some bedside notes, make some lists or pose yourself some bedtime questions. These will serve as sleepy-time homework. When your alarm goes off, you will already know what you're going to work on.

(10) **Keep a well-stocked nightstand:** In her author interview in *January Magazine* (www.januarymagazine.com), bestselling author Luanne Rice says, "I'm so involved that a lot of times I wake up at night and instead of going to my desk I'll just keep a notepad next to the bed."

Sometimes capturing or losing that morning inspiration can be as simple as keeping a good stock of pens, notebooks, or a recording device next to your bed. In one of my creative writing classes, a student of mine told me how, when she wakes up before daybreak, she reaches for her notebook without turning on the light. "If I turn on the bedside light, I just disturb it all. I forget what I woke up thinking." My student pointed out another advantage of writing in the dark: "If I turn on the light, I start wondering if what I'm writing makes sense. By writing in the dark, I just get the words down." A stock of pens, notebooks, a penlight, your reading glasses. Make sure you've got the right equipment at hand.

WRITING EXERCISES TO START YOUR DAY

Exercise 1:

Step 1: Don't wait for the alarm to ring all the way out. Instead, switch it off and reach for your bedside notebook, and record a snippet or image from the dream you were just having. Insert the date of your dream. Don't exaggerate or editorialize or theorize or interpret. Just write down the image or scene while it's fresh in your mind (even going to the bathroom can make you forget your dream scene).

Step 2: Practice writing down your dreams for an entire week, seven mornings.

Step 3: Set yourself a reminder in your planner or cell phone. Set a date with yourself for a day that's *exactly two weeks* from the date of this last writing entry. So if your seventh dream entry is July 2, set your calendar reminder for July 16.

Step 4: When July 16 arrives, reread your old dream writings.

Step 5: Choose your favorite image or scene. Plop it into a new setting or piece of writing. Don't write about you, your dream, and why you dreamed this. Just use the image and its colors, feelings, smells, or conversations to write a new scene. Trust the writing to take you to a new, unexpected place.

Exercise 2:

Finish this sentence. Write lots of other sentences. Let the writing take you wherever it wants to go.

Today, I want to write about ...

Exercise 3:

Part A: Select a daily routine activity (brushing your teeth, making coffee, making lunch for your kids). Now, in third person (he, she), plot your routine activity, step by step, as if you were describing this activity for a space alien who has never witnessed it before and who cannot otherwise know what us silly humanoids do with our limbs, our smiles, our expressions or our household gadgets.

Here's how I might write my morning toothbrushing routine:

> First, she walks across the beige carpet landing to the bathroom sink. The cat, Harry, weaves between her legs, heading hopefully toward the stairs and his food. When he sees that she's actually headed toward the bathroom, he follows her there.
>
> "Ugh," she thinks, glancing at herself in the mirror above the sink. "Morning hair." Above and behind her own reflected image is the bathroom clock on the opposite wall. Eight-thirty. She's late. Again. From the white porcelain jar she picks out the red Oral B toothbrush.

Part B: Later today, or first thing tomorrow, go back and read your morning routine piece. Circle the words that could be strengthened or made more vivid. In my example above, we might replace "she walks across the beige carpet landing" with "she pads." Or let's replace "she picks out" with "she chooses" or "she selects." We're aiming for the most accurate language in which to convey our morning routine to that imaginary space alien. However, while we do want precision, accuracy and vividness, avoid pretentious language ("She *culls* the red Oral B toothbrush?" Noooo!).

Exercise 4:

What is the best thing that could happen to you today? What is the best news you could receive? Imagine that moment when the telephone rings or your e-mail pings with this fantastic news. Now write that live-action scene. For a tutorial on writing lively scenes, see Tutorial 1 on page 13.

Exercise 5:

Choose one of these topics and write about it:

Why I hate (or love) eggs

What I'd change about my past (this one may take several mornings)

The person I love most

When I woke up this morning, my first thought was ...

When I stood in the shower this morning, I was thinking about ...

5

JOURNAL WRITING

Usually, after the initial classroom introductions, I give my writing workshop students a short, easy exercise to get things started and to give us some shared discussion points. After this timed assignment, I encourage students to share these short works with the group. As my students read their pieces aloud, I can nearly always tell who keeps a journal.

"Do you keep a journal?" I ask. This writer often looks at me skeptically. I'm either very nosy or very clairvoyant.

"Well, yes, I do."

At least 90 percent of the time—even when our writing exercise is not based on reflective journal-type writing—I'm right. I've sniffed out another journal writer. Even in a class of fifteen or eighteen people, I can spot one. I can hear it in his or her writing.

This is based on experiential and anecdotal experience only, but there are some common traits among those journal writers. First, even though some will declare and swear that they're beginner writers, their work never sounds or reads that way. Instead, there's a practiced fluidity to it that reveals a familiarity with language and the written word. Second, even in this first get-to-know-you piece, the writing has an unapologetic boldness about it that tells me that this is someone who has already built up his or her writing muscle via regular journal entries. And finally—even when I've assigned something very innocuous or whimsical—the journal writers in my workshops write with an immediacy that can only come with having spent lots of time being up close and personal with the words, and with their own inner selves as they have confronted themselves in the blank pages of a journal.

This is also true when I teach teen writing workshops or presentations—regardless of the school district or the quality or standards or the price of my young students' formal schooling or language arts or English programs.

Sure, well-taught kids from good language arts programs may have a more grandiose vocabulary and the confidence to strut it out on the page, but across the school districts and standards, the young journal writer is always, *always* the stronger writer. Again, it's about practice, familiarity, and courage. Words don't scare these kids. Neither does the blank page. Sitting with an online journaling program or propped up in bed with a notebook or laptop, these kids have an up-close-and-personal relationship with writing. So parents, if you *really* want your kids to be writers, to achieve a mastery over language, plunk down $1.99 for a composition notebook or point them to a free online journaling program like Penzu (listed on page 60). Oh, and make sure they get as many opportunities as possible to hang out with other teen writers. This last part is important—very important.

OK, confession time: I shouldn't write "those journal writers." And I shouldn't write in the third person. I've kept a journal all my life. Quite frankly, I don't know how my life or this adult version of me would have proceeded or evolved without this practice of journal writing.

So you won't get an unbiased answer from me. I strongly advocate for daily journaling as a way to build your daily writing practice and your writing voice. Just as important, I also believe in journaling as a route to discovering *what* and *why* you want to write (See Section 1, "Getting Started.").

As our twenty-first century lives get busier and louder, as our employers and families seem to demand more from us, a pen-and-paper or online journal practice is a great way to check in with yourself, to explore and keep in touch with your quiet inner self. Call it the written version of yoga practice.

REAL MEN (AND REAL WRITERS) CAN KEEP A JOURNAL, TOO

Not into all that personal navel-gazing? Or do you associate journal writing with those little diaries from your teenage years? You know the ones where you wrote your teenage secrets and narrated the adventures of your school day?

For writers, a journal-writing practice is much more than just a written record of their day and its events. In fact, many published authors use their journals as a kind of sandbox in which to play with ideas, explore different plot possibilities, discover what the story is about, or explore their own or their characters' voices. For example, in the book, *Writers and Dreaming: Twenty-six Writers Talk about Their Dreams and the Creative Process* by Naomi Epel, Sue Grafton describes how keeping a journal supports her more formal writing:

"As I write I keep a journal for each novel that I work in. And many journal entries begin: 'R.B. (right brain) told me in the dead of night …' That's much the way I get the story twists, plot connection, strange layering of characters."

In fact, Grafton reports that her journals run four times the length of the actual novel that she completes.

Grafton also uses her journal in the more traditional way—as a diary or a way to document her daily emotional state. She believes this is important because her own life, her own feelings will "come into the writing itself whether I intend for it or not."

Five years ago, when I wrote an article on journal writing for a New England–based arts magazine, I interviewed some authors on how they use their journals.

New Hampshire–based fiction (*Before*) and memoir (*Fields of Light*) author Joseph Hurka (www.josephhurka.com) describes how he uses a journal to create early versions of his published works. He sees those initial journal pages as freewriting, as a chance to get to know his fictional characters and situations. His journal is a place where he can give them free rein to be themselves. Says Hurka: "To me, the greatest danger for a writer is to censor this early creativity. Insisting on an agenda makes certain that art will meet its death."

Alaska-based short-story writer (*Copy Cats, The Man Back There*) David Crouse (www.davidcrousehouse.com), uses a different journaling approach. His journal entries *follow* the first draft to become an informal and quite messy *second* draft. Crouse also believes that a writer uses a journal entry to tease out the story. He often leaves aside the work to scribble in his journal because this is what moves a story forward, gets a writer unstuck. Crouse says: "I don't like to be too formal about it because for me the disorganization is precisely the point. I've always felt that journaling is about creative chaos."

Massachusetts-based poet (*Spin Moves, The Last Miles*) and creative nonfiction author (*Themes For English B: A Professor's Education In and Out of Class*), J.D. Scrimgeour writes in his journal in the evenings, lying in bed, when he likes to recall "the interesting details or curious stories from the day."

Scrimgeour is careful to make the distinction between writing *to* himself, not *for* himself. Far from being a set of throwaway writing, this author sees his journal entries as having a longer shelf life:

"Writing *for* oneself is therapeutic; if one is enraged at one's lover, one writes to get it off one's chest. By contrast, writing *to* oneself implies a split self between author and reader. Later, as a reader, we want to be entertained and surprised. Later still, these journal entries sometimes become the source of finished works, serving as a kind of unconscious first draft, a first attempt to render an experience in language."

"CLEAR YOUR THROAT BEFORE YOU CAN SING:" WRITERS, START YOUR JOURNALS!

Prewriting: I once had a writing professor who, like Joseph Hurka, was a great advocate of those early, unedited drafts. "You have to clear your throat before you can sing," she told us students. This smart professor was also a great advocate of keeping a journal as a companion to our more formal college papers. An online or paper journal is a nonthreatening way in which to sketch that first draft of a story, essay, or novel. In those blank pages, you can doodle and wonder aloud and draw some diagrams or write character bios or pose yourself some questions about where your piece might go and what it might have to tell you, the writer.

Meet and greet your characters: I often use my journal as a way of exploring who my character is—what was her childhood like? What's in her refrigerator? Her closet? What's her favorite food? What's her greatest fear? Her deepest desire? If she were to write a letter to her nemesis or the secondary character, what would that letter say? A journal allows me the kind of unfettered creativity to do this. In my journal, I don't have to be the know-it-all author. I just have to keep scribbling my way toward a deeper knowledge of my story and who's in it.

Record faces and places: Many bookstores stock travel journals. Many globe trekkers keep their family and friends up to date and share their travel adventures via an online blog. For a writer, the travel journal has an added bonus: You can record sounds, memories, smells, faces, voices from your travels—from that exotic trip to southern Italy, to your Saturday jaunt to the local farmers' market. A travel journal has the added bonus of letting you record your own reactions to all these sights and sounds. Later, if you choose to write about your travels—either as a nonfiction memoir or as a setting for a fictional piece—you will need these live-action details and observations.

On her travels, Pat Lowery Collins (www.patlowerycollins.com) (*Hidden Voices, Signs and Wonders, The Fattening Hut*), uses her travel journal to pin down the details, to record the settings, to make notes about period dress and historical facts. For example, when she was working on the YA novel, *The Fattening Hut,* Lowery Collins traveled to Antigua to learn about the birds, flora and fauna, the history of its indigenous tribes. Later, while she was writing *Hidden Voices*, a YA novel set in early 1700s Venice, she brought her journal along on her trip to Italy. Lowery Collins says: "I've kept a journal just to keep track of things and to separate one experience from another, and one church from the next."

Write your way back to you: From your employee ID number to your log-in codes to your quarterly reports or spreadsheets, many jobs are about subsuming the personal or the inner self in service of the corporate or general good. By contrast, journal writing is all about discovering and documenting your individual take on the world. Even amidst deadlines and projects and public presentations, use your journal entries to write your way back to that deeper sense of yourself.

Make journaling your transition between work and home: On any given work day, it's tough to transition from the worker bee you to the creative you. A half hour or two pages of journal writing can bring you back to yourself and your private, personal world. It can help you leave the workplace behind.

The ultimate honesty check: Like short-story author David Crouse, I often use my journal to step out of my current writing draft, to take time out to find out what I'm actually writing about. Sometimes I do this because I'm stuck in that story. So I need to spend some more playful discovery time with a character. But most of all, I use my journal to force myself to be honest. "What's this really about?" I ask myself on that journal page. "Why am I writing this?"

This honesty check is particularly necessary when I'm working on a nonfiction essay. Ask any essayist or memoirist out there: Writing about a personal experience is a dizzying and wonderful waltz between relating a real event (this is what happened to me) and crafting an engaging, reader-accessible story. (This is why you should care about what happened to me.) While leading this personal-public dance, I find it easy to get so focused on the words and the story structure and the (real or imagined) brilliance of my own work that, I need to take time out and force myself back to basics. I need to shut off the computer, step off the vanity train, and go sit in a quiet room or inside a café with my writing journal. In those blank pages, I pose myself the tough questions: "What's this really about?" "What are you holding out on?" "Is there a deeper significance here?" "How could this be better?"

A tool for wellness and stress release: Last winter, I had an adult writing student who was struggling with two concurrent medical issues, requir-

ing multiple trips to two different sets of specialists and hospitals. Both conditions required her to take a very complicated cocktail of medications, some of which were experimental. Long before she came to my class, this feisty woman had begun keeping a journal as a way to track and record her doctor visits, to write down who said what, and that week's recommended medication regime. Between doctor visits, she had used her journal to document and track her daily symptoms, her mood, the medications' possible side effects and interactions. She wrote about good days and bad days. Then, when it was time for the next doctor visit, she presented her doctors with her own daily experiences—her own personal experiences with these medical treatments and medications. It gave her a wonderful sense of control. And this sense of control reduced her stress, which made her feel less like a victim of illness. Soon, her daily journal writing transitioned to the really personal, as a route to writing about the very scary experience of being ill. And she also wrote about her vision of getting better, when she would be fully restored to her beloved family and hobbies and artwork.

You may or may not be struggling with a major medical or emotional issue. But I'm going to bet that you've had days in your job and in your life and in your family life that are downright stressful, sad, or maddening. You've had family, childhood, or workplace experiences that keep you tossing and turning through the night.

In her 2007 *Newsweek* magazine essay, "Write for your Life" best-selling author Anna Quindlen commented on the movie, *Freedom Writers*, which Quindlen describes as being about "the power of writing in the lives of ordinary people."

In *Freedom Writers*, a young, wide-eyed teacher turns an inner city, at-risk classroom experience around by handing her students some marble-covered composition notebooks. In those notebooks, she told her students to write the unabridged version of their lives.

In her *Newsweek* essay on the power of writing, Quindlen writes:

> Ms. G, as the kids called her, embraced a concept that has been lost in modern life: Writing can make pain tolerable, confusion clearer, and the self stronger.

Well, now, I couldn't have said that better myself.

NEVER KEPT A WRITING JOURNAL?
HERE ARE FIVE STEPS TO GET STARTED

1. Writer, know thyself! Are you more comfortable writing on a keyboard or handheld device than using a paper and pen? Or does an online journal remind you too much of workplace writing? Try both styles of journal (electronic and paper) to see what feels more comfortable and natural for you. Which makes you happier? If a big, blank page is scary, buy one of those tiny, 3" × 5" dime-store notebooks. Just fill that first tiny page and see what happens. Equally, if opening up your word processing program to a blank screen seems daunting, consider a personal blog. This format may be less threatening for you. The bottom line? Find your own comfort zone. The journal has to be about you.

2. Write what you feel: What's bugging you today? What's making you happy? Write these words at the top of the page. "Today I feel … " Don't censure yourself. Shut off that chastising voice that tells you to "snap out of it" or "get over it." Just describe how you feel. Now.

3. Pretend you're writing for a blind person: Stumped for something to write about? Just write down the sounds, smells, the atmosphere of the room you're writing in. Write them as if you're describing them to a blind person who really, really wants to know. Describe the sunshine through the window. Describe the color of the floor tiles. For the first week of your journal-writing practice, assign yourself one discrete writing task. This will keep you writing *and* develop your author's eye for detail.

4. Make lists: If you've abandoned writing since school or college, don't start with a "here is my life" composition assignment. Just start with some simple lists. I have included some examples in the writing exercises on pages 61 and 62.

5. Let yourself go: Once you get writing, don't stop to check your spelling, your grammar, or how clever you sound. Just write.

QUESTIONS AND ANSWERS ON PERSONAL OR JOURNAL WRITING

Q *What kind of journal should I buy?*

A There are many, many choices—both online and on your bookstore shelves. In addition to blank journals, there are specialized journals which provide writing prompts for you, such as travel and dream journals. But you know a dime-store notebook is also fine. It's important to get a journal that works for you and that fits your personality.

Q *What about those wellness journals with specialized writing prompts?*

A There are journals which address specific life and wellness issues, such as eating disorders, cancer recovery, depression, addiction recovery, unemployment, parenting, or elder care. If you're considering a topic-specific journal like one of those, I advise you to check the source of the author of those writing prompts. Have the writing prompts been written by someone with clinical expertise in these areas? Also, many national or nonprofit recovery and wellness organizations have a small publishing imprint. These journals are more likely to have been thoroughly researched and written by someone with clinical certification in this specific area of health care or wellness.

Q *I type so much for work that I've lost the art of handwriting. What about online journals?*

A If you're more comfortable writing on a keyboard or portable device, online journals may be an option for you. They're also a great option for those busy people who travel or are on the road. See the list of online journals on page 60.

Q *Won't someone read my secrets and deepest thoughts?*

A You will not write if you fear prying eyes. Keep your hard-copy journal in a safe, secure place. If you choose an online journal, most tend to be password secure. It's a good idea to sign up for the trial version first—and to double-check that security or encryption. If you want to double-check, sign into one online journal site and write one innocuous entry. Then log out and use a reliable search engine (Google, Yahoo, Bing) for some words from that entry. Your name or this topic should not come up in the search.

Isn't this just navel-gazing—not writing?

A I plan my first drafts in my journal. When I'm writing a personal essay, I ask myself tough questions about what my in-draft essay is really about. Sometimes, one of my fictional characters takes over and starts to write in her own voice. In your journal you can write about yourself—or not. Your journal can be written in a formal or informal, conversational tone. Even in this highly personalized writing medium, it's good to practice that art of creating an *I* voice, a sense of yourself and your narrative voice. Write your opinions, your plans, your to-do lists. Oh, and don't forget to check in with that bucket list.

Q *Yeah, but how can my journal writing transition into publishable work?*

A Journal writing is mainly a very personal, introspective practice. Also, because there are no rules, because journals often free us from our left-brain, editing self, they're a great place for that freeflowing first draft. Certainly, this draft can then be redrafted for a more formal, cleaner version of your piece.

Q *How do I turn my journal entries into personal or memoir essays?*

A If you read back through your journal entries, you will notice recurring themes. These are the themes that are uniquely you. And these are the themes that you should be writing about. Write a list of these themes. Or, if you use blogging software or online journals (see the list below), you can tag and track those themes.

ONLINE JOURNALS

The Journal (www.davidrm.com/thejournal) ($49.95) downloadable software for any kind of writing, including dream writing. It also allows you to add images and a search feature. Free, forty-five-day trial available at the website.

Life Journal for Writers, (http://writers.lifejournal.com) ($49.95). Free downloadable demo. Includes general writers or specialized, topic-specific editions.

> **Penzu.** (http://penzu.com/content). "Best Free Software of 2009" (PC Magazine) You can try this one free before signing up. It's also the closest simulation of pen-and-paper writing. When you sign up for the fee-based Penzu Pro version ($19), they promise you the same level of security and encryption as the U.S. government. I love this product because it lets you customize, tag, organize, search, and group your writing entries by topic. You can set a reminder frequency in which the program will remind you that it's time to write. Best of all, the fee for Penzu Pro is donated to nonprofits which support literacy.

ONE WEEK TO THE JOURNALING HABIT: SEVEN JOURNALING EXERCISES

Monday:

Write down your three happiest memories from childhood. Don't think about this, just list them. Now, write at random on what you associate with each memory. Where were you? Was this a single occurrence or something that happened every year? Every month? Who else was there? What kind of weather did you have? What house did you live in back then? What made each memory so happy?

Tuesday:

Go back to yesterday's entry. Of the three you listed yesterday, what is your happiest memory? Write about it until you can't write anymore. Just capture that happy moment.

Wednesday:

I am God (or the Universal power). I can wave a magic wand and eliminate three things from this world. Poof! Just like that. What are my three things? List your three things or creatures. Feel free to write about your selections and why you feel the world would be better off without them.

Thursday:

Finish this line. Write for as long as you can. *"I really hate it when people … "*

Friday:

> If they ever made a movie about my life, I would make sure that they named the movie
>
>
> I want it named this, because

Saturday:

Did someone ever talk you out of doing something? Did someone tell you that you didn't have the money, the talent, or the right background to pursue something? Or that your idea didn't make sense? Write about how you feel about that decision now. Was that person right? Wrong?

Sunday:

Read yesterday's journal entry. Now write a letter to that person who talked you out of an idea or a life change you wanted or proposed. In your letter, will you thank that person? Or let him know how wrong he was? How you regret following his advice? Or will the letter tell him that you went ahead and did it anyway—with what results?

6

WRITING AT THE END
OF YOUR DAY

Writing before bedtime works in basically the same way as writing first thing in the morning. Only now, your workday is over. You're winding down, and the creative, dreamy part of you is ready to write and create. Switch off your TV, your iPad, your Blackberry, and all other devices that connect you to the workaday world. Your partner or roommate or your kids are tucked up asleep. So now it's time for you.

Nighttime writing has two advantages: (a) The day's work, worries, and deadlines are done, so your mind is free to scribble, journal, or pen that next chapter of your book. (b) Bedtime writing can function like nighttime yoga, reading, or meditation. Although you're staying up later, this quiet, contemplative, or creative time can ultimately give you a deeper, more restful night's sleep.

TIPS FOR WRITING AFTER SUNDOWN

1. **Develop a ritual:** Develop a personalized ritual or signal that says, "Time to write." Ten minutes of yoga works great for me. Or get into your pj's and fuzzy slippers and make yourself a cup of hot chocolate.

2. **Set a place:** Devote a place for your nighttime writing session. Simply snuggling up on the couch with the living room lights turned low can jump-start the imagination and unleash your writing voice.

3. **Journal for ten minutes:** Pick up or log into your personal journal and indulge in a nighttime "brain spill" to put that busy, deadline-packed day behind you.

4. **Only write:** No multitasking. We're often tempted to get that last project done before the end of the day. If you're journaling or writing on your computer, close out other computer programs

or windows. No checking e-mail. Finish that load of laundry before you sit down to write.

5. **Make some morning to-write lists:** Eyes drooping shut? Prefer to only write in the mornings? Before you turn out the lights, take five minutes to scribble some lists for tomorrow's writing session. Pose yourself some questions. Set yourself some nocturnal dream homework. When you wake up tomorrow, you'll be ready to just get writing.

TOP TEN CHALLENGES TO WRITING IN THE EVENING— AND HOW YOU CAN OVERCOME THEM

1. **"I'm exhausted!"** Between carpooling, commuting, work, and errands, we seem busier and more stressed than we were ten years ago. If you're too exhausted to pen the next chapter of your novel or memoir, create a more realistic writing plan. Just write one small page, propped against your pillows and just before you go to sleep. Write until your eyes droop shut.

2. **My partner/spouse/family watches TV:** Find a quiet room away from the main family area. Or go to bed before everybody else and bring a small laptop or bedside notebook with you. Or leave the TV on and turn it to mute or put on some headphones. Watch the characters on the TV screen. What are they saying? Write the dialogue.

3. **Once I get home, that's family time:** Stop for a half hour on the way home from work. Find a regular haunt such as a public library or a café. Buy yourself a nice relaxing beverage, observe the world around you. Write a few pages. Write in your journal to put the workday behind you. When you get home, your family will like this calmer, less stressed you.

4. **I just want to kick back and relax:** If your workday is extra busy or stressful, keep the lighter, happier writing chores for nighttime (see the exercises on pages 61 and 62), when you need some escape or comic relief. Use writing as a way to kick back and relax.

5. **I get home late and I'm starving:** Call me antisocial or a woman with poor table manners, but I love to read while I'm eating. I also love to munch away on a plate of food or a bowl of cereal while scribbling

in my journal or editing a draft. Eating and writing can make great companions. Especially if you live alone, your dinnertime may provide the ideal, built-in writing time when you've changed out of your work clothes and your day is over. Or, if you live with someone, can you sacrifice some other luxury to afford an evening meal out so that you can get some writing done?

6. **I have middle-of-the-night insomnia, so I need to get to bed early so I can patch together a full eight hours:** Most sleep experts will advise you not to lie there tossing and turning and fretting. Instead, you can get yourself back to sleep if you get up, go to another room, or switch on your night-light and read. Or … you could switch on your night-light and write.

7. **My company has offices or centers in three time zones, so my Black-berry goes off all night long.** Unless answering after-hours calls is specifically in your job description (if you're customer or help-desk support), turn it off. If someone really needs you, most organizations have their employees' emergency or home numbers.

8. **But this is my time with my kids!** Wait until they're gone to bed, then make yourself some herbal tea, and write until it's your own bedtime. Or encourage your kids to voyage beyond their school assignments to become writers, too. By turning your teens or children into effortless young writers, you will also be preparing them for a life of words and thought and story. There's no reason why creative writing can't become a shared family experience (see page 67).

9. **Between volunteer work and errands and social appointments, my evenings are busier than my days!** Nobody wants to become a hermit (or maybe you do!). But becoming a writer means giving up other things in your life. There is not a way around this. If you're the type of person who's always signing up for community chores, make a list of what you really can and cannot do. Then, practice saying "no."

10. **I don't feel very clever or sharp at night:** Who said anything about being clever or sharp? You've got lots of time tomorrow in which you can revisit your writing or get clever or clean up your draft. Or use those evening writing sessions to just doodle and wonder aloud on the page or to pose yourself questions about a piece you're working on.

NIGHTTIME WRITING EXERCISES

Exercise 1:

Did someone tick you off today? Was it that jerk who cut you off on the highway? Was it that colleague who didn't do what he promised to do? Write him a one-page letter. Keep it to *one page only*. Say what you have to say. Don't hold back. Now take the page, print it, scrunch it up, and put your letter in your freezer, with the rest of those hard, cold, freezer-burned items. You've put your anger in cold storage. Now let's switch to happier writing.

Exercise 2:

Tough day today? Even if today was one you'd rather forget, force yourself to remember and write about the positives.

Write down three things in your life for which you're grateful:
1.
2.
3.

Now expand on one of these. Write five hundred words on something or someone for which or whom you are sincerely thankful. Why? How did you arrive at this point? If you hadn't arrived at this point or met this person, what else might have happened in your life?

Exercise 3:

Here's the best thing that happened to me today:

Exercise 4:

If they ever made a sitcom of your life, what scene would absolutely have to be in there? Write that scene.

Exercise 5:

Tomorrow: What small change can you make that would make tomorrow simpler? Happier? Help you to write more? Write down that small change here.

FUN ASSIGNMENTS FOR THE ADULT AND YOUNG MEMBERS OF YOUR HOUSEHOLD

Exercise 1:

Finish this thought:

"Tonight, if my bed were a magic carpet, I would travel to ..." Write five hundred words. Describe your fantasy escape or vacation.

Exercise 2:

I was just out for my usual evening walk (out playing with my friends) when suddenly, the street outside my house started slanting upward. The street got steeper and steeper, and I kept climbing and climbing, until I was halfway up in the sky, still walking upward. I stopped to look back down at our house. Whoa! Someone had taken the roof off! From up here, our house/apartment looked all different. Our family looked different. This is what I saw in our home ...

Exercise 3:

The sound I hate the most ...
The smell I hate the most ...
The smell that makes me happy ...
My favorite color ...

Exercise 4:

It was just a normal _____ (your family name) vacation. As usual, we had packed up our bags and tents and Dad/Mom drove us into the Amazon jungle for our usual Amazon camping trip. But this summer was different—*way* different. For a start, we forgot to pack the _____. Then our vacation went *really* wrong when _____.

7

WRITERS AND DREAMING

Do you dream about your workplace? Do you have those dreams in which you tell your boss off? Or you solve that problem that your work team has been grappling with for weeks? Or how about that anxiety dream in which you walk into work totally naked because somehow you forgot to get dressed that morning? Or you've left that all-important presentation on the morning train?

Now, what if you could turn this dreaming power to your writing advantage? What if you put in some nocturnal writing overtime?

Don't summon the whacko police, but I like to think of sleeping and dreaming as my bonus writing time. I've dreamed up entire plots. I've written and published a short story which was based on one of those vivid, Technicolor dreams. I woke up so sad and shaken by one dream that I wrote and published a personal essay on this incident from my past.

I'm not alone. Throughout history, many published authors have derived inspiration, ideas, and plot scenes from their dreams.

For a book on writers and how they mine their dreams for inspiration, check out Naomi Epel's book, *Writers Dreaming: Twenty-six Writers Talk about their Dreams and the Creative Process* (Vintage, 1994). In the book, Epel, a writer, dream researcher, radio host, and literary escort, interviews authors such as Stephen King, Maya Angelou, William Styron, and Sue Grafton about their dreams and the roles they play in a writer's work.

In the book, Epel describes how, in 1974, William Styron woke up from a dream of a woman with an armful of books and the blue numbers of a tattoo on her wrist. From the dream, Styron went directly to his writing studio and wrote the opening paragraphs of *Sophie's Choice*.

In 1975, Stephen King drew on a childhood nightmare for the creepy house that's featured in *Salem's Lot*.

Elmore Leonard confesses to having a repeating naked-in-public dream. And Leonard uses his nighttime subconscious creativity to great advantage: "From six P.M. on, I try not to think about my work. I don't want to. I want to let my unconscious or subconscious work on it."

In her interview on writing and dreaming, Anne Rivers Siddons says she doesn't believe it would be possible to write or create without drawing from dreams, and that our creative impulse comes from "that dark old country where dreams come from."

WHY LEAVE IT TO CHANCE?
HARNESSING THE WISDOM OF YOUR DREAMS

Robert Moss (www.mossdreams.com) best-selling novelist and pioneer of Active Dreaming, an original synthesis of shamanism and modern dream work, believes that creative dreaming is not a chance or random happenstance. Instead, he believeswe can develop the art of creative dreaming, and we can actively seek answers from our night dreams.

In his book, *Conscious Dreaming: A Spiritual Path for Everyday Life*, Moss dedicates an entire chapter to creative incubation of dreams. He writes: "You can incubate a dream to solve problems or provide creative inspiration in an intentional way …" In other words, as our working day winds down, we can nudge our dreaming selves or posit pressing questions, life puzzles, or problems for which our dreaming selves may produce solutions or wisdoms.

However, Moss assures us that it's important to remain open-ended and open to the answers to what our dream wisdom provides: "Your deeper self wants more for you than your ego agenda."

Anything sound familiar here? This process of letting go, of stepping aside to let our creative, subconscious minds take over, also describes the early-draft stages of the writing process.

Of course, this is the opposite to what the twenty-first century workplace and lifestyle demand of us. At work, we are required to produce, take charge, push buttons, and make things progress along a defined path to a defined solution or deadline.

But this does not work in writing.

Often if we try to force our writing to a preformulated or tidy ending or ego-driven resolution, the work will read as formulaic and forced.

Conscious Dreaming also includes a chapter on using dreams as writing inspiration:

> As a writer, I have always found dreams a principal source of creative energy and inspiration. On the most basic level, keeping a dream journal gets me started each day: I am writing

before it ever occurs to me to ask myself what I am going to write about. This brings into play the writing "muscles," which may later be applied to specific projects that are waiting.

BUT I DON'T DREAM. OR, IF I DO, I DON'T REMEMBER!

I've had colleagues and friends who tell me they simply don't dream. First, at the risk of delivering a science lecture here, the International Association for the Study of Dreams tells us that everyone dreams. Our most vivid dreams occur during a type of sleep called Rapid Eye Movement (REM) sleep. During REM sleep, the brain is very active, the eyes move back and forth rapidly under the lids, and the large muscles of the body are relaxed. REM sleep occurs every ninety to one hundred minutes, three to four times a night, and lasts longer as the night progresses. The final REM period may last as long as forty-five minutes. Less vivid dreams occur at other times during the night.

So it's not a matter of never dreaming. It's a matter of not remembering your dreams.

According to dream experts, we can nudge ourselves to remember our dreams.

TEN TIPS TO IMPROVE YOUR DREAM RECALL

1. Avoid alcohol which can often affect your REM sleep and dream recall.

2. Before you go to sleep, tell yourself to remember your dreams. Or write yourself a note and put it under your pillow.

3. When you wake up, try to lie still. Just remember.

4. When you wake up, don't start making plans for your working day. Just lie there and remember what you were just dreaming about before you woke.

5. Make sure you have set a notebook, a pen, or a recorder by your bed to record your dream.

6. Sometimes you remember a dream later in the day, when something reminds you of it. Stop to feel and recall the dream.

7. If you can't remember the drama or the details of the dream, write down how it made you feel.

8. Can't remember a complete dream? Write what was on your mind before you woke—even if it's just a fragment.

9. In the beginning, simply record your dreams without interpreting or trying to assign a deeper meaning.

10. Even if you don't remember the events in the dream, write down the images or the voices that come to you.

DREAM JOURNALS

Keeping a dream journal is an easy way to record your dreams and to transition into your daily writing—to build that writing muscle. But here's a case where technology doesn't often work. Getting up and switching on your laptop or computer means you risk losing the dream and its voices and images. So stick with a bedside pen and notebook.

> *Dreamer (and Writer) Beware!* Know where dream recording ends and writing begins. Yes, your dreams can provide a rich source of inspiration, ideas, plot solutions, characters, and a window into your creative and subconscious self. But don't kid yourself that the process of recording or interpreting dreams satisfies your daily writing quota. As Robert Moss points out, a dream journal may be a wonderful way to get your writing going, but then you have to *keep* going and *keep* writing.

PLUNDER YOUR DREAMS WISELY

Have you ever turned to your partner and related your dream, blow by blow? Yeah, it's interesting or funny at first, but then your partner's eyes start to glaze over.

This is why we shouldn't cut and paste dreams into a piece of fiction or creative nonfiction. A fully recycled dream narrative or plot—even a really juicy one—rarely makes for interesting reading.

Instead get into the habit of recording the most vivid or recurring images, settings, or feelings. The feelings are crucial. While the dream's images or events may be baffling or make no sense, how you *felt* in the dream can be a window into those internal fears or desires that will inspire your writing.

Nonfiction and fiction writers alike tell us to write about our greatest fears, to write into the eye of our own personal storms or our own passions. And there's no better window into these personal fears or passions than those recurring dreamscapes.

ONLINE DREAM JOURNALS

www.dreamjournal.net

www.abatons.org

www.dreamstop.com

www.whispy.com

Section 3

INTEGRATING WRITING INTO YOUR WORKDAY

Hopefully the last section helped you to look at your daily schedule to find a half hour or an hour in which you can write a little or a lot—every day.

But as someone who holds down a busy day job, I have to tell you that, despite my best plans and promises, there are days when I know I cannot and will not get to my writing desk. These are the days when my work schedule is simply packed tight with meetings or travel plans or teleconferences or project crises or deadlines. Or I'm trying to cram my dental or medical appointments into those early-morning time slots and just about make it to work on time.

But if there's one lesson that I've learned about the career-writing balance, it's to train myself to turn apparently fallow time into writing time. On those days when I absolutely cannot pen or type some words, I make myself mentally log out of other tasks or concerns and log into and revisit my writing in my mind. I pay my writing a daily visit. I say, "Hello?" and, "How are you?" to my writing. I turn my latest project over in my mind. I pose some questions, tease out some problems, and think up some new ideas.

You should do this, too. Every day. Even if you've just been summoned to the White House for a daytime summit. Or even if NASA has just called and they need you ASAP around that conference table. On the way there, *visit* your writing. This is a minimum requirement.

8

DRIVE TIME: THINKING OUT LOUD ON THE ROAD

Far from being wasted time, your daily car commute provides an uninterrupted time slot for this "visiting" process. Often, it's when we're not actually typing or writing that we can set our minds free to come up with solutions and ideas. When I was planning this book, I got most of my ideas while driving to and from work.

In his book on writing, *The Elements of Mystery Fiction: Writing a Modern Whodunit,* the late William Tapply, author of the Brady Coyne mystery series, described his planning process as "disciplined free association, at once random and purposeful."

Here's how William Tapply describes his writer's planning process:

> Planning your story requires more than the inspiration of a good idea. The creative process that precedes actual writing is unique to each writer ... If anyone watched me do it, they'd accuse me of daydreaming. I do it on long automobile trips. I tend to miss highway exits when I'm driving.

TURN YOUR DRIVING INTO WRITING TIME

The key word in Tapply's self-described process? *Disciplined.* As we say in Section 2, as a writer with a day job, accomplishing your writing goals requires some real discipline. So the minute you fasten that seatbelt and turn that key in the ignition, develop the habit of setting yourself some creative or imaginative assignments. Develop the habit of using your drive time well.

I've assigned myself a particular milestone along my morning commute—the part where I enter the three-lane highway that brings me to work. Once I pass that milestone, it's time to start the drive-write.

Before this, between my home and the highway, along those narrower roads and back roads through town, I allow myself to hear news headlines, to think about the workday ahead, to complete a mental inventory of what I have to do when I reach my workplace. But the minute I merge onto the southbound highway, this is my cue to shut off those other thoughts and switch to thinking about writing. It doesn't always work. By the next two exits, my mind has wandered. But I try to harness my thoughts and draw my concentration back to the draft I'm working on.

Here are some typical tasks I set myself while driving:

1. **Openings:** Does my piece really open where I think it does, where that rough draft opens (probably not). If not, where could it open? If I'm going to ditch the current opening scene, should it be saved and included elsewhere?

2. **Honesty checks:** I discussed this in the chapter on journal writing. When I take some time away from the work, when my mind is in this kind of disciplined freewriting, I often check back in with myself: "Is this really what you want to write about?" "Why?" "Could you take the piece up a notch?"

3. **Who is this character?** Currently, I'm working on two short pieces—a short story about a home-care nurse in Florida and a personal essay about my first summer as a new immigrant to the United States. For the short story, I am still wrestling with my main character the nurse. I don't know who she really is. In fact, she's rapidly emerging as a male nurse, which shifts this story dramatically. Why has (s)he chosen home-care nursing? Why Florida? What has brought him or her to this point? Why is (s)he having an illicit affair with his/her elderly patient's married son or daughter? Who is the son? When he comes to visit his ailing mother in her beachfront air-conditioned condo, where has this adult child flown in from? Most mornings, as I drive along the highway in New England, I'm watching the traffic in New England, but I'm really in a beachfront condo in Florida.

4. **Recalling scenes:** In completing the first draft of my essay about my first summer in the United States, I can retrace my geographical steps and look up the Chamber of Commerce website in a small New York town. This will help me to get the facts and the geography correct, and these are details that I don't want to leave to memory alone. But knowing and checking these details about a place I once lived in will not capture the essence of the place. And it will not evoke my memory of it, the sights, sounds, and smells. For these details, I must hit the

rewind and play buttons in my mind. I must let these memories run through my head. So as I drive along, I let myself remember.

5. **Finding the voice:** Driving is also a great time to let the voice of a story or piece of writing come. Writing depends on a strong voice—a narrative voice that's strong enough to engage the reader and to carry the story right through to the end. There is no library, no resource, no website in which to find your story's voice. It must come from within you, like a breath. Give it time and space, and let it come.

6. **Rearranging the plot:** Often, establishing the what-happened-next or the overall arc of your narrative is like a jigsaw. It's a matter of mentally moving your scenes around the imaginary page, playing musical chairs with them in your head. Or you have to make some honest and brutal decisions: to cut that piece of lyrical narrative you just wrote because, deep down, you know that it's gratuitous and it will stall the plot and lose your reader. As you commute to work, you can set yourself these kinds of jigsaw assignments.

7. **Find the closing lines:** Again, like the narrative voice, the line or lines that will conclude your piece of writing can come when you least expect them. You have to be ready. You have to clear that mental space and get your ego out of the way, and let that closing scene and language come seeping up from within you.

Give Yourself Mental Space for Drive-Time Writing

Do touch that dial

Are those morning news bulletins on the Dow Jones going to help your creative process? Can't they wait until later? Would unobtrusive background music work better? How about some rap music? A Strauss waltz? Pretty soon, you'll be sitting in a noisy office with ringing phones and chattering colleagues. So for now, how about turning off everything in your car to treat yourself to some creative, productive silence? Or play some familiar music or white noise that serve as a backdrop to this productive creativity.

Put your cell phone in the backseat

That's right. If your partner is calling to tell you the house is burning down, he or she will keep calling, and you will know to pull over to the side of the road for this news. But other than that, how important are those early-morning or after-work calls anyway? If you customarily use your driving time as an opportunity to get a jump-start on your day job, now is the time to let your boss know that until you walk through those office doors, you're out of range.

Record your drive-time genius

Just as those dream images or middle-of-the night inspirations can disappear in seconds, so can your ideas behind the wheel. To prevent this, I purchased a microcassette recorder, a 4" × 2" battery-operated recorder that fits in the front pocket of my briefcase. Now when I'm highway inspired, I reach for my little gadget and record live memos to myself. Yes, I feel like a doctor giving dictation as I whiz along. But when I play my ideas or reminders back later, I'm glad I did it.

Put your cell phone to work

If you must keep your cell phone with you, use it to capture those brilliant ideas. Sign up for a free or paid subscription to www.reqall.com. reQall is founded on the knowledge that we often get our best ideas, or we often remember that all-important errand when we're on the go, away from home, or away from our offices. Based on this, reQall lets you call a central number to record your own reminders. It will store your ideas, reminders, or appointments for later retrieval, either via your cell phone, text message, or will even synchronize your reminders with your Outlook or Google calendars. Because it's voice activated, you can use it anywhere you have access to a telephone. And you categorize your tasks and reminders for greater organization.

Chill out and kick back: Avoid road rage

Do I need to say it? Swearing or shaking your fist or hissing nasty names at that driver in front of you is *not* conducive to the creative process. If you're an impatient driver (and who isn't at times?), adjust your driving patterns. Adjust your thinking and your automatic reactions to delays, roadwork, and gridlocks. Or, even if it takes a little longer, is there a more tranquil, less stressful route you can take to and from work?

THE GRIDLOCK SAFARI

Look at those two women over there in the blue SUV. Are they friends, sisters, or carpool buddies? Watch the woman in the red jacket, how her mouth moves in that glassed-in animation. What's she saying to her sister/friend/colleague? Is she telling the truth? Lying? Or is she just being nice and making small talk? How can you, the stranger in the next car, tell this? Isn't this a little voyeuristic?

You bet it's voyeuristic. That's the whole point. Writers are voyeurs. We're observers to and eavesdroppers on human behavior. We're writing about it, so we better have gone on safari and watched it up close and in the wild. If you commute to work every day, there's no wilder place than an American thoroughfare or highway. So as you're driving (safely, of course), watch for the body language and expressions. Watch for the fast-talking liars, the animated actors, the innocents, the earnest, the quietly sincere. That's your job.

Later, back at your writing desk or on your lunch hour—either today or next week—you will be writing dialogue. You will not just be putting comic bubbles in your characters' mouths. You will also be giving your characters some idiosyncratic, inadvertent movements, facial expressions, or habits. These tics and gestures will make your characters real, three-dimensional, and believable.

I don't know if Annie Proulx honed her skills of human observation and replication from the driver's seat of her car. In her 1993 novel, *The Shipping News,* she uses up close descriptions to introduce us to the book's main character, Quoyle. Look at this excerpt from the second page of *The Shipping News,* where we first meet the hapless, homely Quoyle as a sixteen-year-old boy who is being raised "in a shuffle of dreary upstate towns":

> At sixteen he was buried under a casement of flesh. Head
> shaped like a Crenshaw, no neck, reddish hair ruched back.
> Features as bunched as kissed fingertips. Eyes the color of
> plastic. The monstrous chin, a freakish shelf jutting out from
> the lower face.

Twenty pages later, after a disastrous relationship, Quoyle's paternal Aunt Agnis Hamm turns up to take him and his kids to their ancestral homeland of Newfoundland.

Here's Proulx's portrait of Aunt Agnis:

> The aunt, in a black and white checked pantsuit, sat on the
> sofa, listened to Quoyle sob. Made tea in a never-used pot.
> A stiff-figured woman, gingery hair streaked with white. Presented a profile like a target in a shooting gallery. A buff mole
> on her neck.

Proulx's fine-brush technique makes us, the reader, feel as if we've actually met Quoyle and his Aunt Agnis. We feel as if we know them. And, more than just knowing, we care what happens to them as they drive up the New England coast to take the ferry to start a new life in Newfoundland.

Look Left. Look Right: Here's Your Next Great Character

I'm sure the American Automobile Association would give you this message, so I'm going to repeat it here, too: Don't let your mind wander while driving. Pay 100 percent attention to the road and the traffic around you. No exceptions.

But see that license plate up ahead? It's hard to miss, really—that tiny blue hatchback, whose license plate says K-I-T-T-E-N? While keeping your eyes on the road and the traffic, let your imagination meander. Hmm ... who is this driver? And why does she love her nickname so much that she actually commissioned this vanity plate? Let your imagination run free here. Where does this woman live (*pull*lease, you can do better than a trailer park!)? With whom? How does her boyfriend or husband or girlfriends feel about this license plate? Or does she live with a husband? How old is she? What's Kitten's real name? What's her real hair color?

You get the point. From the way they talk on their cell phones to that deadpan expression on their faces to the idiosyncratic license plates, characters can be found just outside your windshields.

Come On Baby Drive My Car

Cars (in fiction or nonfiction) can also serve to quickly place your character or characters within a given social class—or portray your characters' struggle to rise above that class. Gulp! Social class? We don't talk about that in America, right? Wrong. We most certainly do. And should—especially in our literature, theater, and film. A movie like *Trading Places* would have had no plot, no reason to hit the big screen if it weren't for that great, yawning chasm between one social class and another. Ditto for a movie like *Pretty Woman*. Or a bestselling novel like *The Help*.

But wait, you say. My writing is not about the class wars. Fair enough.

But as a reader, I like to know, instantly, who I'm reading about. Within the first page or page-and-a-half, I want to know which hemisphere I'm in, whether the narrator is male or female, the main character's approximate age, the story's central conflict, and, yes, his or her (or this family's) social class.

There are, of course, many ways to convey this information. The naming and description of a car model is one of them. So why not use it?

Just as our workplace cubicles can showcase or hint at our subversions or our secret selves, ditto for our choice of car. As you study roadside humanoids, observe who drives certain cars. That pink Volkswagen van with the peace sign on the doors? That black Chevrolet with the oddball rear red door? That sleek black BMW? That little red sports car? That huge blue pickup with the "My kid beat up your honors student" bumper sticker? The car make, model, and its accoutrements can provide a window into your story and into the lives of your characters.

Cars also create a collusive nudge-wink between what the reader knows and what you, the author knows *what the* reader knows. When we do this, we are exploiting our shared cultural reference points. (Dodge Omnis are cheap cars; older Americans favor Cadillacs.) In the hands of a skilled, thoughtful writer, the characters can either be indigenous to or grossly mismatched with their vehicles. Or the car can define and deepen our sense of the characters. In *The Shipping News*, Quoyle and Aunt Agnis set off for Newfoundland in an old station wagon.

Writing Tutorial 3:
CREATING MEMORABLE CHARACTERS

Creating memorable characters—characters that your readers will love, re-member, and care enough about to keep reading—is a two-step process.

First, we have to get the idea. We have to imagine up or invent the charac-ter. Next, we have to give that character an entire life, habits, a house, a family, a situation. We also have to give her an interior life, and we have to know her past, her fears, and her desires. As an author, you may not reveal all these facts. You may not present all of this character information in your story. But you, as the writer, should know these details.

A NOTE FOR NONFICTION WRITERS

Nonfiction authors often eschew the word *characters*, because it smacks of the concocted or invented. You're writing real-life portraits. You're writing about you and your family, partner, or ex-partner—not some Alice-in-Won-derland stuff.

But in your nonfiction writing, you still have to draw these real-life people accurately and interestingly. For example, if you're going to write about the high-school sweetheart who stole your heart, you have to find a way to bring him to us, the readers, to render him on the page in a way that will make us interested and care. And you must make us care about you—both as a jilted teenager and as the wise adult, writing from memory, telling this retrospec-tive story. As the first-person, real-life narrator—the *I* voice of your own narrative—you cast yourself as a character in your own story. Therefore, you cannot be inert, passive, or simply boring. Otherwise I won't really care about your high-school love affairs.

(A) INVENTING CHARACTERS

First, you must invent or conceive your fictional characters, let them materi-alize, come to life in your mind. You may be inspired by someone along the highway, in a store, on a bus. Or you may base a character on one of your rela-tives, a friend, or a neighbor. You may be inspired by your own experiences. Most authors say that certain characters are actually composites of people from their own lives. For many writers, the entire idea for a book comes from a character sketch.

(B) GIVING YOUR CHARACTERS LIFE

This is where your driving time, your walking, your tennis, your vacuuming, those boring boardroom meetings start to count as writing time. The only way to get to know your characters is to spend time with them. As you drive or walk or daydream, ask your characters all kinds of details about themselves. What's in their fridge? How was their childhood? Do they drink coffee or tea in the morning? Milk or cream? What kind of school did they attend?

Ask your characters these two crucial questions: What is your greatest desire? What is your greatest fear? Then, rather than playing stage director, let your characters romp and play and interact with one another. Let them surprise you. Back off and give them space.

FIVE TIPS TO CREATE MEMORABLE CHARACTERS

1. **Love:** Fall in love with them—even the bank robbers and murderers and liars. As their creator, you must love them enough to have them stick with you for the length of your project. And you must make us, the reader, love them, too.

2. **Physical traits:** Give your character a subtle physical quirk or facial tic. For example, in *The Shipping News,* when Quoyle is perplexed or stressed, he has a habit of passing his hand over his chin. This familiar, up close tic makes readers feel like they know the character.

3. **Distinctive speech:** Give your character her own speech pattern or voice. It doesn't need to be bizarre or exotic, but make her speech patterns subtly distinguishable from the other people in the story. In *The Shipping News,* Quoyle's aunt, the native Newfoundlander, speaks differently from her nephew, the native New Yorker. Or read Kathryn Stockett's *The Help* to see how the author uses speech patterns to distinguish the characters from each other.

4. **Avoid cliché:** Boy meets girl. Poor boy makes good. Man sells his soul to the devil. Girl goes on journey to learn more about life. Since the first cavemen sat around their campfires, there have been few new story ideas. But there are lots of new character twists to give these ideas new life. Give your characters room to breathe. Don't make them fit some overdone cookie-cutter version.

5. Interior world: Live inside your character's skin. Discover and get to know his interior world, his thoughts, dreams, hopes, fears, his memories of childhood, and his hopes for the future.

> *Here's a Tip!* Nothing annoys and offends readers more than an author who misrepresents other social, ethnic, or national groups. Want to create a character from a different ethnic, national, social class, or gender group from you? Then, get ready to do your research. *Lots of* research. If you're a trust-fund kid writing about a homeless person, grab your sleeping bag and get ready to live in the streets. I hate it when non-Irish writers cast their academic or made-up version of Irishness onto the big screen, the stage, or the page. I especially despise the botched speech patterns and the clichéd assumptions about my country—and about me as an Irish person.

CHARACTER WRITING EXERCISES

Exercise 1:

Here are four short car scenes, each from a best-selling book. Don't skip ahead to find out the author or the book title. Read each excerpt. Then, based on these short snippets, write down everything you know or think you know about each narrator—her homeland, her social class, her education, her era, her state of mind.

Excerpt 1:

> "I drive my Mama's Cadillac fast on the gravel road, headed home. Patsy Cline can't even be heard on the radio anymore, for all the rocks banging the side of the car. Mother would be furious, but I just drive faster. I can't stop thinking about what Holly said to me today at bridge club."

Excerpt 2:

> "Elvis was as long and sleek as a racing yacht. It had air-conditioning, gold shag upholstery, windows that went up and down with the push of a button, and a working turn signal, so Dad didn't have to stick his arm

out. Every time we drove through town in Elvis, I'd nod graciously and smile at the people on the sidewalk, feeling like an heiress."

Excerpt 3:

"It was a dusty minicab, whose rear seat was covered in nylon fur with a zebra pattern. But the driver, Michael, was a cheerful West Indian lad who took my case and made a fuss of sliding the front passenger seat forward for me. Once it was established that I would not tolerate the thumping music at any volume from the speakers on the ledge behind my head, and he had recovered from a little sulkiness, we got along well and talked about families."

Excerpt 4:

"How much this kind of farmhouse, this kind of afternoon seems to me to belong to that one decade in time, just as my father's hat does, his bright flared tie, our car with its wide running board (an Essex, and long past its prime). Cars somewhat like it, many older, none dustier, sit in farmyards. Some are past running and have their doors pulled off, their seats removed for use on porches. No living things can be seen, chickens or cattle. Except dogs."

Written your notes? Good. Now turn to page 85 to see just how accurate you were.

Exercise 2:

Choose your favorite fairy tale or fable. Is it *Cinderella? Little Red Riding Hood? Rapunzel? The Three Little Pigs?* Choose one character from the fairy tale. If she's innocent and kind (Cinderella), make her cunning and vicious. If she's the wicked stepmother, make her into a kind, indulgent motherly type. Give her a contemporary, twenty-first century voice and speech patterns. Dress her up in twenty-first century clothes and accessories. Now rewrite a scene from the fairy tale with your newly cast character.

Exercise 3: Fiction Writers

Set yourself a daily character-creation task. As you set out for work each morning, train yourself to see and select one interesting character. Do this for a full work week. Give each of your characters a name (Cadillac Man? The woman in the black raincoat). At the end of the week, who's your most interesting character? Write five hundred words about him. Let this writing take you where it will.

Exercise 4: Nonfiction Writers

Is there an incident from your childhood or youth that you regret, that you wish you could undo, or make good on? Write that scene in which you are the villain, not the innocent child. Make it more than a mea culpa confession. Give us a vivid sense of you. Make yourself come alive on the page.

Exercise 5: Nonfiction Writers

Did your parents or extended family tell you one repeated story about their youth? Choose one story. Now write one or two lively scenes from this "back in the day" story. (See Tutorial 1 for a refresher on writing scenes.) Go beyond the repeated nature of this family story to give life to these "characters." Make them come alive on the page and render a vivid portrait of your mother, father, or uncle.

Answers to Exercise 1

Excerpt 1 is from Kathryn Stockett's best-selling novel, *The Help,* set in 1962 Mississippi. In this scene, a female white college graduate has just left a luncheon house party with her friends.

Excerpt 2 is from Jeannette Wall's memoir, *The Glass Castle,* about her and her family's impoverished, artistic, and nomadic existence. In this scene, set in a dreary town in the Appalachians, Jeannette's father has won the Cadillac in a poker game.

Excerpt 3 is from British novelist, Ian McEwan's *Atonement.* In this scene, the minicab driver is moving through London, and his passenger is a seventy-seven-year-old woman author setting out to revisit her past.

Excerpt 4 is from Alice Munro's short story, "Walker Brothers Cowboy." In the first-person story, set in the 1930s, a door-to-door salesman takes his two young children on an afternoon drive as he peddles his wares to farmers in rural Ontario.

9

ALL ABOARD! TURN YOUR TRAIN OR BUS RIDE INTO WRITING TIME

While she was working as an associate creative director at a Manhattan advertising agency, historical fiction author Susanne Dunlap (www .susannedunlap.com) (*In the Shadow of the Lamp, Anastasia's Secret*) got a lot of her writing done on the New York subway. Dunlap says, "I was able to do a lot of writing on the subway, to and from work. I found a route where I could be certain of getting a seat, and there was/is something about having to tune out the distractions and having no Internet access that made it very easy for me to get in the writing 'zone.' "

Riding the rails to work can double as your writing time—and very productive writing time at that! Your train commute provides a defined time span in which to write or let your imagination wander.

But like using your drive time, it means getting into the habit and discipline to use your commute time well.

Of course, it also helps to have the right tools.

WRITING THE RAILS: TIPS AND GADGETS FOR WRITING ON THE TRAIN

Earplugs: Yes, that cell-phone conversation in the next seat is interesting (or not), but when your writing's really cranking, that idiot who is loudly retelling the details of last night's beer bong party is a giant interruption. When the dirty looks don't work, go to your local drugstore and buy yourself a package of industrial-strength earplugs.

Music and headphones: Okay, you iPod people, don't laugh at me when I say that my tiny transistor radio (does anyone even call them that anymore?) has become one of my best traveling companions. This tiny radio fits in my pocket, and I like it better than a CD player—though this could work, too—because I just keep it switched to a classical music station that provides nonintrusive background music.

Composition notebooks: Remember these from your school days? They're the ones with the mottled pattern on the hard cover? These are ideal for train writes, and it's all because of that hard cover. Also, the inside pages have wide lines, which make it easier to write on that jiggling train ride.

A mini laptop and notebooks: These have become more affordable and popular, and many have a substantial battery life. And of course, there's the iPad. Pop a small laptop or iPad on top of your hard-cover composition notebook, and you've got yourself a sturdy and portable writing desk.

Penzu.com: Penzu, the online journal-writing people, have released a mobile version of their writing product. Now you can carry your fully encrypted writing in your pocket, on the train, bus, or anywhere you go. You will need the fee-based ($19) Penzu Pro to use the mobile version.

A pocket-sized notebook, a mini cassette, a small camera, or ReQall.com: Carry some device in which you can record your own bright ideas, what you see out the train window, and your thoughts on them. Really want to capture that elegiac piece of graffiti or that strangely shaped tree trunk or the light against that city rooftop? Use your cell-phone camera. If it helps you to recall the scene for future use, record some personal commentary with your landscape photo. However, if that man or woman or child sitting in the seat opposite yours is too intriguing not to study and remember, you may want to think twice about taking a photo. There are laws around taking photos of people in a public place. Generally speaking, the laws center around what you're going to do with the photo (editorial use versus advertising) and if the photo shows your subject in an offensive light. Also, beyond the legal aspects of photographing people in public places, it's best to apply the do-unto-others rule. How would you feel if, buried in your morning commuter newspaper, someone suddenly without permission snapped your picture? As a writer, real-life people's facial features and physical details only come alive on the page when they've been filtered through your own imagination and rendered in your unique writer's voice. So play nice and play safe, and do your character sketches in a notebook.

> *Writer Beware!* Many of us carry our company laptops to and from work each day. But unless you have written permission from your company, it's not a good idea to use your company

laptop to write on the train. If you must do this, check your employer's equipment use policies. Also, many research, software,
and educational organizations have an intellectual property
policy which states that anything you create on company time
or equipment belongs to the company.

WHAT'S OUT YOUR TRAIN (OR BUS) WINDOW?

Because they nudge through traffic or trundle through tunnels or speed
along overpasses, buses and trains provide a fleeting but vivid snapshot of a
particular setting or swatch of landscape.

When we write narrative scenes, when we place the action or character
or plot within a certain geographic or physical setting, we replicate this
viewfinder technique. As writers, we want to give the reader a very real and
authentic sense of place—even if it's a fantasy place in an invented galaxy.
But we don't want to bog down the story with long, ponderous descriptions
that bore the reader and detract from the story.

Of course, you're not always going to be writing about the great or the
gritty outdoors. But to hone your writer craft means developing a painter's
eye for the vivid, pertinent details around us. We must also develop the
art of quickly and vividly conveying the setting to the reader. So get off
your cell phone or Blackberry and sit up and look out the train window.
Pay attention.

Clacking along at over forty miles per hour, you're not going to see
every detail. So notice and remember the important ones: the morning sun
behind that skyscraper, the upstairs bathroom window in that house, the
gray sheen on the river, or the lights in the underground station.

Here's one of my favorite train-window settings or scenes. It's from British author William Trevor's 1999 novel, *Felicia's Journey.*

> The train judders on, rattling on the rails, slowing almost to
> a halt, gathering speed again. Felicia opens her eyes. A hazy
> dawn is distributing farmhouses and silos and humped barns
> in shadowy fields. Later, there are long lines of motor cars
> creeping slowly on nearby roads, and blank early-morning
> faces at railway stations. Pylons and aerials clutter a skyline,

> birds scavenge at a rubbish tip. There's never a stretch of
> empty countryside.

Notice how, although this train is traveling through miles and miles of the English countryside, the author presents only those details which will quickly and deftly convey the morning landscape to the reader?

Here's a second excerpt from Jeannette Walls' *The Glass Castle.* Here the young Jeannette has taken the bus from her impoverished and bohemian West Virginia existence and headed for New York. This is her first bus-window portrait of Manhattan:

> All I could see were the spires and blocky tops of buildings.
> And then we reached the crest of the ridge, and there, across a
> wide river, was a huge island jammed tip to top with skyscrap-
> ers, their glass glowing like fire in the setting sun.

Again, in the hands of a skillful writer, one of the world's busiest and most cosmopolitan cities is rendered quickly, vividly, and in a way that we will remember—and all from the window of a Greyhound bus.

Writing Tutorial 4:
WRITING GREAT SETTINGS

Here's a little quiz: If you haven't read the book or seen the adapted movie, what does this train scene from *Felicia's Journey* tell you about Felicia's state of mind? Notice that the scene is told in third-person limited point of view—Felicia's. Is she happy? Sad? Excited? Where is she headed? Is she going on vacation or someplace she'd rather not be?

Or look at the bus scene from *The Glass Castle*. See how the narrator's depiction of Manhattan evokes the city *and also* echoes her own state of mind.

In literature, setting your story or scene involves far, far more than just fabricating a backdrop against which you will let your characters move, speak, quarrel, laugh, and live.

I don't know about you, but I've attended my share of school plays or community theater productions in which the volunteer stage manager unfurls a crudely painted backdrop of impossibly blue skies and puffy clouds and gray church steeples. As the audience, we don't really "believe" those scenes. Instead we look to the actors—who are drawn (we hope) with a finer brush and more detailed nuances—to deliver the story, to carry the drama, and to keep us from fidgeting in our theater chairs.

On the page, the setting carries more weight than these stage sets. As we see in the train and bus scenes above, the geography or setting heightens and mirrors the central drama, emotion, or conflict of your story (notice how the nervous, excited Jeannette Walls describes the Manhattan skyscrapers as "glowing like fire in the setting sun").

THE FIVE SENSES

Creating a setting is more than just plopping your story into a small town in New Jersey, circa 1973. It's about giving an authentic sense of the small-town neighborhood, the houses, the season, the weather, the smell of freshly cut grass, or the sounds of kids' voices as they ride their bicycles home. Of course, your setting can be an imagined or fantasy place—a planet on a yet-to-be-discovered galaxy, a retirement home overlooking the lunar Sea of Tranquility. Wherever it is, whatever it is, you must write and rewrite in a way that brings the reader there. And the best way to draw your reader in is to appeal to our senses: sight, sound, smell, taste, and touch.

SIGNIFICANT DETAIL: LESS IS MORE

I'm going to bet that an amateur video account of the train scene from William Trevor's novel would show us many, many more things and details than the excerpt from his book. But the excerpt above isn't an amateur video account. It's narrative fiction. So as that British train "judders" on through the rural landscape, the author lets us see only certain, well-chosen details.

Without going back to reread the excerpt, which details can you recall now? Write them down.

When you're writing your first drafts, load up your scenes with all sorts of visual, auditory, or other details. Give it your kitchen-sink all. Then, as you redraft and polish your work, look at the setting you've created. Examine and weigh each detail to decide which can stay and which should get cut. By overloading the reader with too much detail, you will end up with a cluttered scene in which all details carry equal weight. When you redraft, cut the extras and keep the details that matter.

CREATING AND MIRRORING YOUR CHARACTERS' MOOD AND POINT OF VIEW

I know a woman who hates the beach. She rarely goes there. When she does, she won't get out of the car. She thinks it's a dirty, sweaty place. Yet, all over the world, families and individuals save up and plan for their yearly vacation by the seaside. Travel agencies and Internet travel sites hire entire staffs of copywriters to sell beach-vacation packages, in which these writers wax poetic about golden sunsets and the warm sand between our toes. Now imagine if my beach-hating friend were hired to write those beach-resort blurbs. She'd write about the stench of seaweed, the kids peeing in the water, your picnic basket full of sand. The setting and its details depend on who is holding the camera—the point-of-view character or narrator.

In the train scene from *Felicia's Journey*, Felicia is an unmarried pregnant girl who has traveled to England to find the runaway father of her unborn child, even though she has no actual address for him. If Felicia were traveling on vacation, or if she were off to live happily ever after with her lover, wouldn't we see a different set of landscape details from that train window?

DESCRIPTIONS AND ACTION: HOW LONG IS TOO LONG?

Each of your stories will have its own pace. Depending on the individual piece, the genre, and your writing style, some narratives are ponderous, slow, and thoughtful. Others, such as thrillers or mysteries, move snappily along. Those snappy, action-oriented pieces still give a sense of the place and scene, but it's usually a high-impact well-chosen vista. Then we're back into the action, the characters, or their dialogue. Some books or stories open with a description of scene. Others open right in the middle of the action or the dialogue. Depending on your piece and your preference, either scenario is correct.

"Whoa! Wait!" I hear you say. "What about those novels or memoirs in which I'm forced to skip several pages before I can get back to the actual story, to the part where something's actually happening?"

Certainly. Let's avoid those long, static passages of description of the weather, the landscape, or a seedy motel room. You will bore your reader, and she will feel angry for having paid thirty dollars for a book in which she keeps skipping over chunks of it. Make your story a well-chosen tapestry of description, action, and dialogue—a tapestry that suits your style of story.

Above all, avoid those descriptive passages which do nothing else except describe or showcase your powers of description.

Let me be the proverbial cracked record here: Write and redraft your settings so that they're relevant, vivid, sensual. Make them not only mirror, but be a part of what actually happens in your story.

SETTING: GETTING THE DETAILS RIGHT

When my first novel was published, one reviewer in a small local newspaper accused me of having placed the book's fictional town too close to the local airport. Based on the real-life town (my hometown) and the real-life airport (which exists about twenty miles from my hometown), the reviewer cited the exact mileage from airport to town. And … guess what? As a local girl-turned-writer, I'd gotten it all wrong.

I regret that slipup. But then, my book *was* fiction. And, while I drew upon some of the atmospheric details of my hometown, my fictional town was completely invented. So I could, in fact, have made the journey from airport to town as short or as long as I wanted or needed for that story.

Equally, if you're writing a memoir, I'll bet that one of your siblings will find something to quibble or contradict. Your sister will tell you that the front windows in your childhood house were actually three-paned, not two. Or that it was your Aunt Julia, not your Uncle Jack, who came for Thanksgiving in 1967. So, as a memoirist, does this mean you are lying?

Let's talk about fiction first: I believe that the details should be well researched and checked thoroughly enough to make your reader believe in the story on the page. In other words, the geographic or weather or landscape details should be authentic to that story—not necessarily to the actual place that exists in a Fodor's guide book or a Rand McNally map. This is why I usually make up names for my fictional places—even if I'm broadly basing the atmosphere and lifestyle of that place on an actual location. By making up the name, I can play LEGOs and move the river closer to the housing development, plop the village school into a completely different location, or make the town nearer the airport. If it's written well enough and all the other cultural details are correct, even someone from my hometown can suspend his actual knowledge to enjoy this new fictional world that I've fabricated.

In the case of nonfiction, I do my very best to ensure that I'm telling a journalist's truth. Sometimes it cannot be a journalist's fact-checked truth. But it has to be *my* truth to the very best of *my* remembering. In other words, I've made a very thorough and good-faith effort to replicate my childhood home as it was. Yes, of course, my sister will remember certain details differently. Or she will remember certain details that I've forgotten (that portrait of my great-uncle that hung over the parlor mantelpiece). But it is my story. And remember, as we saw in the excerpts from the train and bus windows, writing the setting is an interplay of actual physical details and the character's point of view. So while I may remember the sepia portrait of Great-Uncle Charlie as looking dour and forbidding, my sister may remember a very cheerful, chipper little Uncle Charlie. In fact, I don't know where that portrait is now. I have no reliable way to check my facts. So the best I can do is to check my own memory and my childhood impressions. Then, if I choose to write about this family portrait, I must replicate it as honestly as I can. And, in a nonfiction essay or memoir, I can actually ponder or second-guess the accuracy of my recollections—out loud, right there on the page.

AVOIDING CLICHÉS OR CONDESCENSION

In the last tutorial, on writing characters, I warned against creating characters who are very different from you—unless you've done your research thoroughly, and unless you've spent time with those characters. The same goes for placing your characters in settings which smack of cliché or condescension. For example, if you've been raised or always lived in a five-bedroom Colonial in the suburbs, be very, very careful about putting your characters in a fourth-floor inner city public-housing apartment. And, before you place your characters in that slum, ask yourself if there isn't someplace more interesting they could be. A place more authentic to your fictional story—not cut and pasted to match your assumptions based on what you know—or think you know—about these people.

If you're going to place your characters in a milieu that's totally different from your own life experiences, don't play social worker and insert yourself, as writer, between the story and the reader. If your story has some social commentary, let the reader draw his own conclusions from the characters.

WRITING EXERCISES: SETTING

Exercise 1: Fiction and Nonfiction Writers

Rewrite the train scene from *Felicia's Journey*. If you like, replace this setting in a geography more familiar to you, either in an urban or a rural train ride. Or make up a setting or landscape. Wherever you send that train, write it from the point of view of a train passenger who has just won a once-in-a-lifetime vacation. As she watches the passing landscape, she's giddy with excitement. What does she see?

Exercise 2: Fiction Writers

This is a two-step exercise for you commuters out there.

(A) In five hundred words, describe each of the following:

> A boys' college dormitory
> A public men's room
> The U.S. President's bedroom
> The courtyard of a hospital
> The inside of a RV camper

(B) Now insert this character into each of the above settings. Don't describe your character. Just rewrite your setting through the character's point of view.

A boys' college dormitory where Jake, a sophomore, lies on his bunk bed just after his lover, Tiffany, has dumped him by text message.

A public men's restroom where fifteen-year-old Ryan is standing on the toilet seat, hiding, because he has just witnessed an alleyway murder.

The U.S. President's bedroom during the President's first night in the White House. He has just won the election and the moving trucks have left.

The courtyard of a hospital on a warm August afternoon, where Margaret, a seventy-two-year-old grandmother, has gone to sit and wait while her husband is in heart surgery.

The inside of a RV camper where Julie, a law professor in town for an overnight conference, has accepted the hotel barman Rick's invitation to "come back to my place."

Exercise 3: Nonfiction Writers

Describe your first day in a new place

Remember your first day in a new school? Your first night alone after you moved out of your lover's or partner's apartment? Your first day in a new job? Write about that experience and that setting (school, apartment, workplace). Write it from the point of view of you, as a child, teenager, or adult at that time. Write it in present ("I open that creaky door") or in past tense ("I opened that creaky door"). Choose the tense that feels most automatic and natural for this piece.

Draft 1: Just write and remember that first day. Write down everything. Don't stop to fact-check yourself. Don't stop to censure or self-edit. Just remember this place, this experience, and write it down.

Draft 2: Now read your piece. What can be moved around to create a better balance between description and action? How can you heighten the piece's feeling of fear or delight or nervousness?

Exercise 4: Uncomfortable Places

Draft 1: Think of a place that makes or made you feel really uncomfortable. Now describe that place. Don't stop to fact-check yourself or to check your spelling, grammar, or the quality of your writing. Just remember and write. Or write to remember. If it helps, start with this line:

"I always hate(d) going there because …"

Draft 2: Now read your piece. Can you make it more sensual? Can you bring us, the reader, in one step closer so that we can see and feel your discomfort or fear? What details can you cut? What details can you keep and make even more vivid and sensual?

10

BEFORE, DURING, AND AFTER WORK: GRAB YOUR WRITING TIME WHEN YOU CAN

Glen Cook is the author of more than forty science fiction and fantasy novels, including the Dread Empire trilogy and the Black Company series. Cook completed most of his books while employed at General Motors, where he worked for more than thirty years. In an interview in *Strange Horizons,* (www.strangehorizons.com), an online magazine devoted to speculative writing, Cook describes his very full life.

> At the old plant (GM assembly plant) I was working six days a week, helping coach Little League, and still getting three books done a year. Now I'm retired, theoretically. I've got nothing else to do and a book every fifteen months is a miracle, it seems like. Of course, they [the books] have gotten fatter because now we've got computers. There always seems to be something else that needs to get done first.

All that and over forty books!

I've noticed that the writers that I interviewed for this book have additional commitments beyond their jobs and their writing (coaching Little League), including their families or volunteer work. I also notice that these authors share three traits: (1) They accepted and embraced the realities and competing demands of their working and writing lives. (2) Whether the writing happens in the evening, morning, on the train, or in the bedroom, each author has established a habitual writing schedule that works for him or her. (3) In addition to their scheduled writing habits, each day job author is alert for those quick, unplanned writing opportunities that present themselves throughout the working day.

Sometimes availing of these quick, incidental writing stints is as easy or as hard as adjusting your attitude to how you use time. It's also all about keeping your backpack or briefcase or shoulder bag or car organized and equipped so that you can always work on your writing—even if it's just for fifteen minutes while you're waiting for the dental hygienist to call your name. Like your train commute or your lunch hour, this defined, limited time—and the fact that you're trapped there and removed from the other aspects of your life—can be really motivating.

CAN I HAVE THAT TO GO? TEN GREAT PLACES (AND TIMES) TO WRITE ON THE FLY

1. Doctor's or dentist's waiting room (my favorite)
2. Under the hair dryer in the beauty salon (my second favorite)
3. On the sidelines at your kids' sporting events
4. In the car waiting for your kids after school
5. In the car or in a café between your kids' after-school events
6. At the airport between flights (very productive)
7. Waiting for the taxi to take you from your hotel to the airport
8. Between school drop-off and departure for work
9. While your children are taking naps
10. On the job

GULP! ON THE JOB? CAN YOU? SHOULD YOU?

When I told some writing associates that I was writing this book, they assumed I was penning a manual on how to sneak in some creative writing while actually on the job—as in, how to sit there in your cubicle or work station and pretend.

In fact, my associates' misunderstanding earned me a certain cachet. With a roguish wink, they inquired in a gleeful voice, "How's that writing-at-work book coming along?" I felt like I was writing a book on how to hoodwink the IRS or a blueprint for tapping into the national grid.

Here's the reality: Unless you're on your legitimate coffee break or lunch hour, or unless you have actually cleared it with your boss, you should not do any extensive creative writing while on the job. I say this not as a moralist or puritan, but as someone who believes in honoring your commitment to produce what you're being paid to produce. And I say it as someone who believes in keeping on the right side of a pink slip or dismissal.

EVERYTHING YOU WRITE CAN AND WILL BE USED AGAINST YOU

There are trillions of online writing opportunities out there. When we join or contribute to one of these online writer exchanges, we develop a kind of imagined cyber-immunity. After all, we're communicating and writing and work shopping and writer-chatting in cyberspace—not via our office's e-mail or project management program (Outlook, Lotus Notes). Online, we can meet, befriend, and collaborate with an entire cast of online writing buddies, who are happily sitting at their own computers, on another coast, in another time zone. We can join any number of online writing workshops. We can sign up for a poem per day, a writer's prompt per day, a daily or hourly journaling prompt. Ping! Here's your next reason and motivation to abandon that work project and catch up on your writing.

Even when we're not in active writing mode, we can check out other writers' blogs or tweets. We can listen to a podcast of our favorite author. Or we can just log onto any one of the many, many literary e-zines out there, and read enough essays, short stories, reviews, and poetry submissions to last us from now until retirement.

In fact, we could spend our entire working lives frolicking in that galaxy of online literary playgrounds—all from our corporate office chairs, without ever moving from our work station. And, so long as we look busy and talk a good game and remember to periodically delete our online browsing history, what employer is going to be any the wiser?

How you use your work time and conduct yourself as an employee is up to you. But as any computer forensics experts will tell you, every keystroke you make on that computer—on- or off-site—can be monitored, tracked, and, possibly, used against you.

And employers can and will use your online activities against you.

According to the Privacy Rights Clearinghouse (www.privacyrights.org), a California-based nonprofit organization with a central mission to raise consumers' awareness of how technology affects personal privacy, employers are fully in their rights to monitor your online activities

> Most computer monitoring equipment allows employers to monitor without the employees' knowledge. However, some

employers do notify employees that monitoring takes place. This information may be communicated in memos, employee handbooks, union contracts, at meetings, or on a sticker attached to the computer. In most cases, employees find out about computer monitoring during a performance evaluation when the information collected is used to evaluate the employee's work.

The same goes for those personal, nonwork-related e-mails, even when you send them from Web-based accounts such as Yahoo or Hotmail. And ditto for your deleted e-mails, which can be retrieved and are generally backed up via electronic tape.

As part of its advice to employees, the Privacy Rights Clearinghouse offers this general rule of thumb: "In general, employees should not assume that these activities are not being monitored and are private."

Let's take a look at this from the employer's point of view. According to the website of the American Management Association (AMA) (www.amanet .org), 66 percent of all employers who responded to the organization's 2007 Electronic Monitoring and Surveillance Survey monitor their employees' Internet connections at work.

And, as one last word of warning, The ePolicy Institute (www.epolicy institute.com) offers these words of wisdom: "Workers' e-mail and other electronically stored information create written business records that are the electronic equivalent of DNA evidence."

So you get the point. Don't use your working hours to write that next chapter of your novel—either online or offline.

By the way, for a really scary glimpse of where workplace Internet excursions can actually land you, check out the The ePolicy Institute's "101 E-Mail and Internet Disaster Stories," or the organization's "CyberLove Disasters." But check them on your home computer or at an Internet café. Who knows? These cyber boo-boos may provide inspiration for your next great fictional character.

NO ... BUT ... REALLY!

Okay, let's be honest, here. Which of us has not taken a few minutes to read a personal e-mail or check the local weather forecast or logged onto an airline's website to verify a flight arrival time? As workdays get longer and our work

schedules grow more demanding, many employers' Internet-use policies specifically allow for the kind of limited personal use that lets us keep up with
family and other commitments.

For many day job writers, the extent to which you use work time or company equipment really depends on your relationship and written agreement
with your employer.

In her author-interview, New York author Stephanie Cowell writes: "People from the president of the company to the head of the mailroom read my
novels. There could never have been a more supportive day job ... I took my
disk in and wrote in my office during downtimes."

If you're just starting a new job, read your employee manual and the organization's written policy on Internet use carefully. If this policy is not included
in the manual, ask for a copy of the policy. In writing.

If you've been in your current job for a while, dust off that employee hand-
book or log onto your company's corporate human resources page and check
for the most updated Internet use policy. If your employer has a "limited use"
policy (occasional family e-mails, check the weather, you child's school-closing
notices), ask exactly what that means. Ask for actual examples of permitted
use. Ask for it in writing.

In chapter 2, I write about the advantage of one consistent job (part or full
time) over the hodgepodge of funky, bohemian gigs. One premium advantage
is that, as a longer-term and trusted employee, you are in a much stronger position to negotiate for privileges such as using the company laptop or, indeed,
reaching an agreement with your organization that, so long as the work gets
done and you reach your benchmarks, you're free to use those downtimes to
edit a typed-up draft or create a new one.

WORKPLACE EQUIPMENT USE POLICIES

So you cannot write online during working hours. But after a busy weekend
or morning's writing at your home writing desk, there's no harm in e-mailing
yourself a draft of your work and then storing it in some word processing files
on your work station desktop. You're not really using the Internet, and, during
your downtimes, you can always go in for a quick review and edit. Right?

Check this out with your employer. Many employers have an equipment
use policy which limits or completely restricts the use of company-owned
equipment to work-related tasks. As companies become more virtual and as
more and more employees telecommute, many organizations have amended

their equipment-use policies to cover off-site, on-the-road, and telecommuting employees. Again, before you pen that best-seller on company time or on a company computer, double-check your employer's most recent equipment use policy.

Depending on where you work, your employer may love having a creative writer on board. Or the organization may regard your creative work with suspicion or as the direct antithesis of your paid work.

WHAT YOU *CAN* DO AT WORK

Despite all these employer thou-shall-not's, there are things that you can do at work to make your writing life better and easier.

Buying writing time: Use your sanctioned, allowed telephone or Internet use to buy you some writing time for later on your lunch break or when you've clocked out for the day. Use your personal cell phone or one of those prepaid calling cards if you must, but that quick, workplace call can save you time, stress, and chaos later. For example, can you call ahead and order your groceries to be delivered to your house? If you need to set up an informational interview to support your writing, can you make that call now from your desk, so that it's scheduled and set up for you to do on your way home from work? If you need to borrow research materials from your local library, order them online via the library's website. Call your child's school or log onto the school's website to get any bulletins about homework, weather, fund raisers, or other parental announcements. If you're going to grab a bite and get some writing done on your way home from work, check the restaurant's online menu and call ahead so your food is ready and waiting when you get there.

Writing on your downtimes: I have a lawyer friend who's a mystery writer. Some days, her law job takes her to court where there are periods of downtime between cases. She can't leave. But she can't do anything, either. This is a writer who always, *always* keeps a notebook with her. Some jobs have naturally occurring, built-in downtimes, when you need to be there, when you need to be on call, but there's nothing to do but sit and wait. Stores have slow periods. Midafternoons in a restaurant or bar can resemble a ghost town. When your office equipment breaks and you're waiting for the help desk to call you back, there's not much else to do. If it's not going to get you in trouble and if it's not dishonest, use your downtime wisely.

Making notes and lists: The best writing ideas or solutions often come when we're doing something unrelated to writing—when we're doing the laundry, out for a walk, grocery shopping, or sitting in a staff meeting. It's a shame to lose these lightbulb moments. And why risk that they'll still be there, fresh in your memory, when you get home or get to take your workplace lunch hour?

Even the strictest workplaces allow you to get up and walk away from your computer or production line. Use this time to jot down your ideas, to scribble some handwritten notes in a notebook or your personal portable device—even if you have to do it in the bathroom.

I like to keep these daytime aha moments in a specific notebook (mine is dollar store bright pink) in the front pocket of my briefcase. Or use a battery-powered, handheld microcassette recorder.

If you work in an office, your colleagues will probably grow suspicious if you're always the one at the meeting who's furiously writing or typing—even when there are no minutes to record. But that weekly office meeting could be a place in which to make short handwritten lists. Again, like the doctor's waiting room or the train ride to work, it's captive time.

Watch, listen, and learn: New Orleans-based author M.A. Harper (www.ma-harperauthor.com) (*The Worst Day of My Life So Far, The Year of Past Things*) has worked as a window dresser, a law office receptionist, a stage manager, and a commercial artist. Currently, she works retail, selling high-end walking shoes. About her shoe sales position she says:

> Holding a pleasant but dumb job allows me to interact daily with all kinds of people I wouldn't be among if I just stayed home in front of the word processor. It benefits my ear for dialogue as well as deepens my understanding of human nature.

We may not cast our colleagues, unedited, in our writing (see chapter 12 on libel), but sharing a work space and a schedule and a sense of shared commitment to deadlines or sales figures or production quotes brings many of us up close and personal with people with whom we would not normally associate in our personal lives. Like it or not, this kind of exposure to humanity develops our sense of that humanity, in all its idiosyncratic weirdness.

My first American job as a waitress and bartender taught me the most about people and life, hands down. It showed me the extraordinary diversity of human sensibility—and the huge contradiction between our public and private personae. The woman in the prim suit and stockings often had deplorable table manners. Give the executive guy in the Oxford shirt and the designer tie a few beers and he turned into a lecherous, profane lout. The rich. The depraved. The lonely. The pretentious. The insecure. The power hungry. The addicted. The kind hearted. The optimistic. The insane. The control freak. All of my jobs, from waitress to secretary to editor to communications director, have deepened my sense of humanity in all its quirks and mutations. Also, my day jobs have given me a mirror into myself, as a person. And as a person writing about people.

Manage your notes and ideas and printouts: Because your writing is taking place at different times, in places away from your formal writing desk, one of the biggest challenges can be in getting and keeping your work organized— keeping all those morning drafts and quick notes and sticky notes and aha ideas in a central spot.

Paper drafts: If you use a journal during your workday, leave the first few pages of the journal blank for a handwritten or pasted-in table of contents. Then number your journal's blank pages by hand. As you complete your journal, create a general topic list of your writing. This will make it easier to go back and find your rough drafts.

Printouts: If you bring your printouts to work for quick reviews or editing, keep a special folder for these in your briefcase. Use this folder for your creative writing printouts only. This way, when you go to lunch, you can just grab your folder and go. Also, remember to do some spring cleaning on your printout folder. Everything in there should be a work in progress.

Electronic documents: Do you really want to carry those flash drives or CDs back and forth to work? Why run the risk of losing some of your precious drafts in transit? Avail yourself of some online document storage websites. Most are free or offer a no-fee option.

> **Google Docs (www.google.com):** This free service from Google lets you create, store, share, and save your drafts, without using space on your laptop hard drive and without using a flash drive or disk. If you're creating a document which will be appended to a longer, fuller manuscript on your home computer, make sure you save your temporary, daytime document under the same name. Larger files don't work.

Office Web Apps from Microsoft Office Live (www.officelive.com): These free apps allow you to create, edit, and store simple documents from any computer or your mobile device.

MediaFire (www.mediafire.com): MediaFire offers unlimited storage, and lets you upload an unlimited number of files, and if you're having someone review your writing, it lets you grant sharing rights to others.

ADrive (www.Adrive.com): The free basic plan offers 50GB of storage capacity and a search function.

Penzu (http://penzu.com): This is a free online journaling software that you can access from your mobile device or you can upgrade to the paid version, which has added security and a mobile feature.

11

WRITERS, TAKE BACK YOUR LUNCH HOUR

In the Introduction to this book, I told you about an ex-student of mine, a man named John. He was the novelist who, five days per week, left his office cubicle to go sit in his car and write the next part of his novel. Like many of my adult students, John had a busy job and family life, but he also wanted to finish his novel, and the daily lunchtime car write was his best and only solution.

Lunchtime can be used to your advantage. First, if you're an exempt (salaried and not entitled to overtime pay) employee, this is an hour in your day that you can use to get more writing done. The trick is to make sure, no matter how busy you are, to really take that hour. As our workplaces get busier, as our day job schedules grow more packed with tasks, deadlines, and onsite and intertime-zone telemeetings, more and more employees tell me that they're lucky if they manage a midafternoon trip to the snack machine.

I'm not a dietician. But listen to me when I say that this is downright unhealthy (read: brain fog, sugar imbalances, rapid weight gain, and perpetual grumpiness). In addition to the physical effects to your overall health, this kind of enforced or voluntary starvation will turn you into an embittered, disgruntled employee. And that's not the attitude that benefits either your work or your writing career.

Think that working and fasting through your lunch hour will help you keep your job and score some brownie points? Even the most dim-witted boss knows that a hungry employee may *look* busy, but she's actually sitting there fantasizing about a triple cheeseburger or … you guessed it … a big pan of luscious chocolate brownies.

So let me play your mother here. Writers! Workers of the world! Whatever you actually use your lunchtime for get up, stand up, and take back your lunch hour!

If you're a nonexempt employee (entitled to overtime pay for working beyond your assigned paid hours), it's highly unlikely that your employer will let you skip your lunch hour. In most cases, this controverts the labor laws and counts as overtime.

WRITERS, MAKE YOUR LUNCH HOUR WORK FOR YOU

As a writer, the traditional midday or midafternoon lunch hour can work for you in one of three ways:

1. **Trade the hour:** If you have a relatively flexible work schedule, trade in this hour for a later start or an earlier quitting time. This gives you an extra hour for your writing—either at home at your writing desk or in a local café or library on the way home.

2. **Write on your lunch break:** Like our friend John, use your lunchtime to produce new writing or to read and edit last night's or this morning's draft.

3. **Take a class, workshop, or webinar:** More and more downtown and suburban organizations (public libraries, YMCAs, writers coalitions, university extension programs) are catering to the busy lunchtime crowd by offering short workshops, reading series, or writer-discussion groups.

4. **Jog, walk, visit the company gym, or run errands:** Use this midday hour to get in your daily exercise or to run errands. This will improve your mood and energy level. And, by using your lunchtime wisely and efficiently, you leave the evening hours free for you.

> *Here's a Tip!* To really take back your lunch hour, practice these lines of dialogue. Or better yet, write your own.
>
> Standing there in your office door, your colleague looks friendly, well meaning, and hungry. "Wanna go to lunch?" she asks.
>
> "Thank you. But I'm afraid I have plans for lunch," you say—the disciplined writer.

DING! DING! IT'S LUNCH TIME!

If at all possible, take your lunch hour off-site. By eating and writing in your workplace cafeteria, you leave yourself vulnerable to those come-join-us invitations. Or you're too available for those on-the-fly work questions or discussions.

I eat six times per day or more. I'm hungry every two or three hours, or even more often than that. It's just how my metabolism works. So most days, I'm on my third snack or mini meal by 11 A.M., and my next mini meal is not until about 2 P.M.—right in the middle of that mid-afternoon slump. So I rarely or never use my actual lunch hour as a mealtime.

You may not have this luxury or dietary preference. But if your lunch hour doubles as a writing hour and if it works for you, try this snacking-on-the-job routine. It frees you from standing at that deli counter or waiting for that waiter to bring you the daily special.

On Your Lunch Break or After Work: Where Can You Write?

Writing in a café

In her 1990 biography, *Simone de Beauvoir,* about the French author who wrote *The Second Sex*, existential philosopher and feminist, Deirdre Bair describes how, during World War II, Beauvoir turned the Café de Flore into her Parisian writing studio:

> She quickly noted that two tables in particular were almost touching the stove, and decided that from now on, she would hurry over to the Flore as early as possible in the morning, claiming the table closest to the stove as her own. There she would write until it was time to go to the Bibliothèque each afternoon. Thus, from a desire to keep warm and write without interruption, both rumor and reality about Beauvoir were born. The reality was quite simply that throughout the war, she wrote two philosophical essays, another novel, and a play, mostly in the Café de Flore.

Is there a café as bohemian and exotic near your workplace? If so, good for you. But if you work in your average, urban, suburban, or American downtown, you may have to settle for something more pedestrian. Often pedestrian works just fine.

When it comes to writing in a café, I've found that not all eateries are created equal. There are some—even some national chains—that work for me. There are others that simply do not.

Here are some tips for finding your writer-friendly place:

> **Music:** Unless this is your preferred writer-muse, avoid the headbanger hangouts. If the music always sets the dishes jiggling, it will drive you

to distraction, not creativity. But if you like everything else about the place, visit at different times of the day to see if it's just certain counter staff who play certain music. You can also ask to have the volume turned down.

Brown bag: You're willing to pay for the overpriced Coolatas, but ask if you can discreetly bring your own lunch. If it's one of those beverage-only java joints, they may let you bring in your own food. Or, even if the place does sell some lunches, catch the manager during a slow afternoon shift and explain that you're a writer who's looking to become a loyal, daily customer. Who knows? His place may become the next Café de Flore. Many coffee shops are flattered that you've chosen their place. And writers add to the overall ambiance and appeal.

Discounts and freebies: If you're going to actually eat there five days per week, do they have any preferred-customer coupons or freebies? Some lunch spots offer a free lunch for every four or five you purchase.

Service: The entire choreography of waiting for a waiter and placing your order and stressing about getting back to work in time can distract you from your writing. Does your spot offer ready-to-go salads or soups?

Scope out your table: At my local coffee joint, I have a favorite table inside the front window that looks out onto the town square. I'm not Simone de Beauvoir, but I do think of it as "my table." When I'm at my table, I know I'm there to write.

Cell-phone policy: If your lunch spot has and enforces a cell-phone policy, so much the better. Those "can you hear me now" conversations can inspire great dialogue or fictional character development. Or they can be downright annoying.

Leave your own phone and Blackberry at the office: Do I need to say this? You're on your lunch hour. Or you've just logged out for the day. If your colleagues or your boss need you that urgently, they'll leave an e-mail or voice mail.

Other writers: Even if you don't introduce yourself to the other writers at other tables, it can be really inspiring to be one of many writers, all of whom are sitting there, typing or scribbling away.

General ambiance and layout: If the tables are crushed together, if the lunchtime counter queue overflows into your table space, or if the place smells of last night's fry-o-lator grease, look elsewhere.

It must fit you: If you're just starting to write or if your office has moved or if you're starting a new job, scope out a few different neighborhood locations. Appearances can be deceiving. One writer's haven is another writer's hell. Hip isn't always happening. (I had one student writer who could and would write no place else except in her neighborhood McDonald's). It has to feel right and work for you.

Headphones: If you want to block out some conversations, listen to some online music, or if you're taking a writer's workshop via webinar, don't forget your headphones. In his author-interview, Mark Greaney talks about using downloads and uses free iPad apps of background noise to block out the café noises around him. While he's typing his next international thriller, he listens to the sound of rain in his headphones.

Writing in the library

If you work near a public library, then you may have a no-cost easy-access writing studio just around the corner. Here are some tips for writing at the library:

Hectic is the new hush: If you're thinking staid rooms and the bespectacled, disapproving librarians, think again. Today's public libraries are busy, wired, and interactive places. In fact, they often serve as a kind of community center and no-cost Internet café. They also serve as an after-school homework hangout. If you want quiet, avoid the teen loft and the public-access Internet room.

Cell phones: Except for in the lobby, most libraries ban them—and all other devices that bleep or squeal or ring. Leave yours at work, in your car, or switch it off.

Eat first: Most libraries do not allow food or drinks inside the library.

Sign yourself up: Some public libraries offer small study rooms, which you can book for an hour or two. By booking ahead, at the same time each day, you give yourself a fixed commitment, a quiet comfortable room, and a regular, daily schedule.

Use the computers: If you write via an online program (see pages 60 and 61 for a list of online journal or writing sites), sign yourself up for the library's Internet computer time. It saves you hauling your laptop there and back. Just like your employer, many libraries have installed firewalls and software which blocks access to X-rated sites. But it's unlikely that they will block your personal blog or secured journaling sites. Most libraries also offer some Internet-free computers for word processing only. You can sign yourself up for a given time slot. Don't forget to bring a flash drive or a disk to back up your work.

Brown-bag writers workshops or lunchtime readings: Many writers organizations, bookstores, or writers coalitions offer lunchtime readings, discussion groups, or brown-bag lunch programs. Many university extension programs are looking for new ways to engage the noncampus community. If your town or the town you work in has nothing like this, consider starting a lunchtime library program of your own. All you need is an easy-access location, a willing coordinator (you?), and a few like-minded writers or readers. It has to be a program that's lively and attractive to busy working people, and it has to be doable within a one-hour time slot. But make sure organizing it wouldn't distract you from your true goal: writing.

Here are some ways you can check on lunchtime writers events: Visit your statewide writers organizations or coalitions. Most of these statewide organizations list local or regional writers groups and projects. For example, the New Hampshire Writers' Project (www.nhwritersproject.org) serves writers who live in or near the state of New Hampshire. The California Writers Collective (www.californiawriterscollective.com) serves writers from the San Francisco Bay and greater Los Angeles areas. The New York State Literary Tree (www.nyslittree.org) serves New York State writers, while the New York Writers Coalition (www.nywriterscoalition.org) provides opportunities, workshops, and readings in New York City, with a focus on "groups that have been historically deprived of a voice." In Florida, the Florida Writers Association (www.floridawriters.net) serves as a central resource for beginner and advanced writers in the Sunshine State.

Wherever you live, check if there's a statewide organization. Its website will list city-specific groups, programs, or workshops near you. Also, although it's not a complete listing, Big Hat Press (www.bighatpress.com) lists writers groups by state.

START YOUR OWN LUNCHTIME WRITING OR READING SERIES

Libraries: Contact your local library and ask for the adult program director. Ask if she or he would consider reviewing a brief written proposal for a daytime program to engage local adults. But remember, most public libraries will not allow you to brownbag it. Also, as municipally funded and staffed organizations, public libraries typically plan their yearly programming well in advance. So don't expect to propose your idea tomorrow and schedule your first writers session next week.

Universities or community colleges: Contact your local college's continuing education or the university extension program. Again, research and query the right person—the person who has the power to consider your proposal and actually put the concept in motion. Assure her that the cost to the department will be minimal, if any. Push for the brown-bag idea—simply because it will appeal to daytime employees and be more worker friendly.

Your local YMCA or YWCA: Some Ys have thriving writing and reading programs. Find and contact your local Y. As a writer, your proposal for a lunchtime writers or public reading group may be just what the center needs to diversify their programming and serve a broader and more diverse constituency.

Be creative with that corporate plaza: If you work in an industrial park or a corporate plaza, speak with the building manager about unused or community-shared space. Post a flyer in the cafeteria, where all employees—not just your company—can see it. Use your first posting to elicit input on interest levels, time preferences, and general group suggestions around the hours, rules, leadership, and how the group will function.

Shopping malls: They're not Simone de Beauvoir or Ernest Hemingway's Paris, but they're an easy-access, free-parking location where shrinking retail rentals can mean cheap, available space. It may not look very academic or literary, but a small, Spartan room can quickly become one rockin' writers salon when you have the right people participating.

Art galleries, empty storefronts, church basements, hospital community rooms: The possibilities are endless. If a lunchtime or after-work writers group or reading series will jump-start your writing and keep you connected to your area's writer community, then forget the snack machine or the office lunchroom. Get creative. Get out there. Get writing.

LUNCHTIME WRITING: HOW MUCH CAN I REALLY WRITE?

I know some teachers who surprise themselves by how much class prep or how many student papers they can grade during a midday free class period. Or, remember your own high school or college days. Remember how much homework you could complete during that a free period between classes—work that would take you twice that long at home? Or did you ever surprise yourself by how much work you accomplished at 37,000 feet, stuck in a cramped seat on an airplane?

When writing on your lunch hour, the key word is *hour*. There's something really motivating about having a limited time in which to complete a defined task. Also, when we effortlessly completed that homework during free periods during school, we were motivated by the fact that we were buying ourselves some free time in the evenings.

Wherever you decide to spend your lunch hour, this timed writing approach can really work to your advantage. And it works best if you develop some kind of system, which includes knowing what you're going to write and where.

What will I write or work on? You probably wouldn't want to eat an egg salad sandwich for lunch five days in a row, but I advise you to dedicate lunchtime to a specific, habitual writing task, such as writing the first draft, completing a journal entry, editing, or rewriting.

When I worked in one of those awful corporate tower buildings, I got a lot more accomplished when I knew that the minute that elevator hit the ground floor and pinged open, I was crossing that concourse to work on a specific task. Some weeks I dedicated to idea gathering and very rough handwritten first drafts. For others, I made sure I had a printout completed and a pen in my pocket so I was ready to do some serious editing.

Feel free to change your lunchtime plan from week to week. But before you log out or clock out for your lunch break, have a plan.

(1) Editing: If you're going to use this time to read and mark up a previously written draft, get yourself on a schedule of saving, printing, and stapling drafts in advance. Really! It can be as simple as that. Then the minute you unwrap your lunch, you're already reading and reviewing that first line of your own writing. Better yet, develop a write-and-edit schedule which allows a lag time of twenty-four hours or more between writing and editing. For example, Tuesday's lunch is spent editing Monday morning's draft. Or Thursday's lunch is always spent editing Wednesday morning's draft. The more defined, predictable, and planned your lunchtime schedule is, the more you will get out of it.

New York author Stephanie Cowell (www.stephaniecowell.com), worked as a production manager in the publications department of a nonprofit research organization, while penning five historical novels. Cowell says that she wrote "in my office during my downtime and on lunch hours." She would take her printouts on the subway to work. In fact, she recalls one day when she walked down a New York City street "editing my manuscript as I went."

(2) Writing: This hour can produce a fast and furious first draft. Again, before you reach that café or park bench, make sure you've got what you will need (writing idea or assignment, laptop, notebook, pen). Because once you're out there, once you've left the service counter or the office or the assembly line, you can't or won't schlep back to the office.

(3) Character ideas and sketches: Stroll downtown or visit your workplace cafeteria or pop around the corner to any lunchtime café. Or take a walk through a nearby park. At lunchtime, especially in good weather, buttoned-up adults spill out of elevators and stores and corporate buildings like schoolkids let out on recess. In the cafés or at the street vendors' food carts, watch and listen to how people order their food (that woman who barks her order while still gabbling to her friend on her cell phone). Watch how people actually eat (that burger gobbler), and *what* they eat (the fastidious salad picker). Look at what they're wearing (the conformist, the rebel, the fashionista). Block out their chatter, switch the imaginary sound dial to *mute*, and just watch how these people interact with one another.

I don't know about you, but I find the socializing-colleagues syndrome as fascinating as watching any action-packed movie. I like to watch how these contrived friendships play out over a lunchtime salad or a fast-food meal. Often it's an assemblage of mismatched or reluctant people. Are those two at the end of the table really friends? Who's the workplace heartthrob? Who's the snitch? Who's the boss? Is she a good or a bad boss? Despite the simpering smiles, do her colleagues actually like her? How do the women interact with the men?

The Guardian, Britain's leading daily newspaper, published a 2010 series, "Your Rules for Writing," in which the newspaper invited famous writers to submit their top ten "rules." In her submission, internationally acclaimed mystery writer P.D. James offered this advice: "Open your mind to new experiences, particularly to the study of other people. Nothing that happens to a writer—however happy, however tragic—is ever wasted."

Gabriel Valjan is an award-winning short-story writer and a nurse at a busy metro hospital in greater Boston. In his author interview, he cites an interesting link between his nursing career and his writing. "Nurses are listeners and observers. So I'm observant of body language, particularly when what the person has said does not accord with his or her body positioning."

Valjan suggests an exercise for observant writers: "Watch two people in public talking to each other, examine their body language, and create the dialog. Is the person with her arms crossed listening or tolerating being spoken to?"

(4) Rewriting or inputting edits: Of all the writing chores, I find that inputting or typing edits on a previously marked-up page requires the least creative input or creative juices. If it's hard for you to transition from your working self to your relaxed, lunchtime self, dedicate this time to inputting or typing in the edits that you have already made—that morning or the night before. "It's just typing," I tell myself—although I often go away beyond my previously marked edits. But this is a task that I can undertake easily, even in a noisy cafeteria, and even when I'm tired or distracted.

(5) Reading through background research: Depending on your work schedule and demands, it may be hard for you to switch off your job, to switch from the day job you to the writer you. Then allocate your lunch hour to simply reading—preferably reading the background research you will need for the piece you're working on. For example, if you're writing a personal essay on the experience of dropping your oldest son off at college, your personal essay will benefit from a larger view, such as a set of regional or nationwide statistics. Thanks to the Internet, and thanks to our many government or university-affiliated think tanks and offices and centers of research, statistical facts and figures are now at our fingertips. As you munch on the daily lunch special, read up on information that can be used in your writing.

Writing Tutorial 5:
WRITING DIALOGUE

As you sit there on your commuter bus or train, or as you scribble away in your café, diner, or bagel joint, you're going to overhear some conversations around you. Especially when you just catch that last, out-of-context snippet, these can be downright juicy and evocative. And writers can and should be downright nosy. It's our job to observe, listen, and depict humanity in all its delight, flaws, trials, and tribulations. So … all you have to do is eavesdrop, record, and presto! You can just cut and paste some dialogue onto the page. Right?

No. Written dialogue is never a replication of actual human speech—the sort of chatter you overhear at work or in the supermarket queue. Go on and try it. Simply record and write down every pause and *um* and *ah* and *gee, I dunno* that you hear around you and what have you got? Pretty boring dialogue—the sort of dialogue that makes the reader skip forward to the next page.

Instead written dialogue is a highly stylized composite of everyday human speech, and there's a real art to writing it. We never just plop a few paragraphs of dialogue into our story—just to get people talking. And there are, of course, stories and essays that have no dialogue at all. For some stories, no dialogue is just fine.

WHY WRITE DIALOGUE?

1. It can move your story's action forward ("Is that fire I see coming from that house?" Joe asked.)

2. Reveal something about the character ("Look, I fear commitment, just like my runaway father," she said.)

3. Distinguish the characters from each other ("I ain't sittin' here for no more of this crap," he told Dr. Smith, his new philosophy professor.)

4. Reveal other needed information about the story or about the character's past (Carl just blurted this out without meeting my eyes. "I've never told you this before," he said, "but my dad never came back from the war.")

THE ART AND CRAFT OF WRITING DIALOGUE

I'm going to keep this part of the tutorial brief. Why? Because I believe that the best way to learn how to write dialogue is to (1) Listen to people. Pay attention to how they talk and fidget, lie, pause, and hesitate. (2) Read and study lots of written dialogue. I tell my adult students that it's like taking apart a hard drive to see how a computer works inside. To study the craft of writing dialogue, read lots of it. Listen to lots of it. Study how experienced authors do it.

A good place to start is Hemingway's short story, "A Clean Well-Lighted Place," which is rendered almost completely in dialogue. James Joyce's short story collection, *Dubliners,* is another good one. Or look at how the characters converse and reveal themselves in E. M. Forster's *A Passage to India.* Or choose from among your own favorite authors. Read closely and study how they manage the dialogue on the page.

SOME BASIC, GENERAL RULES FOR WRITING DIALOGUE

(1) Dialogue is never gratuitous. If you're going to break the narrative to have someone talk, there better be a darned good reason for doing so. See the list of reasons above.

(2) Each time someone talks, you must begin a new line of text.

> "I hate you," said Julia.
>> "Not as much as I despise you," said Tom.

(3) Capture the rhythm and cadence of each speaker's voice, language, and words. To learn this skill, read and study lots of dialogue. Note how experienced authors can make you actually "hear" their characters speaking.

(4) Avoid heavy use of dialect: Some authors use heavy regional dialects, including Mark Twain in *The Adventures of Huckleberry Finn* or Kathryn Stockett in *The Help.* When it comes to replicating accents or racial or nationally influenced speech patterns, less is more. First, overuse of dialect calls attention to itself and can stand between the reader and the actual story. Second, it can confuse the reader who is not familiar with that region and how people speak there. And third, if you replicate too many *ain'ts* and *gonnas* and other assorted grammar mistakes, you run the risk of sounding snooty and condescending—as if you're mocking your characters. Remember Tutorial 3 on Creating Memorable Characters? The first rule of thumb is to love them. It's not very loving to mock their speech patterns. As the writer, you may come across as a grammatical smarty-pants.

(5) Instead of dialect, use these techniques. (1) The first time someone speaks, I give a sense of his speech pattern, so that the reader knows who this is and where he's from. After that, each time that character speaks, I reduce the number of regionally influenced speech boo-boos. **(2)** Capture the rhythm and cadence (speed, intonations, music, inflections) of the character's speech. Then you really only need one or two dialect-specific words.

(6) Use simple dialogue tags. He said. She said. Stick to simple verbs. Avoid other verbs ("I hate you," she panted.). If the actual line of speech is written well, the verb (said) should be almost invisible. In well-crafted dialogue exchanges, you don't even need to insert the *said* every time. Study how authors manage this.

The Guardian newspaper modeled its "Ten Rules for Writing" series based on the book, *Ten Rules for Writing*, by Elmore Leonard. Here's what Leonard has to say about using verbs in dialogue:

> Never use a verb other than 'said' to carry dialogue. The line of dialogue belongs to the character; the verb is the writer sticking his nose in. But 'said' is far less intrusive than 'grumbled,' 'gasped,' 'cautioned,' 'lied'.

(7) Make them move and talk and twitch—all at the same time: As you study written dialogue, note that characters are also moving, fidgeting, squirming, or petting the cat as they talk to each other. Writing this is an art and a skill you can master. You must study it widely and practice it often.

Here's an example from Janet Fitch's second novel, *Paint it Black*. The main character, Josie, is an art model, punk rocker, and runaway in 1980s Los Angeles. The story opens when she has to identify the body of her artist lover, Michael Faraday, who has committed suicide. After the funeral, Josie agrees to have a drink with Michael's absentee father, Calvin, who has flown across country for the funeral. In this roadside bar scene, Calvin and Josie are discussing Michael's relationship with his possessive mother, Meredith:

> "I only saw them together once. When he told her he was moving in with me. That we'd rented a place together."
> Calvin Faraday stared at the bottles behind the bar, his blue eyes watering, a smile playing around his worn mouth. "God I would have loved to see that. The storming of the Bastille. Vive la Liberté." A tear dripped down his cheek, stubble-dotted, he brushed at it absently.
> "She was really pissed."

> "I can imagine. You don't know how they used to be. Just the two of them, in their own little world. No intruders welcome. Meaning me, of course." He coughed and drank, went back to turning the glass in his hands.

In this high-impact scene, notice how Fitch intersperses the words with small, incidental, and up-close actions? What effect does this have on you, the reader?

DIALOGUE-WRITING EXERCISES

Exercise 1:

In chapter 2, you followed a fellow commuter home from work and created the setting in which she lives. Now make that person arrive home again—this time to an apartment or house in which her partner has rearranged the furniture—yet again. Make her tired and stressed and angry. Make her stub her toe on a misplaced armchair. Set her and her partner talking.

Exercise 2: Nonfiction Writers

When you were a child, what arguments did your parents have? If you didn't actually overhear any, you can make up. Place your parents (or grandparents) in that setting. Give us a strong sense of them as people. Make it authentic for that era and place. Now write the argument you think they had.

Exercise 3: Fiction Writers

Here's the start of some dialogue between two people named Izzy and Margaret. Finish it. Take their conversation as far as you can.

> "How many times have I asked you not to do that?" Izzy's voice filled the tiny downstairs hallway.
>
> > "Do what?" Margaret asked. She flashed Izzy that maddening smile, as is she didn't already know what was bugging her.

Exercise 4:

On your lunch break, pick up a newspaper. Choose one of the headlines ("Sewer Committee Agrees to Townwide Strike"). Show us what happened ("The three men and four women, all members of the sewer committee, sat around a tiny, smoky room"). And let's hear those men and women talking, arguing, and plotting.

12

TRUTH AND FICTION: WRITING ABOUT OTHER PEOPLE— INCLUDING YOUR COLLEAGUES

The popular Public Broadcast Service (PBS) TV program, *All Creatures Great and Small* (check it out on YouTube) is a series of funny and heartwarming stories about a small-town veterinary practice in rural England. The opening credits feature a close-up of the series' main characters, Siegfried and James, two happy colleagues driving down a country road after a successful veterinary case.

All Creatures is based on the series of books by the late author Alfred Wight, and the book, movie, and TV series are all based on Wight's real-life experiences as a country vet. James Herriot is a pen name. The character of Siegfried Farnon, the charming but often irascible owner of the veterinary practice, is based on Wight's real-life colleague, Donald Sinclair.

In the 1970s, when a film crew moved into small-town England to start filming the movie version of Wight's (aka Herriot) best-selling books, the happy-go-lucky veterinary colleagues turned less happy. Sinclair objected to how he was being portrayed as the fictional Siegfried. And then, just before the film cameras started to roll, Sinclair threatened to sue Wight, his colleague and close friend of more than thirty years.

In the memoir, *The Real James Herriot: A Memoir of My Father,* Wight's son Jim Wight describes the effect of an impending libel lawsuit on his author-father:

> ... now his greatest fear had materialized: that his writing would not only hurt someone but that he would be taken to court over it. Even worse, it was one of his oldest friends raising objections. I remember him saying to me at the time, "I have lain awake these last two nights wishing that I had never written the bloody books!"

Eventually Mr. Sinclair dropped the lawsuit, and Alfred Wight went on to write other veterinary books—all of which inspired the longer PBS

TV series. But the threat of libel litigation impacted how he wrote these later books. Over the objections of his U.S. publisher, Wight changed the character of Siegfried: "After this episode, Alf trod very warily when writing about Siegfried, toning down his character considerably in future books."

There are two takeaway messages here: This all happened more than thirty years ago, when our society was much less litigious than now. And, when he sat down to write his series of semifictional stories, this vet-turned-author used a pen name and he gave all of his characters fictional names—including his colleagues.

FICTIONAL CHARACTERS: FIGMENTS OF YOUR IMAGINATION OR CLONES FROM OUR REAL LIVES?

Most fiction writers will tell you that their characters are pure invention. The Annie Wilkes and the Miss Havishams, and the Hannibal Lecters and the Bart Simpsons of the world are entirely made up. But over the life cycle of a fiction writer's work, from novel one to novel ten, at least one character (probably more) will have been modeled after a real-life character. For example, there is a theory that Dickens modeled his Miss Havisham, his fictional character in *Great Expectations*, on the real-life Eliza Emily Donnithorne (1826–1886), an Australian women who was jilted by her groom on her wedding day and spent the rest of her life in a darkened house, her rotting wedding cake left as it was on the table. Sound familiar?

The 2007 national best-selling novel, *Then We Came to the End* is set in a declining advertising agency and features a cast of office cubicle characters. When he started the novel, Joshua Ferris was working at a Chicago ad agency. Yet, in an author interview on Powells.com, Ferris reported that "the book is not autobiographical, almost at all. Most of the characters are completely created. But one thing that *is* autobiographical is the feeling I had when I worked in advertising that everyone had an opinion about everyone else."

From preschool to high school to college, we've all encountered teachers (great and small): the boring, the acerbic, the crazy, the lazy, the kind hearted, the inspirational. So if we're going to write a fictional story with a fictional teacher named … oh … let's see … Mr. Zambiski … it's likely that we will set the "rewind" button to let the ghosts of school days past parade through our memories and imaginations. So here comes Mr. Smith, the eighth-grade geography drone. Oh, and there's Mr. Jewett, the principal of our middle school.

To create our fictional Mr. Zambiski, it's unlikely that we will replicate either the real-life Mr. Jewett or Mr. Smith, a verisimilitude of these teachers as they were. But we will use what we know and remember about male teachers. And what if you wanted to? What if Mr. Jewett and his mannerisms were just too, too perfect for your story? Could you? Should you?

Many authors believe that the "This is a work of fiction and any resemblance to actual people is purely coincidental" statement gives them automatic immunity from a late-life Mr. Jewett taking offense or worse, suing them for libel. But the truth is that fictionalizing your story and your characters is not an automatic protection from a libel lawsuit. Neither does it excuse you, as an author, from a kind of artist's Hippocratic duty to "do no harm."

From memoirists to poets to fantasy novelists, there is this issue at stake in our work: how to create authentic people on the page without exploiting or hurting or outing the real-life people in our own lives?

FICTION WRITERS BEWARE!
LIBEL IN FICTION CASES

As far back as the 1970s, there have been lawsuits in which the creators of fictional stories have been sued for their negative depiction of real people in the author's life. Here are some of the more high-profile cases:

2009. Vickie Stewart successfully sued her longtime friend, the author Haywood Smith. Stewart claimed that Smith's fictional character SuSu in the novel *The Red Hat Club* too closely resembled the real-life Stewart. And this character falsely portrayed Stewart as an alcoholic slut. The court ruled in favor of Stewart, and Smith was forced to pay $100,000 in damages.

2009. Two real estate agents, Scott and Melinda Tamkin, sued the creators of the TV show *CSI* for six million dollars in damages for defamation and invasion of privacy. The suit is based on a CSI episode which depicted fictional real estate agents with the same names. The fictional realtors are depicted as a reckless, drunken couple who engage in sexual bondage, pornography, fraud, and possibly murder. When the real-life Tamkins double-checked, they found that one of the CSI writers had, in fact, worked with them and used their services to find a house—a deal that fell through. Just before the TV broadcast, the TV network changed the fictional couples' last names, but not before descriptions of the episode (including the matching names and the S&M sex) had made it onto the Internet.

2008. Ravi Batra, a Manhattan lawyer sued the creator of the television series, *Law & Order,* because a 2003 episode depicted a corrupt lawyer character that closely paralleled Batra in terms of age, ethnicity, and appearance. The judge refused to dismiss the case against the TV series because (a) the episode made it possible for a viewer to believe that the corrupt fictional lawyer was actually the real-life Batra and (b) it showed the real-life lawyer in a defamatory light.

1991. Author Terry McMillan was cleared of a $4.75 million libel action by a former lover who claimed that a depiction of a character in the novel *Disappearing Acts* too closely resembled and defamed him.

EEEEK! CAN I WRITE ANYTHING NOW?

Yes. You can. And you should. According to the article, "Libel in Fiction," David L. Hudson Jr., a First Amendment scholar, lists the hurdles that a plaintiff (the one accusing) must clear in order to prove and win a libel case. First, the writing must be published or broadcast. Second, it must have defamatory meaning or make a false statement about someone. It must make that real-life someone identifiable. And it must have caused damage. According to Hudson, in fictional writing, the toughest one to prove is "identification," the "it's me" requirement. In other words, any ordinary reader or viewer who knows the real-life person would have to say, "That's him."

In the $100,000 settlement over *The Red Hat Club,* the author and publisher lost their case because it was ultimately proven that readers of this 2003 bestseller could and would recognize the real-life Stewart in the fictional character SuSu.

Fiction Writers: How to Avoid the "It's Me" Syndrome

1. Change the character's name, ethnicity, location, physical attributes, and life circumstances.

2. Change the fictional character's occupation. In the case of the real estate couple and *CSI*, the plaintiffs claimed that the libelous depiction of them affected their real-estate business. In other words, corrupt fictional realtors + TV series = reduced real-life realty sales.

3. Change how the character acts. In the case of *All Creatures Great and Small*, it's safe to assume that the author's colleague didn't mind being given a literary doppelganger. But he minded that that doppelganger made him, the real veterinary surgeon, look bad or silly. So if it doesn't otherwise affect your artistic vision and the story, change what the character does on the page.

4. If you fear that someone may recognize himself, ask the real-life person to read that section of your story. If the real-life person is comfortable with it, then ask him to sign a legal waiver.

5. Write under a pen name.

6. Knowledge is power. Find out more about your rights as an artist at www.firstamendmentcenter.org.

Nonfiction Writers: What You Can Reveal

According to the Centers for Disease Control, 17 percent of people in the United States drink to excess. Yet, these and other public health statistics ring hollow compared to Scott Russell Sanders' nonfiction essay, "Under the Influence" about his father's alcoholism. Joan Didion's *The Year of Magical Thinking* gives us a real-life, first-person insight into sudden death and the experience of loss. Nicholas Dawidoff's *The Crowd Sounds Happy: A Story of Love, Madness, and Baseball*, opens the window into a boyhood love of baseball and a father's struggle with mental illness. Holly Robinson's 2009 memoir, *The Gerbil Farmer's Daughter: A Memoir* (see the author interview on page 226) chronicles a military family's life and adventures while the author's father, a retired navy captain, operated a successful gerbil farm in the 1960s. Meredith Hall's (see author interview, page 218) best-selling memoir, *Without a Map*, is a raw and real look at the loneliness and shame and shunning of a pregnant teenager who is forced to give up her newborn son for adoption. From family mental illness to military life to teenage pregnancy, how can we write about our lives without also writing about the people in them?

In the introductory chapter to *The Glass Castle,* Jeannette Walls' mother, a key character in the nonfiction story, urges her daughter to just "tell the truth."

But for most of us, it's not that simple. As nonfiction writers, the truth-telling dilemma becomes twofold: (1) how to write a journalist's truth about the people in our lives and (2) even when the facts are the facts, what is our duty to protect those people from being exposed or revealed in a bad light?

(1) Writing the factual truth: When the world discovered that large parts of James Frey's 2003 memoir on drug addiction, *A Million Little Pieces*, were either fabricated or embellished, this author fell from grace. Oprah had chosen the book for her book club. But when the facts of the book didn't quite add up, she confronted Frey on her show and told him, "I feel duped." In fact, Oprah echoed my own sentiments about this and other "nonfiction" writers who just make it up. And worse, in my opinion, are the publishers who just don't bother to check.

I once taught a writing class in which two elderly sisters each read their work aloud to the group—to the dismay of the other sister. Each sister had written about a young man, a handsome, charming neighborhood gadfly. Each wrote about Mr. Gadfly as *her* boyfriend. Of course, each sister accused the other of literary embellishment because the man, in her memory, was her boyfriend *only*. As the instructor, I had to intervene and diffuse, wondering like heck why they don't teach you these things in teaching school. Had one sister been consciously lying? I doubt it. According to her recollections, this guy was her sweetheart.

Lee Gutkind, founder and editor of the journal *Creative Nonfiction* and widely credited as the "godfather of creative nonfiction," issues a checklist for nonfiction writers in his essay, "The Creative Nonfiction Police." He urges nonfiction writers to "strive for the truth." Overall, Gutkind says that truth in nonfiction (including memoir) is "a question of doing the right thing, being fair, following the golden rule. Treating others with courtesy and respect and using common sense."

When she wrote her memoir, *The Gerbil Farmer's Daughter,* Holly Robinson spent a year researching and a year writing this family memoir. During the research year, she studied her father's papers and researched old articles about gerbils and interviewed every person in her family. She did this, she says, because "memories are never exact."

(2) **Writing the kind-hearted truth:** In commenting on *The Kiss*, the memoir in which Kathryn Harrison writes about her sexual affair with her father, Lee Gutkind questions the effect of such revelations on the "innocent victims of Harrison's quest to unload her anxieties." In "The Creative Nonfiction Police," Gutkind wonders aloud about the possible effects on the author's children and the possibility of embarrassment and distress—or the fallout for her father's new wife and second family.

In her 2002 book, *The Bookseller of Kabul,* Norwegian journalist Åsne Seierstad depicted the life and family of a bookseller and his middle-class Afghan family based on her three months living in his home as a western observer and a journalist. The book was translated into thirty languages and became an international bestseller. Now the Afghan family has won its defamation lawsuit against Seierstad and her publisher. This family also claimed that the book compromised their safety. In the book, Seierstad gave key family members fictional names. She also handed her manuscript to the family for approval. But the family claimed that parts of the nonfiction book were not true and misrepresented them. Also, by using some real names and one real address, the publication of the book forced some family members to emigrate. So how do you write true stories about your family without either being sued or losing their familial trust or affection?

Holly Robinson consulted with her family all the way. If something in there had upset them, she says she would have omitted the offending part.

Kitty Gogins' family memoir, *My Flag Grew Stars,* chronicles her parents' flight from World War II Hungary to Canada then the United States. When Gogins began writing and researching the family memoir (see the author interview on page 214), the author says that her mother was initially honored to have her life as a refugee and as a mother documented. But, says Gogins, as publication date approached, her mother "became anxious to have her life so publically exposed. She also has a very hard time reading the book because of the painful memories it evokes." But as Kitty the daughter also became Kitty the family memoirist, her mother found the process of telling her story cathartic, and it helped the author's mother to review her life in retrospect and to "come to terms with some nagging aspects." In describing her writing process, Gogins describes how she would interview her mother, write a rough draft, then read that draft to her mother, and ask questions.

So both Robinson and Gogins first consulted their family subjects. They did not write and expose and let the family chips fall where they would.

As a nonfiction essayist or memoirist or journalist, you must do your very best to get the facts right. And, unless this is actually your intent, and you're ready and willing to live with the consequences, you must ensure that the published facts don't injure someone else in the process.

Even when we're writing about the grimmest situations, most writers want to create something beautiful. It's why we become writers in the first place, right? And sometimes, despite our very best intentions, we cannot control or predict how every single reader will interpret our work.

WRITING AND EDITING WITH HONESTY AND DECENCY

Here's a checklist that will help you to review and redraft your work with an eye for factual honesty and a writer's decency:

1. **Fiction and nonfiction:** While casting an engaging or amusing narrative, has my humor or raconteuring inadvertently made my subject (mother, father, friend) look foolish or stereotyped or stupid?

2. **Fiction and nonfiction:** If I'm writing now about a previous, less sophisticated era, have I condescended to or patronized my subjects? For example, if I'm a college-educated writer born to uneducated working class parents, have I described their existence accurately (they were poor) but with empathy and respect?

3. **Nonfiction:** If I'm writing about a different generation, have I acknowledged the different sensibilities and cultural norms of that generation or setting? For example, if I have presented my 1950s father as distant or stoic or absent, have I acknowledged the discrepancy between parenting norms now and back then? If my writing is judging someone by modern and unfair standards, then what can I do to make it fairer and relevant to that place or era?

4. **Fiction:** If your fictional character was inspired by a real-life character, would she (or close relatives) easily recognize herself in my story? If so, what can I do to change this or to mitigate the potential damage to her and to me as the author?

5. **Nonfiction:** Have I balanced my own feelings and emotions with self-reflection, narrative distance and/or factual research? If my first draft is a "poor me" story, then how can I make the second and subsequent drafts richer, fairer and more universal?

6. **Fiction and nonfiction:** If I have presented my subject in an unavoidably negative light, what is my motivation for doing this? For example, in Scott Russell Sanders' essay, "Under the Influence" about his father's alcoholism, he could not have cast his father as a teetotaler (factually incorrect) or even as a moderate drinker. Sanders' essay about a very flawed father is articulate and analytical, and it is void of vindictiveness.

7. **Fiction and nonfiction:** Is there a niggling middle-of-the-night voice urging me to double-check a date, a place, or a significant detail? Or is my writer's conscience bothered by how I have revealed someone else on the page? If so, listen to that voice and act according to your conscience.

Section 4

MAKING YOUR WRITING BETTER: REVIEWING AND REVISING

Let's compare the writing, drafting, and editing process to a new paint job for your living room. Once, on a bright morning in April, you woke up with this ingenious idea for a whole new décor. Mint green walls. Wow! Now *there's* one big, brilliant idea (hereafter called, "the BBI"). Now, fast-forward to a Friday night in mid-April when you invite your friends for cocktails and to admire your finished and beautiful room.

As they stand around, nibbling on canapés and admiring your artistry, you have almost forgotten how, after that initial rush of green genius, there was all that taping and priming and trimming. And what about those mornings when it was all you could do to back in here and back up on that painting ladder? It was hard work!

The reality: Between your BBI and your grand show-off party were a lot of trial-and-error steps along the way. In writing terms, these steps are the rewriting, reorganizing, editing, peer review, copyediting and polishing phases.

Honest, I don't mean to make the revision phase sound like drudgery, but the fact is that very, *very* few writers create a final product with the first draft. And for many writers, revision is actually the fun part; it's where the writing reveals its potential.

This section of the book will help you get back in there—to push in that living room door and take an honest, appraising look at yesterday's handiwork. It will also help you assess your own writing fairly, honestly and with a diagnostician's eye for what's wrong and how you can fix it. It will give you the courage and the tools to reassess, to rearrange and to revise. And finally, this section will give you some resources to get some peer feedback for your writing—the kind of useful input that will help you make that BBI the best that it can be.

13

GOING BACK IN THERE: REVISIT AND REWRITE

The revision process is where the real writing, the courageous writing, takes place. Yes, courage. There are some days when I would much, much prefer to go shopping for a bathing suit or go to a job interview or tune up my car than to open up a first draft to embark on the second draft. Why? Because it can be downright terrifying to sit there, reading your own writing—the words and ideas that, just twenty-four or forty-eight hours ago, seemed so brilliant that you were already selecting your outfit for the Pulitzer Prize ceremony. And now … here it is … on the page. You scroll or read through the first few lines, then the first few pages, and … there's this little voice in your head. Yeah, *that* voice. The voice that starts to whisper, "Yuck! This stinks." And then that louder voice and words: "You stink." And now, for the grand finale in the let's-bash-the-writer overture: "Who the heck told you that you could be a writer?"

Okay, writers. Time out here.

As an aside, let me say that, in comparison to other professions, writers are particularly talented at self-recrimination. We are particularly good at bullying ourselves into a state of doubt about our own abilities—and all based on just a lousy first draft? Among the other artists I know, the musicians or sculptors or dancers, most will have a bad day or hit a creative block. Sure. But they'll shrug their shoulders and go on with the rest of their day and figure that tomorrow will be better. Not creative writers. Don't ask me why, but we seem to turn upon ourselves and our own work (and sometimes each other) with bared teeth and a hissing kind of self-hate that rivals the local cattery. Why? I don't know why. I just know that I do this. Often. And so does almost every writer I know.

Perhaps it's because the price tag and the public respect for the craft of writing are so often diminished (anyone can write) or low-balled (this freebie will be good for your portfolio). Make no mistake:

It takes an extra-tough and courageous writer to go back in there to prune and perfect the work for the sake of the work itself—and for the sake of your own writing goals.

Think of that beautifully painted room. Picking out the color was the sexy, fun, creative part. But when your friends are standing there, praising your blemish-free paint job, they're really praising your tenacity and toughness for sticking with it.

So take a deep breath and take a leap of faith. Let's go back to that first draft to make it better.

DRAFTING AND EDITING: DO I HAVE TO?

Yes. You have to. And not just because I said so. Except for that rare writer whose first draft is also his final draft (he has been drafting in his mind), you must go back in there and make changes, rewrite, edit, or rearrange your first draft. This is not as painful as it sounds. In practice, it can be quite thrilling. And for many writers, including me, this is where the writing begins to reveal itself to you, where *it* begins to tell *you* what it's really all about. But you have to be open to that.

As children or teenagers, we've all submitted those "what I did on my summer vacation" assignments and waited patiently for the teacher's glowing response. We even imagined how she would summon us to the front of the class to read our essay aloud. Because it was so beautiful, so witty, so moving, so eloquent, so perfect. And then, the day comes when she handed back your composition sullenly, and you opened up your beautiful assignment to find it marked up in red pen, complete with that scribbled note: "Could do better."

Whoooaaah! Could do *better*? But … this *was* the best!" You feel hurt, reprimanded, and punished.

But now you're all grown up. And now you're a working writer. So you really can do better than that first draft. You must. The "can-do-better" is not an indictment of your first draft. It's an invitation to go back in there and begin to discover what it's really about—what you've been wanting to say to the world and how to say it better.

And better.

Of course, redrafting your work is a much deeper, organic, and thoughtful process than attending to those snarky grammar corrections in the margins of your school composition. Redrafting means switching your writer's hat for your reader's hat. Usually you are your own first reader. When you reopen that file, you are assessing the work for clarity, consistency of voice, plot, sequencing, structure, character development, dialogue, and pace. (See page 154). And, oh yes, when you've examined all of these aspects of writing, you will reread and reassess the beginnings and the endings. You will be assessing and editing your work at the macro (big picture) and micro (detailed) levels.

REDRAFTING MAKES YOU CLEVER

In addition to reading and assessing and marking up your own manuscript, redrafting often requires inserting some pieces of brand-new writing. In some cases, your essay requires an entire rewrite, in which you hit the "delete" button and start all over, from scratch. From Draft 1, the most you manage to salvage is a central idea, one small scene, or a main character who, you have now decided, is relegated to a minor character. Or you've decided that your family memoir should really start with and focus on the grandparents, not the parents. That's where the story begins. In this first, raw draft the grandparent scenes are where the energy is, where the language is sharper, the voice much stronger. So now you've decided to angle the camera more closely toward the grandparents. Why didn't you see this before? How stupid of you! And now you have to undo an entire six months' worth of work. What a terrible waste!

Wrong.

Not terrible. And certainly not a waste.

First, how could you have *known* that the grandparent story is the real story—the one you really want to tell—unless and until you wrote and experimented with that first draft? And second, between Draft 1 and Draft 2, between the so-called "mistake" and the "right" story, a wonderfully rich creative process has evolved within you, the writer. While churning out your first draft, your idea and voice and words were taking form. Writing the first draft made you clever. It has led you gently or furiously into the real topic and story. It has allowed you to flex and build your writing muscles. It has allowed you to play in the sandbox of language. And now, the cleanup process and the rewriting will make you even cleverer—Einstein clever.

And here's the thing: There are *no shortcuts* to cleverness. There are no shortcuts through this process of writing and pruning and rewriting. Why?

Because there are no shortcuts through this wonderful, organic, and synaptic process that happens while you're writing.

Ever sit down to write in your journal or switched on your computer, today's topic right there in your head? And now you're all primed and ready to get it down? But then … wait! You end up writing about something totally different. Who saw that coming?

"I didn't even know I thought this!" my adult writing students often say to me after one of our in-class writing assignments. They surprise themselves—not just by being better writers than they originally gave themselves credit for, but by what they put on the page.

Why or how does this happen?

I don't know. School- or college-based writing theorists might call it "writing to discover" or "writing to learn." Over and over, in my workshops and in my own writing, I witness this magic, this sorcery of how putting words on a page begets more words on a page. Obviously there's a lot more language in there, in the part of our brains that processes written language than we acknowledge or use in our daily lives. By starting to type, by letting the pen move across the page, we turn on the language faucet. Put simply, the more we write and let ourselves write, the better and easier the flow. And ultimately, the more delightful the surprises.

So that first draft is never "stupid" or "a waste of time." It's that first switch, that first step in a multistep process.

In a November 2009 article, "How to Write a Great Novel" journalist Alexandra Alter profiled the writing processes of eleven top authors in *The Wall Street Journal.*

According to Alter's article, Margaret Atwood has written two hundred pages of two books and then abandoned them. From one book, she saved one sentence. From the other, she salvaged two short stories.

In the same article, author Dan Chaon writes:

> I used to think my average as a short story writer was one completed story out of every twenty." He adds, "I have at least two novels that I think are dead—maybe three if the thing I'm working on right now sputters to a stop.

But are these "dead" or abandoned narratives a waste of time?

I say no. I say that the act of revisiting and revising, pruning and dumping parts or all of your work are all a vital part of the artistic process. These are the parts where you dig and excavate to see what's there and what can be salvaged or dusted off or improved.

Some of my writer friends are a little shocked by how careless and disorganized I am about my computer files. It's true. I should do a better job at backing up and labeling and placing individual files into folders. But deep down, it never bothers me all that much if I lose or accidentally delete a file that contains a first (or even a second) draft. I'd prefer *not to*. But it's not that big a deal if and when I do. And I have. Because the next and better draft lives not on a hard drive or a flash drive, but in that creative space that exists in between the two drafts. This creative space is not in a computer file. It's in the time or days; it's in the walks and middle-of-the night awakenings. It's in those random notes on scraps of paper and in my writing journal.

So penning the next best draft is rarely a linear or tidy process. You must be tolerant of your own revision rhythms.

DRAFTING AND EDITING: WHAT'S THE DIFFERENCE?

Okay, can you stand one more paint-the-room analogy? The first draft was when you decided to go crazy and change the whole look of your room. So you woke up with this BBI for green, vivid green. The subsequent drafts could easily include entire mind changes (oh, my God, it looks like the stage set for a kiddie pantomime about magical leprechauns!) in which you revise and amend your original creative idea. These drafts will also include large-scale fixes to the way you've applied the paint, including making the fireplace wall just a shade lighter in order to balance the light in the room.

The editing part is nearer the end, the finishing touches, when all the big parts are already in place. There! Just to the left of the light sconce, you missed a little spot. And down there, along the baseboard, you dribbled green onto the white gloss. These are fine-brush fixes. These are the missing apostrophes and the misspelled words and the commas in the wrong places. They are not the job of nitpickers or grammar grannies. These are the copyedits that make your writing look professional and complete—that show your mastery of language and its usage. Now … back to that congratulatory dinner party. However beautiful your overall paint job is, if you've dribbled green onto the white window trim, your guests will not be able to get past that. That one sloppy boo-boo will undermine the overall genius of your room.

WHEN IS IT TIME TO REDRAFT? AT THE END
OR AT SPECIFIC STOPPING POINTS ALONG THE WAY?

The National Novel Writing Month program, NaNoWriMo (www.nanowrimo. org), is now an international and high-energy write-a-thon in which writers from around the world are invited to sign up to complete a fifty thousand word novel between November 1 and midnight on November 30. Novelists complete the fifty thousand words and upload their novel for official verification. Once verified, the writer is added to NaNoWriMo's winner's page and receives a winner's certificate and web badge. In 2009, NaNoWriMo had 167,150 participants and 32,178 winners and at the time of this writing, more than fifty authors have sold their manuscripts to publishing houses. You win if you produce fifty thousand words. No other requirement. Nowhere on NaNoWriMo's website does it mention that they have to be articulate words, clever words, arcane words, erudite, interesting, thought-provoking, or earth-shattering words. There just have to be fifty thousand of them.

On the website, the organizers assure participating writers that "the ONLY thing that matters in NaNoWriMo is output. It's all about quantity, not quality. The kamikaze approach forces you to lower your expectations, take risks, and write on the fly."

Whether you accept NaNoWriMo's challenge is up to you. But it's interesting to consider this style of writing and the process by which you defer your second draft until the very end. Just get the words down, without censoring yourself.

In a 1962 letter to Robert Wallsten, John Steinbeck offered his guidelines on writing fiction, including this one, included in the book, *Steinbeck: A Life in Letters*, 1975:

> Write freely and as rapidly as possible and throw the whole thing on paper. Never correct or rewrite until the whole thing is down. Rewrite in process is usually found to be an excuse for not going on. It also interferes with flow and rhythm which can only come from a kind of unconscious association with the material.

In her book, *Bird by Bird: Some Instructions on Writing and Life*, Anne Lamott also comments on the value of unbridled first drafts: "The first draft is the child draft, where you let it all pour out and then let it romp all over the place, knowing that no one is going to see it and that you can shape it later."

THE KAMIKAZE APPROACH

Five Advantages of the Kamikaze Approach

1. Unleashes creativity: Gives your right brain full rein. Anne Lamott compared it to the unleashed creativity of children coloring on paper.

2. Motivates by productivity: A furious first draft motivates you by the sheer volume of writing. "I wrote one thousand words to-day," is more motivating than, "I sat editing yesterday's work."

3. White-water rafting on the page: The adrenaline factor kicks in because you never know what's around that next bend. By not employing your careful editing side, you are—literally—going with the flow of your own ideas and words.

4. Big-picture vista: Good manuscripts are all about seeing where the elements of our narrative connect, intersect, and echo each other. By completing an unedited first draft, you give yourself enough material to work on.

5. Differentiate from your workplace process: If you work in an office or for a corporation, much of your day is spent re-viewing, fixing, and revising. From a simple e-mailed memo to the organizational employee policies, much of workplace writ-ing (even if your job is not actually writing) centers on making your sentences clear and correct. If this review-and-revise pro-cess starts seeping into your creative life, then forcing yourself to write without censorship may work well for you.

Five Disadvantages of the Kamikaze Approach

1. Lose the element of discovery: Reading our own words teaches and inspires along the way. Often it's when we redraft that we discover what the writing wants to say. By engaging in this teaching process earlier rather than later, or at fixed points along the way, we develop a heightened sense of our work and its possibilities.

2. Loss of language: From a linguistic point of view, there's something that happens to the quality and flow of the writing in a twenty-four- or forty-eight-hour period. When we return to our work on day two, we are infinitely better editors, equipped to make yesterday's language better, tighter, sharper. A three hundred–page manuscript of poor or mediocre writing can be discouraging.

3. **Detours to nowhere:** Remember the two hundred pages that Margaret Atwood abandoned? It was probably disheartening—but not as disheartening as it would have been if it was three hundred or four hundred pages. By stopping to assess the story and its viability, she found a way to regroup and recycle.

4. **Disaffection and boredom:** All artists fall in love with the idea of the BBI and its flurry of creative energy. But it's hard to maintain this Eureka factor over the life of a full manuscript. By taking time out to become the reader of our own work, we develop a more nuanced, sustainable love affair with it.

5. **Losing the voice:** As day job writers, we usually get up and leave our writing to commute to work or return to the factory floor or make a phone call about something a million miles removed from our creative writing topic. To reenter the world of our writing, we must go back and reread the last few scenes we wrote. As we reread and tweak and edit, we are also reclaiming the mood and voice of our writing.

Five Signs That Kamikaze May Work for You

1. You love and are motivated by a clearly defined challenge or word count.
2. In all the other areas of your life, you thrive in a crisis, under pressure.
3. You're pretty competitive. You love the idea of a stopwatch and of beating out your averages.
4. You have a little Las Vegas gambler's streak. You enjoy high stakes and racing to a finish line.

> 5. You've snagged a few weeks of free time. This is your chance to bang out that unfettered and complete first draft. Then, when you return to your normal work routine and shorter writing slots, you will have lots of material to edit and redraft.

REVISION AND WRITING EXERCISES

Step 1: Write a first draft of eight hundred words on each of the topics below. Even if you have run out of ideas or even if the piece flags along the way, keep writing until you reach your eight hundred–word quota. It doesn't have to be literary or smart or funny or grammatically correct. There is no other requirement here, except to get eight hundred words down on the page. You can write fiction or nonfiction. Write the topics on separate days.

1. The Stupidest Thing I've Ever Done
2. The Most Shameful Thing I've Ever Done
3. I Wish I Never Said That
4. One Aspect of My Family I'd Like to Wave a Wand and Change

Step 2: Once you've completed your kamikaze first draft for each topic, leave your draft aside.

Step 3: Two days later, read your piece through. Which piece makes you smile or cringe or cry or laugh out loud? Select this piece for further revision (or you might find some thematic overlaps between pieces, so you may want to combine two).

Step 4: You're ready to revise your strongest or favorite piece.

(1) Circle the parts that you wrote effortlessly, almost as if your writing had a mind and speed of its own.

(2) Underline the parts that can be made more vivid. Look for place that you can open up to let the reader in closer.

(3) Cut and paste each scene (or print up the entire story, then cut the paper with a scissors) and drop the text into a separate word-processing page. Print up all the pages, each with just one scene per page. Read them again. As you read, look at the order. Can you rearrange the order of these scenes to build excitement or tension, or to create a more logical sequence for your narrative or story?

(4) Rewrite your chosen story, making the improvements you underlined in number two above.

14

REVIEWING AND REVISING YOUR OWN WORK

At work you're the go-to person when someone wants her memo or report given the once-over for typos or grammar mistakes. Or you're that customer in the restaurant who sits there clicking your teeth over the typos and grammar mistakes in the menu. Or a friend asks you to review his short story and you immediately come up with some clever fixes. Oh, and your eye instantly goes to that egregious misuse of the subjunctive clause, right there in the middle of page three. Tut-tut. Now, how could any decent writer have missed that?

Reviewing and revising your own writing drafts will be a snap. Right?

Hmmm. Maybe not. We have a huge blind spot when it comes to our own work. We've been working on it, slaving over it, immersed in the narrative for so long and so deeply that we can easily overlook the most obvious mistakes—even errors as huge and as damning as a spelling mistake in the first sentence (I've done this). Or a structure that just doesn't carry the story we're trying to tell.

Thankfully, you can become a better editor. You can heighten your own critical and redrafting skills.

In this chapter, we'll look at ways to stand back and assess the large-scale architecture of your piece, with a view to redrafting or rearranging your story for clarity, structure, and readability (think of that process of repainting the living room in a different shade of green to make it match your vision, and your furniture). We'll also look at the fine-brush techniques—that close-up view—to help you perfect the language and story.

DOING DOUBLE TIME: WRITER TURNED EDITOR

In the 2009 *Wall Street Journal* article, "How to Write a Great Novel," Colum McCann, National Book Award Winner for his 2009 novel, *Let the Great World Spin*, says that he sometimes prints up his book in huge type and sits in the park pretending that he's reading a book written by someone else. According to the article, this act of "changing the way the words look physically gives him more critical distance."

In this same article Edwidge Danticat tapes herself reading her entire novel aloud. While reading, she listens for places where the work falters. After the reading, these are the places where she makes corrections.

Somewhere toward the almost-final draft, I read tracts of my story aloud. Like Danticat, this helps me hear where the writing has grown insipid or forced. And here's a secret that most of my colleagues or professional associates don't know about me: I'm an amateur singer, someone who could always pick up a melody or a tune or a song after hearing it once. So when I read my work aloud, as well as listening for obvious boo-boos, I'm also listening for the piece's musicality. Most important, I'm listening for where my sentences end. I believe that there's a certain sound that a sentence is supposed to close on—just like the lines of a ballad. So when it doesn't sound "right," I make a mental note to change it on the manuscript. There's absolutely no science to this. Like learning or listening to someone sing a folk song, I simply trust my own ear.

But long before the read-aloud part, I do my first cursory review on-screen. Then I print up a hard-copy draft for the "real" reading. I bring these hard-copy drafts to the doctor's office, to work for a quick lunchtime edit, or for under the dryer at the beauty salon. I find that these drafts are often best read in limited, defined time slots.

As a day job writer, I find that the on-screen first reading carries the double duty of getting me back into the piece and trawling for errors or places to make changes. As I read, I make changes along the way up to the point where I finished yesterday. Then I proceed onto that day's new writing.

EDITING AND REVISING UNDER DEADLINE

The only time that I write straight through is when it's a piece, say an essay or a feature article, that's under 3,000 words, and for which I'm under a really, really tight deadline. For example, I once came back from a trip overseas with a personal essay deadline hanging over my head. My plane landed on American soil on a Saturday afternoon, and my essay was due to the editor by that Monday around noon.

A week before this, I left on my trip assuring myself that "I can write the first draft on the plane." But if you've ever sat scrunched into one of those coach-class seats on a transatlantic flight, you know that, between keeping your legs from a permanent state of pins and needles and eating the airline crappy meal, there's little or no chance of writing.

The day after my homecoming, Sunday, I was jetlagged, fighting a head cold, and suffering a particularly bad bout of what I'll call linguistic constipation. Sitting at my writing desk, it took me half the morning just to come up with the opening line and scene. It was a very lousy opening line and scene, but I was under deadline so I kept writing without stopping, all the way through to the end, writing well over my required word count. In those places where I knew I was missing some background information, I simply put an asterisk and made a note to myself, in the document, in capital letters. "Better to have some draft than no draft at all," I told myself, as I reached for yet another tissue.

Then I took a long nap and some more aspirin. When I woke, I printed up my lousy draft and made some changes. Then I made some more changes. Then I shut off my laptop and went and ate some home-cooked food. And then, I went to sleep again, knowing that jetlag would be my friend and have me up and at my desk earlier than usual.

Next morning, I woke with a good opening line and scene right there in my head. So I redrafted, made more changes, and pruned the essay down to size. I made more on-screen edits, then printed it up and went downstairs to sit at my kitchen table. There I did a thorough review and copyedit. Sure, I knew that the magazine would copyedit, too. But as a part-time editor myself, I hate to submit work that looks sloppy—even if it's one little mistake. I made these final changes to the document. Then I did something that had saved my deadline-frantic skin in the past. Around 11 A.M. I opened my e-mail program and typed a cheery little note to the magazine editor saying that I was send-ing the essay via an attached file and as a cut and paste into the body of the e-mail—"to make it easier for you." But instead of hitting the "send" button, I chose the "save as draft" option. Then I sent a second e-mail of this cut and pasted file—this time to myself.

Ping! I had mail. Reading through this cut and pasted e-mailed version, I noticed some things and made some changes that I had missed before—both in the printout and in the on-screen word-processing file. Finally I cut and pasted this final-edit version back into my word-processing file to save it. I opened my draft and made the changes there, too. Then I sent it off to my editor.

For shorter pieces, whether I'm submitting to a lifestyle magazine—as in the case I have described above—or to a literary magazine or contest, I always, *always* send myself an e-mailed version before I send it into cyberspace. This e-mailed version becomes my last, fine-brush edit. I have discovered amazing things there.

I think this technique works because, like Colum McCann and the large-font version of his book, it forces me to switch from writer to reader. And, because of the changed format (e-mail), I am reading as if I am the editor, the person on the other end. It's a quick and efficient way to have that final look, to weed out those extra words, to smarten up the language, and to catch any boo-boos.

TEN WAYS TO BECOME YOUR OWN BEST REVIEWER AND EDITOR

(1) Read like a writer: Whatever genre you have chosen to work in, I'm betting that you are and have been reading lots of work in that same genre—and in other genres, too. Of course, you read for the sheer pleasure and enjoyment. You read before you go to sleep at night, or while sitting on the beach, or to pass the time on your train commute. But leisure reading can also teach you how to read your own work with a closer, more critical eye.

Gabriel Valjan, the nurse and short-story writer interviewed in the back of this book, recommends this read-to-learn process:

"Reading other writers makes one start to notice what works and what doesn't work … If you continue to return to a particular writer time and again, then analyze why."

I compare this to a beginner computer technician who dismantles a hard drive to learn what's in there and to study the component parts. As you read for pleasure and instruction, here are some particular aspects of the narrative craft to notice and learn from:

    (a) Openings: What makes you buy certain books and not others? If it was the first few lines of the first chapter, ask yourself why? What is it about this opening that convinced you to plunk down your dollars or download the Kindle version of this particular book? Was it the narrative voice? The immediacy of the writing? The pace of the plot? A narrative hook that immediately brought you into the story?

    (b) Structure and architecture: Whether it's a collection of essays or a mainstream blockbuster novel or one of those oddly structured or nonlinear novels that interweaves several story lines, take a closer look at how the book is organized. Don't look at the text. Just look at the overall architecture of this book or story. How did this author manage and organize all this information or narrative? Are there different parts to the book? Is it organized by sequenced chapters? If it's a short story or essay, are there double white spaces between the scenes? Or are there subtitles? I once read a short story about a young son killing his father. The author had organized this entire dark tale of teenage pathology by using the twenty-six letters of the alphabet: "A is for Axe." Whatever organizing device or architecture the author uses, you may not like it or ever choose to replicate it. But it opens you up to the choices—and to the fact that, sooner or later as you redraft, you are going to have to devise a way to organize and present your material on those pages.

(c) **Scene and time switches:** Read through a chapter of a favorite book and pencil the first lines of paragraphs only. See how this author manages time shifts between the story's present, past, and distant past. See how much space he allocates to the story's main action, flashbacks, explication, and dialogue.

(d) **Dialogue:** Read lots of dialogue in many types of writing. Read dialogue in books and essays that are set in various regions of the country or in other countries. Read dialogue between characters of different social classes. Read male dialogue. Read female dialogue. Study how the author weaves in other actions and movements and interior dialogue around the actual spoken dialogue.

(e) **Study a favorite author's career trajectory:** If you're one of those readers who reads everything that a certain author writes, then look at the entire progression of her books from the early publications to the more recent ones. Which are better (it's not always the more recent books)? And why? What is she doing differently in later books that she did not do in her earlier works?

(2) Go to the movies: Just as you can learn a lot from other writers' published works, take yourself along to the movies and watch how the filmmaker unfolds the story on the screen. Certainly narrative writing draws on different devices from film (though there are some overlaps), but it's useful to watch how the filmmaker manages the material—the structure or arc he uses to tell this story. When teaching yourself through movies, study two particular film devices:

(a) The opening scene and how it brings us in, while also delivering key information about these characters and the story's central conflict

(b) The time switches that waltz back and forth between the main story and the what-happened-before

(3) Know your real estate: If you're going to paint a room or landscape a garden, it's good to know what square footage or acreage you've got to work with. Granted, the typical, required length of your particular genre—what the publishers generally accept and publish—may not affect you when you're happily banging out that first draft. In fact, the more words the merrier, so that you have a rich and panoramic sampling to prune and rework. But as you develop your revision skills, it's good to know what's expected of you—how much real estate you're working with. Of course, the allowed space will not factor into your pruning decisions (Oh, I must keep this; otherwise, the piece will be too short), but it's helpful to know your genre. Seasoned, multibook authors have more clout or wiggle room when it comes to submitting a book or short piece that's dramatically over or under the general length. If you're a first-time author, publishers will not be as understanding or as willing to work with you to cut or expand the text.

THE APPROXIMATE LENGTH OF VARIOUS NARRATIVE GENRES

Personal or nonfiction essay: *The Christian Science Monitor* looks for essays between 400 and 800 words. The literary magazine *Creative Nonfiction* (www.creativenonfiction.org) has a word limit of 5,000 words. Generally most multigenre literary magazines (those that accept poetry, fiction, and essays) require first-person essay submissions to be somewhere between 2,000 and 4,000 words. If you're pitching your essay to a particular publication, research that publication's required word count. When the editors issue a desired word count, they're not kidding. This is what they want. They, too, are working with a given amount of real estate. So don't waste their time with pieces that are too long or too short.

Novella: A novella is a shorter version of the novel. It's anywhere from fifty to one hundred pages or up to 25,000 words. For some publishers, seventy pages is the approximate magic number for a novella or novelette.

Young Adult (YA) Novel: Novels which are generally pitched at teenagers. They range from 125 to 250 pages, though contemporary YA novels can be much longer.

Adult Novel: Again this varies by subgenre and by the actual writer, but most editors look for the three hundred page or 75,000- to 120,000-word ballpark.

Full-length memoir: Again, it varies, but publishers generally look for 40,000 words or more before they can consider it a book-length memoir. Generally 75,000 to 120,000 is the approximate length.

Short (fictional) story: There are many subgenres within the short-story category, such as speculative, science fiction, western, detective, crime, romance, fantasy, and literary. Different publishers have different required lengths. For literary short stories, most U.S. literary journals issue a 2,000- to 4,000-word count requirement.

Short shorts or flash fiction: These generally weigh in under 1,000 words. Though some are as short as 100 or 300 words.

(4) Learn your genre's conventions: Ask yourself, "If I walked into a large bookstore tomorrow, what section would I find my book or story in?" If it's not on its own display in the front of the store—complete with neon flashing lights, of course—where would the bookstore staff shelve your work? Would it be shelved under memoir, local interest, crime, romance, mystery? Or would it belong in one of the literary magazines just next to Periodicals? Or would it be in one of those glossy lifestyle magazines inside the front door? Once you figure this out, research the conventions of the genre. For example, in mystery fiction, the crime should be introduced within the first three chapters of your novel. The detective should appear very early in the book. If you're writing romance, by the midpoint of the novel, there should be an (ahem) coming together, a physical intimacy between your two protagonists. Before you set about cutting, pasting, and strengthening your work, learn and know what's expected of you in this genre. At a minimum, if you're going to break or stretch the rules, know that you're breaking or stretching the rules. And know why you're doing it.

(5) Develop your mapping skills: As you write and redraft, you'll tweak and change your story map over time. But for the second or third draft, it's useful to have a sense of your story's waltz in time, how your narrative moves forward and backward from the story's present (forward) to its past (what happened before the opening sentence). If you overuse flashback, or if each flashback is too long, your piece will lose momentum, and your reader will lose interest. Are there ways in which you can deliver the backstory or the necessary details about a character without going into flashback? Dialogue can often fill in some background. As can visual details or prompts (if, say, your grandfather sorts through his box of war medals every morning, we know that he once went to war). To map the forward momentum and the background flashback of your story or essay or memoir, print up at least twenty pages and take a pencil or a marker and map its backward and forward movements.

For example, here's how I would map this excerpt from "The Boarding House," a short story from James Joyce's *Dubliners*. In this scene, set in an urban Irish boarding house, a young man named Mr. Doran is about to be summoned downstairs by the boarding house landlady, Mrs. Mooney. Doran has impregnated Polly, Mrs. Mooney's young daughter, and the sly, parsimonious landlady expects to benefit from this. (The forward arrows indicate forward motion in the story and the backward arrows indicate backward motion.

FORWARD ➔ While he was sitting helplessly on the side of the bed in shirt and trousers she tapped lightly at his door and entered. She told him all, that she had made a clean breast of it to her mother and that her mother would speak with him that morning. She cried and threw her arms round his neck, saying: "O Bob! Bob! What am I to do? What am I to do at all?"

➔ She would put an end to herself, she said.

➔ He comforted her feebly, telling her not to cry, that it would be all right, never fear. He felt against his shirt the agitation of her bosom.

BACKWARD ⬅ It was not altogether his fault that it had happened. He remembered well, with the curious patient memory of the celibate, the first casual caresses her dress, her breath, her fingers had given him. Then late one night as he was undressing for bed, she had tapped at his door, timidly. She wanted to relight her candle at his for hers had been blown out by a gust. It was her bath night. She wore a loose open combing-jacket of printed flannel. Her white instep shone in the opening of her furry slippers and the blood glowed warmly behind her perfumed skin. From her hands and wrists too as she lit and steadied her candle a faint perfume arose.

↩   On nights when he came in very late it was she who warmed up his dinner. He scarcely knew what he was eating feeling her beside him alone, at night, in the sleeping house. And her thoughtfulness! If the night was anyway cold or wet or windy there was sure to be a little tumbler of punch ready for him. Perhaps they could be happy together ...

↩   They used to go upstairs together on tiptoe, each with a candle, and on the third landing exchange reluctant goodnights. They used to kiss. He remembered well her eyes, the touch of her hand and his delirium ...

→   But delirium passes. He echoed her phrase, applying it to himself: "What am I to do?" The instinct of the celibate warned him to hold back. But the sin was there; even his sense of honour told him that reparation must be made for such a sin.

→   While he was sitting with her on the side of the bed Mary came to the door and said that the missus wanted to see him in the parlour. He stood up to put on his coat and waistcoat, more helpless than ever. When he was dressed he went over to her to comfort her. It would be all right, never fear. He left her crying on the bed and moaning softly: "O my God!"

→   Going down the stairs his glasses became so dimmed with moisture that he had to take them off and polish them. He longed to ascend through the roof and fly away to another country where he would never hear again of his trouble, and yet a force pushed him downstairs step by step. The implacable faces of his employer and of the Madam stared upon his discomfiture. On the last flight of stairs he passed Jack Mooney who was coming up from the pantry nursing two bottles of Bass. They saluted coldly; and the lover's eyes rested for a second or two on a thick bulldog face and a pair of thick short arms. When he reached the foot of the staircase he glanced up and saw Jack regarding him from the door of the return-room.

Suddenly he remembered the night when one of the music-hall artistes, a little blond Londoner, had made a rather free allusion to Polly. The reunion had been almost broken up on account of Jack's violence. Everyone tried to quiet him. The music-hall artiste, a little paler than usual, kept smiling and saying that there was no harm meant: but Jack kept shouting at him that if any fellow tried that sort of a game on with his sister he'd bloody well put his teeth down his throat, so he would.

Polly sat for a little time on the side of the bed, crying. Then she dried her eyes and went over to the looking-glass. She dipped the end of the towel in the water-jug and refreshed her eyes with the cool water. She looked at herself in profile and readjusted a hairpin above her ear.

Notice how Joyce, the master short-story writer, creates a balanced tapestry between the main story (forward arrows) with the flashbacks (backward arrows)?

Now study the architecture of your own drafts. Mark the backward and forward movements. Then hold the pages at a distance from you (as career counselors often advise us to do with résumés). Are there too many back arrows? Or is each back arrow way too long? Or worst of all, did you start out with all forward arrows (your story's present tense), but then, once you went into flashback (backward-facing arrows), you forgot to return to the present of the story? If so, your story needs a drastic restructuring. For techniques on how to diagnose and fix this, see page 149, "Stat! Stat! Diagnose and Treat the 'This Stinks!' Sybdrome."

(6) Write the *TV Guide* blurb: So you've written a wild and wonderful first draft. Now take a brisk walk during which you ask yourself, "If the piece were a made-for-TV movie, how would the cable people describe it in an on-screen blurb? How would it be written up in *TV Guide*? You can always change it later, but start to sharpen your skills at getting to the heart of your story—fiction or nonfiction—by telling yourself, the author, what it's all about. Of course, it will be about more than this one sentence description. But as you redraft your piece, as you made decisions about what to prune, cut, or expand, it's useful to have this central, guiding context. Once you know what it's about, all your revision decisions will be guided by that knowledge.

(7) Okay, people! Out of the way! It's one of the trickiest things to manage: the dual personas of writer you and regular-person you (the daughter/sister/wife/husband/employee). Some creative writers find it easy. But I've seen other writers—myself included—really struggle with this. When it comes to making big-picture decisions about what to keep and strengthen and what to cut or delete from your writing, these dueling personas can get in the way of smart editing decisions.

This also applies when you're writing nonfiction memoir or a personal essay. Even when it's you telling a true story, you still need to develop your persona as a writer. You need to know who's the writer and who's the narrator and how these are different from each other. In nonfiction, who are you on that page? What is your voice? What is your writer's sensibility? In your family and in your neighborhood, you might be the kind of guy who helps old ladies with their lawn care. But as a writer, you may (or not) have a much sharper or acerbic edge. Step out of the way of your own writing and allow yourself the freedom to be that writer. If you're always revising as the person (Oh, but I *want* old ladies to like my work!"), then these will not be smart editorial decisions. Edit as the writer you.

(8) Take a walk or feed the canary: Learn how to leave your manuscript or piece in cold storage—preferably for at least a week. Sometimes, depending on our impending deadlines, we simply don't have the luxury of a week's distance from the work. But believe me when I tell you that it's never, *ever* a good idea to type the last sentence and then click the "Send" key. Never. At a minimum, give your work the benefit of an overnight resting phase. "Sleep on it," is a cliché of problem solving or decision making in our personal lives. It's also a very good guideline for gaining perspective and finding inspiration for how to fix your writing drafts.

(9) Read aloud and develop your ear: It may feel awkward in the beginning, and you may very well scare your cat into a different corner of the house, but reading your piece aloud is one of the best tools I know for reviewing your own work. It gives a sense of the rhythm and sound and tempo of your sentences. While reading aloud, any slow or lagging parts of the narrative will be instantly audible to you. Reading aloud is also a good way to weed out those errors of grammar, usage, or spelling. Just as you can teach yourself a lot about writing by reading smartly, you can also develop your own ear for good writing in a number of ways: (a) Attend lots of other writers' readings—preferably those who are writing in your genre. For at least part of the reading, try to listen beyond the individual writer's charm or onstage theatrics. Instead listen to the movement and rhythm of the narrative. Has she got it right? If this were your piece, where would you shorten or add more? (b) Listen to books on tapes. They take the pain and boredom out of a long car journey. They also develop your ear for spoken language and how it sounds out loud. Listen for where the reader or the story loses you, where you zone out to start thinking about other things. (c) Online stories: Listen via podcast or on your iPhone or online. StoryCorps, an independent non-profit organization (www.storycorps.org), is a collection of personal stories from people across America. As you listen, develop your ear for really good stories. Or visit your favorite author's website (or YouTube) for links to his or her public readings. Listen and learn.

(10) Know your basic grammar and usage rules: When you're hard at work on Draft 1 or 2 or even Draft 3, you will not need to care about those missing apostrophes or wrongly used words. But as you work toward that final draft, grammatical, spelling, or usage errors will draw attention to themselves and cause a distraction from the rest of the work. And, if and when you send your work out for publication, these kinds of boo-boos will create a sloppy impression of you, the writer. In some cases, an error on the first or second page will make an editor stop reading any further. Why? Because in a highly competitive market in which editors or agents receive lots of manuscripts per week, they will not be encouraged to invest precious time on a writer who doesn't know the basics or who hasn't taken the time to learn the rules of the English language. The tutorial at the end of this chapter will help you develop a copyeditor's eye and talent.

STAT! STAT! DIAGNOSE AND TREAT THE "THIS STINKS!" SYNDROME

> **8 A.M.** Writer awakes before alarm. Very distracted. Pupils dilated. Breathing fast. Attempts breakfast but abandons it to go to writing desk. No doodling. No games of solitaire. No e-mail check. Just writing.
> **Vital signs:** Fast, loud typing. Writer growing flushed.
> **Diagnosis:** Writer showing symptoms of a BBI (big, brilliant idea).

12 P.M. Writer pacing around the room. Some muttering. Three swear words. Writer back at desk. Sighs.

Vital signs: Typing has slowed. Frown lines forming between eyebrows.

Diagnosis: Still bright-eyed with inspiration and the BBI.

2 P.M. Loud flourish of typing as writer finishes Draft 1.

Vital signs: Grinning. uttering: "Brilliant!" "Fantastic!" "Nobel Prize!"

Diagnosis: Brilliant. Fantastic. Nobel Prize.

2:15 P.M. Writer's lips moving as he reads aloud. Shoulders visibly dipping. Posture scrunched slightly. Writer begins biting nails. Three more swearwords.

3 P.M. Writer in fetal position on floor. Moaning. Not responding to questions. Pulse slowed. Finally, writer gets up on all fours and crawls to writing table. Mutters, "This stinks!"

Diagnosis: First bad-draft syndrome. Stat! Writer in distress!

Rx for a "This Stinks!" (T.S.) Draft

First, remind yourself that this is a draft. And, except for a lucky few authors, most of us have to generate multiple drafts before we uncover what the piece is really about. Remember: First, second, or third drafts are the literary equivalent of a singer practicing scales or clearing her throat.

Second, there's a simple but true mathematical formula that guides and governs the T.S. syndrome. The shorter the time lapse between first draft and first reading, the higher the risk for the T.S. factor. Wait twenty-four hours, take a long walk, go upstairs and get ready for work. Tomorrow your draft will seem better. I promise.

Resuscitation Techniques for That T.S. Draft

Take a pulse: Stop the self-flagellation. Get up off the floor and go back and read with an eye for the scenes that have the most vitality, where the words flow, where the sentences have a steady and vital pulse.

Remove and save the good pieces: Either on-screen or on your printed-up, hard-copy version, highlight these good pieces. Or create a new word-processing file into which you cut and paste these keepers. Fantastic. You're doing well. Remember to breathe.

Find overlaps or themes: As you reread your salvaged goodies, watch for similarities or overlaps. Are these good pieces about a given character or subtheme or secondary story line? Let's take a simple example. You're writing an essay about how you, a city girl, became an avid gardener. When you started your draft, you planned to write an upbeat "Portrait of the Gardener as a Young Girl" piece. But now, when you reread your highlighted keeper pieces, you find that these lively excerpts (who is this writer? Dang! These are good!) are all about the third-floor walk-up apartment of your childhood—its smells and its antique wallpaper and the hot city nights your family spent having makeshift, rooftop barbecues. And whoa! What's this? In more than one salvaged excerpt, there's a vivid, lively scene in which your mother, a farm girl from Iowa, always seemed confined and unhappy in this city apartment. By contrast, the parts that tell your own gardening tale—the original story you intended—are drab and lackluster. So consider redirecting your essay topic, your BBI. For now, save your salvaged pieces about your mother and set yourself a new task of mentally redrafting how you might tell a new story about a kid and a lonely mother in a third-floor apartment.

Change the time of day: When I'm writing fiction, this has often saved a scene or chapter or story that was otherwise gasping for oxygen. Don't ask me why, but resetting your day scene in darkest night or your midnight scene at high noon gives it new energy—and often revitalizes the entire story in the process.

Change gender: You're a woman so you must always write as a woman or use a female narrator to tell the story, right? Not necessarily. Try writing from the opposite gender point of view. It can change the tenor of your story and give you and the story the distance and energy it needs to survive and thrive.

Narrow your focus: If your draft loses focus or direction, or if the scenes keep telling, not showing, ask yourself, "Can I move the camera in closer here?" More often than not, our grand, panoramic BBI gains traction and energy when we focus more closely. We may want to write the great American novel or the entire memoir of our lives, birth to death, but the more interesting stories are those that take a nuanced, close-up view of a finite period of time or one aspect of our humanity.

Switch the narrative distance: If you're faced with a T.S. story, open a new file or turn the page and try writing just one short scene from a different narrative distance or from a different point of view. For example, in our city-girl-turned-gardener story above, you tried to tell the story in vivid scenes, rendered in the present tense. (I am eight years old and standing on a chair at the sink, peeling carrots for supper. Mama says, "What I wouldn't give for a real, farm-raised carrot with the clumps of damp, wormy earth still clinging to the ends.") Now try writing this carrot-peeling scene in past tense, from the perspective of the fifty-six-year-old woman that you are now, with the sensibility of someone who has lived for more than five decades and who has found her true spiritual home in the countryside. ("Even now, in these warm late-summer days of harvest, I cannot pull a new carrot from the ground without thinking of Mama and that little apartment.") In this new excerpt, see what happens. If this retrospective, adult version sets your hand moving faster, if the voice feels more authentic and better suited to this story, then write from this narrative perspective.

The truth check: Sure, you woke with a vision of reading your BBI piece at the next writer's get-together, where everyone raved over it and someone stepped forth to offer you an instant movie deal. But put your ego aside and focus on the true strenths of your writing. Look more closely at those parts of your writing that you have decided to salvage. Do any of your salvaged pieces hint at a deeper story? A deeper truth that's more aligned with your own poetics or your personal worldview? If so, go with the true and authentic idea.

Switch genres: To extend the sample gardening story above, try writing one of the scenes as fiction, not memoir. Make yourself, the child in the urban apartment, quite different from how you really were (if you were shy, create a precocious, demanding child character). Make the family different by giving the mother a different job. Add a few fictional children. Introduce a fictional nosy neighbor. Or is this topic more suited to a prose poem? A short short story? Among the salvaged scenes, choose your favorite one. Now write it in a different genre and see if this story gets some colors in its cheeks.

Take the temperature: As a general rule, it's not a good idea to write about something traumatic or sad or infuriating immediately after it has happened. Why? Because you have not yet established enough emotional distance from the event itself to be in a position to read or render its deeper, literary truth on the page. You are not yet ready to play writer. You know that this draft will throb with rage or hurt or heartbreak. And while brimming with emotion, this draft will be short on texture and dimensionality (including an intellectual component). It will also stop short of universality. Being dumped by your lover is the most pressing thing in your life right now. But your broken love affair becomes universally interesting only when you've taken the time and distance to filter this real-life event through your daily consciousness. For an excellent essay on this topic, read Christiane Alsop's, "The Incident with the Dog in the Early Evening—Taking the Emotional Temperature of Your Work" at the writers blog, *Beyond the Margins* (www.beyondthemargins.com). In her essay, Alsop writes:

> But we writers cannot afford to be dizzy or have a narrowing perspective and, most of all, we cannot afford self-righteousness. Why? Because we need to look at an event through the eyes of each and every character and examine their situation, their take on things. Not our writing, but our minds have to be analytical in order to take their perspective.

Heighten the conflict: Even in memoir-style pieces, stories are built around conflict—either conflict between characters or between a character (or narrator) and the larger world in which they find themselves. In *The Three Little Pigs*, it's the pigs versus the big bad wolf. In the 1997 movie *The Full Monty* the central conflict lies between the hopes and aspirations of six British men and the harsh realities of unemployment. In this film, there are also the sub-conflicts of fathers' rights, homosexuality, the demise of industrial cities, and the various relationships and marriages depicted in the movie. In each TV episode of *Law & Order*, the conflict lies between the criminal and the criminal justice system, between crime and punishment. To revive your writing project, consider heightening the conflict. Can you move the two opposing points of conflict (little pigs versus big bad wolf) one step farther apart? Heighten the stakes and see if this resuscitates your story.

Writing Tutorial 6:
EDITING FOR CREATIVE WRITERS

I've heard some creative writers say that it's their job to spin wonderful and spell-binding stories, not to hunt down commas and apostrophes. So you write. And let the dang publishers earn their keep and do all that red-pen nitpicky stuff.

Stop. Right there. Dangerous attitude ahead! A dangerous attitude that will rob your writing of its own energy and potential. If you ignore the conventions of modern writing and English usage, you won't have to worry about the publisher's investment in copyediting your work. The publisher's acquisitions editor will know a slacker when he sees one and simply relegate your work to the recycling pile. If you were going to become a carpenter (maybe you are!), you'd learn all about different wood and how it can be cut, bent, sculpted, and fixed. You'd also teach yourself how to use a hammer, nails, joists, and wood glue. You'd know how wood bears up under certain climactic episodes—and how to fix any breaks and cracks when they happen.

HOW TO EDIT YOUR OWN NARRATIVE WORK

Adverbs: There are some cases where adverbs are needed, but among all the parts of speech, adverbs are the most disposable, so watch for these pesky, overwrought little words that end in *-ly* (quickly, madly, beautifully). Adverbs are the first sign that your writing needs to be revised and strengthened.

Here's an over-the-top example: I've exaggerated the use of adverbs so that you can see just how much havoc these pesky little things can wreak.

> We heard the car door banging loudly. Then, here came Dad, stomping heavily across the back porch. In the kitchen, he avoided looking at Mom and me, just made a beeline for the fridge. He stood there with the door open, sighing angrily and clicking his teeth impatiently when he saw that Mom had forgotten to buy beer. It seemed like ten minutes while he just stood there, ten minutes of me busily pretending to do homework and Mom pretending to nonchalantly peel the potatoes, while he did his Dad-stare at the carton of milk and the wilted bag of lettuce. Then, he slapped the fridge door furiously. We couldn't and wouldn't look up. At last, he cleared his throat gustily before he announced: "I just got laid off today. Just got

> cruelly marched out the goddamn office door." Strange thing
> was, after all that stomping and huffing, Dad announced his
> unemployment timidly, almost shyly.

See just how much these adverbs weaken the writing? Delete them.

Adjectives: In the general food pyramid of editable items, adjective rank higher than adverbs. Most of the time, they carry their own weight and pay their own way. But again, if your writing is vivid and strong, it does not always need to be qualified. Also, give your reader credit for what she already knows about the world. For example, if you write a scene set in the grounds of a perfectly manicured country club, I have a fairly good expectation that the swimming pool is a "perfect, shimmering blue." Unless one of the pool boys has played a prank with some food coloring, I wouldn't expect the pool to be any other color. Check your draft for adjectives that you don't need.

Check your time switches: Nothing exasperates a reader more than a narrative in which he has to keep flipping backward to understand where he's at in the story. "Is this the here and now? Or is this flashback?" Make him do this one too many times, and you've lost him. To edit your work, go through and circle or highlight the major time switches in the narrative. Each time there's a shift from present to past and back again, read it aloud to make sure that you've transitioned smoothly. Check your tenses (present, past, and past perfect). Here's an example:

> Marilyn speeds past the "Welcome to Branville" sign as she
> drives her black BMW south along Route 50, past the gas
> stations and the strip malls and the pizza joints outside town.
> She's smoking a cigarette. As she slows in traffic, she checks
> her blonde hair and her makeup in the rearview mirror. She
> takes another puff of her cigarette, then sets it in the ashtray
> to smooth down her red designer dress. It's her first time back
> in Branville since she first left all those years ago. And now,
> here she is, The Honorable Marilyn Ducannon, High Court
> Judge and the toast of Washington legal circles, reduced to
> this nervous, fidgety woman.
>
> Fifteen years ago, Marilyn drove this same route, except
> in the opposite direction and without looking behind her. That
> was the day she left Jake Mahoney.

> And six months before that fateful day, Jake had come
> home fired from yet another job.

In this example, I created a story about a woman returning to her hometown after a fifteen-year estrangement. So the present of the story is told in present tense (Marilyn speeds). Then we learn a little more about Marilyn's departure and estrangement in the flashback (Fifteen years ago, Marilyn drove). Also, we learn what led up to her departure (Jake had come home fired).

To edit the time switches in your work, study the verbs, the tenses, and the transitions (fifteen years ago). They must be clear and smooth and correct. The reader must never be lost in time.

Fancy, pretentious words: You're a writer, so you live and breathe and use language, and you want to show off your splendid vocabulary. But by showing off your vocabulary, you put an automatic barrier between you and your reader. It's not that your reader is dumb or has a limited vocabulary and can't understand. It's just that he wants to hear and experience your story—not experience your cleverness. Review your work with a newspaper editor's eye for clear, immediate prose.

For example, if you're writing about your first day in a new school, simply show us you there in that new classroom. Let us feel your fear and shyness, your interior dialogue, and the sounds and smells around you. Please don't tell us that, at sixteen, you were "embarking upon a plethora of educational and social challenges that would, ultimately, engender a lifelong resolve to pursue a career in pedagogy." Yuck. Who cares?

Imprecise Verbs: Okay, verbs. You're up next. I knew we'd get to you sooner or later. As you review your draft, ask yourself: "Is there a better, more vivid verb I could use here?" A strong verb carries its own weight, because strong verbs eliminate the need for those pesky adverbs. They can also tell us more about the character or the setting.

For example, look at how the stronger, more accurate verbs change these sentences:

Version 1:

> At eighty-three and suffering painfully with arthritis, Sister
> Lucy Ayers walked unsteadily along the convent's main av-
> enue. She stopped by the azalea bush, leaning on her cane
> and half closing her eyes against the Florida sun.

Version 2:

> At eighty-three and plagued by arthritis, Sister Lucy Ayers tottered along the convent's main avenue. She stopped by the azalea bush, leaning on her cane and squinting into the Florida sun.

Which version is more vivid to you? Which creates the stronger image of Sister Lucy Ayers?

Editing dialogue: Who's speaking? As you revise and redraft, scroll through your lines of dialogue and read them aloud if you have to. Examine the transitions between the lead-in description and the dialogue. Make sure that it's always clear who's speaking. Make sure that, when possible, your dialogue verbs are simple (he said, she said).

Overdescriptions of landscape or characters: Choose a few vivid items. Read through your descriptive passages of setting, buildings, towns, and countryside. How much is too much? If you describe and explain for too long, your reader will long to get back to the story. Also, by being heavy-handed in your descriptions, you begin to insert yourself between the work and the reader. If you're describing a shabby roadside motel room, give us a frayed lampshade and maybe a few cigarette burns on the carpet. Okay, maybe throw in a whiff of mildew. We'll get the point. Now let's get back to the action in the Roach Motel. There's an old saying that when you leave unnecessary writing uncut, your writing bears the burden of not just all those extra, unpruned words, but those extra words also weaken the words around them. It really is like pruning a rosebush. You need to get rid of the dead branches so that the other branches can grow healthier.

Proverbs and clichés: Not everything you write will be original. But avoid phrases or comparisons or metaphors that are over used in everyday dialogue. These include phrases like "there really are no free lunches." Or "A penny saved is a penny earned." It's not that these phrases don't have their uses in everyday life and speech. Often they act as a kind of shorthand for our shared experiences. But when you use them in writing, they reveal you to be a lazy and two-dimensional writer.

There is an exception to this. For example, the main character in Anna Quindlen's 2010 novel, *Every Last One*, compares herself to her father-in-law: "I have become Glen's father, who thinks and talks in clichés: A little hard work never hurt anyone. Make hay while the sun shines." In this case, the clichés work because it's not the narrator who is saying them. They also give us a small glimpse into her father-in-law's character and age.

Punctuation, grammar, and usage: You probably already know them, but those rules about plurals and apostrophes and possessives and dangling modifiers really don't matter in your early drafts. But they matter a lot as you take that finer brush to the work, as you begin to polish it to make it perfect. If you don't know the rules, look them up (see the resources listed below). Learn the rules of English usage, grammar, and punctuation. Or employ a freelance copyeditor who will check all these things for you. And, even if your day job involves lots of editing of other people's work, it's easy to make or overlook mistakes in our own creative writing.

RESOURCE LIST

Here are some resources to sharpen your skills with punctuation, grammar, and usage:

- *The Elements of Style* (Strunk & White, Longman Publishers)
- *A Pocket Style Manual* (Diane Hacker, Bedford Books of St. Martin's Press)
- *The Associated Press Stylebook and Libel Manual* (Addison Wesley)
- *Eats, Shoots & Leaves: The Zero Tolerance Approach to Punctuation,* (Lynne Truss, Gotham Books)
- Northeastern University's online style guide at www.north eastern.edu/toolkit/messaging/style1.html
- Common errors in English: www.wsu.edu/%7Ebrians/ errors/errors.html#errors.

WRITING EXERCISES

Below is an excerpt from "The Adventures of a Shilling" by the eighteenth-century British essayist Joseph Addison. As you can see, the essay was written in the now-archaic British English of that era. (A shilling was a unit of British currency. Its circumference was a little smaller than a U.S. quarter.)

The Adventures of a Shilling

I was last night visited by a friend of mine, who has an inexhaustible fund of discourse, and never fails to entertain his company with a variety of thoughts and hints that are altogether new and uncommon. Whether it were in complaisance to my way of living, or his real opinion, he advanced the following paradox, "That it required much greater talents to fill up and become a retired life, than a life of business." Upon this occasion he rallied very agreeably the busy men of the age, who only valued themselves for being in motion, and passing through a series of trifling and insignificant actions. In the heat of his discourse, seeing a piece of money lying on my table, "I defy (says he) any of these active persons to produce half the adventures that this twelve penny piece has been engaged in, were it possible for him to give us an account of his life."

My friend's talk made so odd an impression upon my mind, that soon after I was a-bed I fell insensibly into a most unaccountable reverie, that had neither moral nor design in it, and cannot be so properly called a dream as a delirium.

Methoughts the shilling that lay upon the table reared itself upon its edge, and turning the face towards me, opened its mouth, and in a soft silver sound, gave me the following account of his life and adventures:

Exercise 1:

Without changing the topic or without adding your own thoughts or opinions, edit and rewrite this excerpt in modern, twenty-first-century American prose.

Exercise 2:

When you have completed an edited, twenty-first century version of Addison's excerpt, finish the story of the shilling (or quarter), his "life and adventures."

Exercise 3:

Now write the *TV Guide* summary of the story: *"This is a story about ..."*

Exercise 4:

If you were going to choose an inanimate object with which to compare and satirize our "busy men of the age," what would you choose?

Exercise 5:

Turn over a new page or open a new word-processing document. Write a response to Mr. Addison, showing and telling examples from your twenty-first-century life and work and acquaintances and experiences. Do not check back on your first version of the essay. Simply write this new version. If you can, write your first draft all the way through. Then go back and revise this most recent version for clarity, language, voice, and vividness.

Exercise 6:

In your versions of the essay, which were easier to write? How much did your draft change between Version 1 (Exercise 2) and Version 2 (Exercise 5)? Why?

15

ENLISTING OTHERS
TO REVIEW YOUR WORK

PART 1: SHARING YOUR WRITING WITH COLLEAGUES

Depending on the industry you work in, your role at work, your relationship with your colleagues and your own personal comfort level, your workplace may or may not provide a quick and instant audience for those early writing drafts. It also depends on just how separate and distinct you want to keep your day job and your working lives.

Some workplaces present an automatic and supportive set of cheerleaders for your creative work. Some just don't.

Personally, I tend *not* to share my creative work with colleagues. In fact, I rarely even mention my work and feel awkward even discussing my role or "other life" there. Granted, and especially in this age of LinkedIn and Google searches, they know anyway—usually because they have seen my name listed in the local newspaper for public readings or panel participations or a book publication. But as a general rule, I like to keep my working and writing lives as separate as possible.

Your work setting and relationships might be quite different. However, before you start organizing a writing group in the workplace lunchroom, there are some considerations about mixing your creative writing with your day job life.

Your Writing Topic May Undermine
Your Workplace Reputation

I am a strong advocate for free expression and artistic freedom. So my writing students are often surprised at my bandwidth and tolerance for just about any kind of writing. Romance. Science fiction. Mystery. Fantasy. Literary. Humor. Erotica. If it's what my student wants to write, and if it falls within that day's instructional topic, then have at it. But I draw the line at gratuitous physical or sexual violence or profanity. *Gratuitous* is the operative word here. Violence or other human nasties can be *in* a participant's work; they can even be the most important part of it. But I draw the line at violence or sex or profanity that's just plopped in there and shared with the group for the shock value or for the author's own titillation. Otherwise, I believe that you should have the freedom to create what you want to create.

But then … there's that … ahem … little issue of the day job and the paycheck and paying the rent. Our twenty-first century companies and organizations are particularly careful about their brand and reputations—as they should be. Equally there have never been so many, many ways in which to check up on employees and their nonwork activities. A quick employer or potential employer search can reveal almost everything that an employee is writing, posting, and publishing. So if you write and publish erotica, will your employer be impressed? Will this impact your promotion or employability? If you've built a strong online presence as the creator of a series of SF stories about a (fictional) Martian with an insatiable appetite for busybody corporate humanoids, will this impact your next annual employment review? Your prospects for promotion? If you're willing to take this risk, or if you simply don't care, then by all means keep writing and posting and sharing your writing successes with your workplace friends. But if you love your job and need your paycheck, and if your writing persona or publications will impact your day job, then I advise you to keep your two lives as separate as possible. One way to do this is to write under a pseudonym.

Making Friends or Creating Enemies

Some readers will insert themselves into your story. So you've written a novel where a loveable, but not-very-bright character named Sarah makes a walk-on appearance in chapter nine. Meanwhile, back at the office, Susie from the marketing department (also a brunette and … jeez! Coincidence! Her name also starts with S!) is convinced that you have cast her—that she's the real-life inspiration for Sarah even though you barely know Susie from marketing. Depending on the degree of real, identifiable, and provable parallels between Susie and Sarah, this will probably not create a legal problem for you. But it may impact your working relationship with Susie from marketing.

Public Opinion

More than once, my job interview would be going along nicely until the *W* reared its head. *Writer.* There it was, right there on my résumé. It would have been dishonest to leave it off. I watched the frowns of trepidation across that interview desk. Sure, I had a well-rounded résumé and a nice interview suit and a practiced, articulate way of presenting information (or so they told me). But when it came to securing some paying gigs, my writing career and publications registered as a distinct negative. And, though I have no proof of this, I strongly suspect that being a writer sent an otherwise positive job interview down the don't-call-us-we'll-call-you route. In fact, one interviewer said, "Look, as soon as you land yourself some big best-seller, you won't care about me or this job." Later, I ran into this man during a literary festival where I was participating in one of the festival's author panels. He recognized, and then greeted me with a smug little sniff that said, "See? I was right."

Actually, he was wrong. Dead wrong. Bear with me as I get on my pet peeve pulpit here. Creative writers are perfectly capable of meeting annual goals or building houses or creating spreadsheets or curing the sick or hitting annual sales targets. But let's face it, there is a prevailing stereotype of writers as a bunch of scatterbrained, feckless, and self-serving creatures who exist in some rarefied world that add little or no value to the commerce of daily life. Read the author interviews in the back of this book. You will meet a group of authors who successfully balance writing and working and parenting and home ownership and community volunteer work. In my opinion, we are all too eager to pigeonhole people these days and to label people as "left brained" and "right brained" or as "the science type" or the "artsie type."

That said, until an employer actually knows you and your work performance, the writer stereotype is a tough one to offset. So why feed this by standing around the office watercooler loudly discussing your current problems with a piece of dialogue you're writing? You don't have to keep your writing life a secret. And lying on your résumé is never, ever the right thing to do. But in the workplace, if you share your writing successes, failures, and foibles, keep it to a few trusted friends and well-wishers.

Keeping It Clean On Social Media Sites and the Blogosphere

In Charlotte, North Carolina, a waitress was fired from her job because she posted an angry message about two lunchtime customers on her Facebook page. In the U.K., a sixteen-year-old woman was fired because she posted that she was "bored at work." In Texas, a Delta flight attendant was fired for posting inappropriate photos of herself in her uniform on her online diary.

Books and literature are quickly migrating from the bookshelves to the blogosphere and beyond. So when your creative or other writing damages your employer's reputation—or when it damages your reputation as an employee—organizations are not amused. Bottom line: If you own or post to a writers blog, or if you use a social networking site to stay in touch with your writers group, post nothing on there that you wouldn't want your employer to read and know about you.

Sharing Personal Nonfiction Writing

Workplace relationships and friendships evolve under a different set of norms from the friendships we form in our personal lives. In an increasingly competitive, volatile, and changing work environment, these friendships exist against a backdrop of promotions and layoffs and shifting workloads. Therefore, even when your creative writing does not and cannot compromise your actual job, it can influence colleagues' unspoken impression or opinion of you. Want to write a personal essay or a full-length memoir about your struggles with depression? By all means do so. And you should write about family estrangement, an impoverished childhood, or an abusive parent. But if you're going to actively share your personal writing with your colleagues, you will be giving them a window into your past or your current personal life. If you choose to share, make sure that you consciously decide to do so—and that this is a decision you will not regret if and when your workplace relationships change.

PART 2: SHARING YOUR WORK WITH STRANGERS: FINDING AND JOINING A WRITERS GROUP

Writing can be a lonely life. Most of the time, it's just you and the computer or a notebook. And, most of the time, we wouldn't really want it otherwise. But it can also be an uncharted course, when it's often easy to lose sight of the starting or ending point. Or it's easy to lose faith, to feel overwhelmed by the dual challenges of fitting some writing into an already busy day. Add to this that there's a general "no whine" gag order on writers. For starters, many nonwriters consider our work as a hobby or luxury. Or the long process from first to final draft is just an unknown, baffling process that has few counterparts across other fields of work or commerce. So when we're invited to the high school reunion or for the neighborhood dinner party, we often grow shy about our own work—the successes, failures, and rejections. Enter: The writers group, a chance to be with like-minded people who can share your joys and sorrows, who really know what you mean when you say that the ending of your story is keeping you awake at night. And, if you choose a peer review setup, a writers group will give you a team of readers to offer feedback and suggestions on how to make your work better.

Day Job Writer Be Warned! Joining a writers group may seem like fun way to socialize with like-minded friends. But participation in a writers group—especially a peer review group—is a substantial time commitment. As a writer with a day job, every hour you take away from your writing needs to carry its own creative and productive weight. So before you sign up for a group, make sure it's the type of group for you, and that it's going to be worth the time invested.

SIGNS THAT A WRITERS GROUP WILL WORK FOR YOU

You are ...

1. Ready and confident enough to have your work reviewed by other writers
2. A group person—someone who enjoys the camaraderie and conversation of other people
3. Open to and see the value of other writers' input to your work
4. Accepting of other genres or subgenres that are different from yours
5. Accepting of various personalities and individual approaches to writing
6. Good at accepting constructive, honest feedback with kindness and diplomacy
7. Good at giving constructive, honest feedback with kindness and diplomacy

You have ...

1. Time in your schedule to devote at least one or two evenings per month to a meeting
2. Time in your schedule to read, review, and provide constructive written and oral commentary on a number of manuscripts from other writers

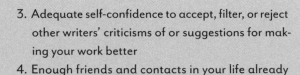

3. Adequate self-confidence to accept, filter, or reject other writers' criticisms of or suggestions for making your work better

4. Enough friends and contacts in your life already so that you do not look to this group as your only outside socialization or way of making friends

A WRITERS GROUP: WHAT TYPE?

Peer led: The most common type of writers group is one in which five, six, or seven (or even ten) writers meet to present their respective work and to critique each other's drafts. Unless someone collects a fee to pay for drinks and snacks, there is usually no fee to join.

Instructor or mentor led: These often grow out of a more formal or instructional writing workshop. In effect, this is a teaching workshop that continues over a long period of time—often with the same core group of students or writers. The teacher or workshop leader sets many of the group's guidelines and rules around how the group exchanges work and how critiques are returned to the writer. Unless the teacher is volunteering his time, these groups generally have a fee which pays for the workshop space and the teacher's or leader's expertise.

Social only: Sometimes you become your own best editor or you hire a literary coach or professional editor. So you simply want to meet other writers to chat and socialize, and talk a little shop about the process of writing. Often there's a potluck or restaurant-based dinner involved, there may be a guest speaker, and the evening or afternoon may be structured around a specific agenda or topic. Or there can be no agenda, and everyone just has a good time among people who are also writing. Generally, except for donations of food or the cost of your dinner, there is no fee for these groups.

Topic-specific writers groups: Some groups are organized around a specific topic or genre of writing, and, therefore, only include writers who work in this genre or format. For example, there are many active, working poetry groups. Or there are journal-writing groups which are based in or emerge from a wellness facility such as a hospice or hospital, or a support group which caters to people in recovery from a specific condition or who are in a certain life situation such as cancer, addiction, or family trauma. Or the group may be affiliated with a church. Generally speaking, the focus of these groups is not on the actual structure or content or style of the writing. Instead, the focus (as it should be) is on personal expression, recovery, and fellowship among people who share a similar life crisis or situation. These kinds of writers groups are often facilitated or led by someone with clinical licensure or training—or a lot of experience or training in personal or journal writing. In fact, if you join a writing or journaling group that is focused around wellness or recovery, inquire from the sponsoring organization (hospital or community service organization) who the workshop leader will be and what her credentials are in terms of leading a group that will more than likely be sharing writing around difficult and painful topics.

Online workshops: Online writers groups are generally moderated, peer-conducted workshops in which you submit excerpts of your writing for review by a group of writers who are working in the same genre as you are. The writers could live across the country or across the world. It doesn't matter. Or online groups can be led by a writing teacher or facilitator, who has been hired by the online school to provide feedback and encouragement to the participating writers. In addition to online writers groups, some authors are also launching their own coaching schools, in which you can send the author excerpts of your work for their expert review and suggestions. There are many advantages to joining an online versus an in-person writers group: (1) You gain feedback from and exposure to writers from diverse geographic and demographic backgrounds. (2) If you're on the road, an online group is more accessible in terms of scheduling and accessibility. (3) If you're not by nature a joiner or a people person, an online group may give you the anonymity you need. See the list of online writers groups and communities on page 176.

Blend of in-person and online: Some in-person writing groups also establish an online platform (blog or website or a distribution list) to support group communication and to create an easy way to share manuscripts at a distance. Similar to an in-person-only gathering, the most successful writers groups set and enforce some general ground rules.

HOW TO FIND A WRITERS GROUP

New in town? Just starting to write and could use some motivation or support or qualified feedback? Established or new writers groups often recruit for new members. Here's how to find a group (or advertise for a new group) near you:

1. Check the bulletin board at your local public library.

2. Ask the librarians at your local library if they know of any writers groups in the area. Some public libraries host writers groups.

3. Ask the assistants at your local independent bookstore. Writers generally hang out in bookstores and often share information about groups they belong to. Some bookstores host writers groups.

4. Check the Classified sections of writers magazines such as *Writer's Digest* or *Poets & Writers*.

5. Check out www.craigslist.org > Select your closest city > Community > Groups.

6. Word of mouth. Ask around. If you know some writers or if you attend a reading, let people know you're looking for or looking to establish a writers group.

7. Bulletin board at your local café. Or, if you notice that a writers group regularly meets there, wait until the group takes a coffee break and ask the facilitator if the group is accepting new members.

8. Check your local community college or adult education facilities. If they offer creative writing classes, e-mail the instructor and ask if she knows of any local writers groups.

9. Local or statewide writers organizations or collaboratives often allow various groups to list their

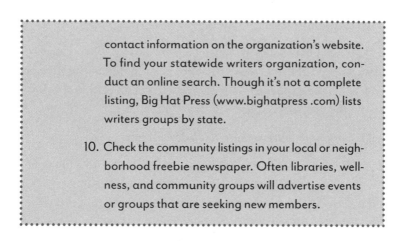

contact information on the organization's website. To find your statewide writers organization, conduct an online search. Though it's not a complete listing, Big Hat Press (www.bighatpress .com) lists writers groups by state.

10. Check the community listings in your local or neighborhood freebie newspaper. Often libraries, wellness, and community groups will advertise events or groups that are seeking new members.

WHAT TO LOOK FOR IN A PEER-REVIEW WRITERS GROUP

Once you locate an established writers group in your area, ask if you can visit for one meeting (without signing up for the review roster)—just to see if you fit the group and if the group fits you. If the organizer or group members are offended by your try-it-before-you-buy-it request, then ask—diplomatically of course—why. Or take this as a sign that the touchy, hypersensitive, or egotistical writers group is not for you.

BASIC QUESTIONS TO ASK BEFORE THAT TRY-IT VISIT

Q *What genres are the group members working in?*

A As a general rule, it's best if the group members are working in either narrative writing (nonfiction or fiction) or poetry. This means that you can establish and share a common critique language. But within these common categories, I find that a healthy dose of diversity benefits the work and keeps the group lively. Genre writers can really benefit from and cross-pollinate between respective works. For example, the mystery or thriller writer in your group will tell you when your plot is lagging or when your opening is trudging along. Equally, the group's literary writer will always read and critique for language and the musicality of a given piece of writing. If you have someone who has a background in writing for theater or TV, he may provide wonderful input on dialogue. Reading and critiquing each other's work is more than trading review services. We really learn a lot about writing and the writing craft by reading the work of other writers.

Q *What do the members do when they're not writing?*

A It's best if at least some group members are also balancing a part- or full-time day job—just like you. You will have more in common with these writers than you will if the group is entirely comprised of retirees or people who have all day and the financial resources to write full time.

Q *Is this a beginner, intermediate, or all-level group?*

A If you've worked hard on honing your writing craft, you will not be grappling with the same challenges as a beginning writer. Also, it's unlikely that a beginner can give you the same level of feedback that a midlevel writer can. Equally, if most of your group is working with the rudimentary aspects of the craft, you will end up feeling like an unpaid teacher, not a peer. You're looking for shared competence in creative writing and critiquing skills—not necessarily a set of writing degrees from a name-brand campus or writing program.

Q *How and how much writing is shared per session? What format?*

A Do member writers send drafts via e-mail and then discuss within the group? Or do writers make multiple copies of their work for distribution? Will this format work for you and your work schedule? Can each writer distribute ten pages? Twenty? One hundred? How many group members are submitting at the same time? If your cumulative, weekly page-reading count totals three hundred, consider if this will be doable, without costing you your own writing and creative time.

WHEN YOU VISIT: WATCH AND LISTEN

Here's the thing: From church groups to book clubs to neighborhood mothers clubs to family reunions, no social group will accurately describe themselves and their group dynamics. This is because group dynamics—including the between-the-lines and unspoken rules—just happen, and the general flavor or feeling of a group is often invisible to the members, from the inside out.

No writers group will function flawlessly and happily all the time. And ultimately a writers group is … well, only a writers group. Even after the most productive or raucous or joyous meeting, you're going to have to go home to your writing desk where it's just you and the work. Ultimately, while your writers group may act as your cheerleaders and readers and critics, the largest and final editorial decisions will be up to you.

So set up a visit. Have fun. Expect the best. But as you sit there, observe the unspoken clues. There are some telltale hints that will indicate whether this is a happy, functional writers group:

The initial meet and greet: Are the group members genuinely happy to see one another? Is there a sense of warmth and welcome and camaraderie in the room (or restaurant or at that member's house)? Also, while not all members of the writers group will be equally friendly or effusive, watch for an overall sense of respect and inclusiveness. If certain members receive a more muted or reluctant welcome, or if one member seems outside of the initial, premeeting chatter, just make sure that this group has not splintered (or is about to splinter) into subgroups of the "in crowd" and the "not-so-in crowd."

Punctuality: We've all run a little late or taken a wrong turn or had to take a last-minute call before leaving work. But if members drift in fifteen minutes late or even at various times during the meeting, this is going to present a problem—especially if and when it's your turn to share your writing. Overall, a late arrival and a banging door are distracting to the group and interrupt the flow of thought, conversation, reading, or critique. If someone does arrive really late, assess whether this is just a once-off (we've all been there) or part of the group's overall habit.

Is an established group open and welcoming to you? As the members arrive and you are introduced around, try to observe how open this group *really* is to a new, unknown writer. Some groups advertise for new blood (an extra reader and reviewer), but in terms of friendship and in-person interactions, they're actually a closed clique. Do their facial expressions show genuine interest in you? In your work? If there's a social part to the evening, do they include you in familiar or shared topics, or the chatter about each other's kids, spouses, partners, or projects?

A room of your own: If the group meets in a café or a restaurant, is it easy to hear the group discussion? Or are you all shouting above the sounds of the café's stereo or a blaring TV in the corner? If this first meeting is at someone's home, does the host seem comfortable as a host? Can you hear the host's family TV through the kitchen walls? Or does the host keep leaving the group to check on children or pets? Either scenario may be okay for this one meeting, but if the group always meets at this person's house because of babysitting or other family issues, then ask yourself how this stop-and-go style will affect your own participation and the quality of the discussion.

After you, my dear: Is the discussion equally weighted among group members? Or does one person persistently hog the conversation? And, more important, is there an unspoken group agreement that one person automatically has the final and definitive word, that her opinion counts more? If so, then this is not a writers group at all. This is a bunch of literary groupies who have been drafted to feed one member's already inflated ego. Trust me, I've suffered through this experience. Both as a writer and as a human being, it leaves you feeling angry and resentful—on your own behalf and on behalf of your fellow writers.

Specific, usable feedback: Listen to how the group offers input on each other's writing. Is it all gushy positive? Is it all negative? Either scenario is a problem. Also, try to get a sense of whether the group reviews in a big-picture way, in which they look at overall structure, plot, or the coherence of the work, or if the discussion gets bogged down in close-up, fine-brush editing ("I think you should use a semicolon here") at the expense of large-format feedback or input. Remember: If you're joining a writers group to gain a first-reader audience, you really are just looking for this macro or big-picture feedback. If you feel you really need editing, you can always hire a professional copy editor when you've reached the copyediting phase of the manuscript.

Specificity: While nobody expects a writers group to rewrite your next draft for you, the critiques and commentary need to be specific to certain aspects or parts of the work under discussion. "This didThis scene in the hotel room didn't work for me because in terms of voice and language, it didn't seem to fit the rest of the story," or, "I'm not sure the scene in the hotel room was actually necessary to this story. In fact, it took me out of this piece's suspended reality. I felt that the writer was interjecting here. Would it be possible to shorten it or even delete this scene and still tell this story?" is much more useful to a writer.

Objectivity: Often members of a writers group become personal friends. Some writers groups endure for years (see the "Anatomy of a Thriving Writers Group" on page 179), and the dialogue goes way beyond writing or editorial input on each other's work. Instead the camaraderie that starts with a love of writing and books extends into each other's lives, relationships, jobs, parenting, and life issues. This is great. However, when it comes to actually critiquing each other's work, keep it as objective as possible. This can be particularly challenging when the group is reviewing nonfiction or fiction that is partially autobiographical. So, as you observe your new or potential writers group, listen to the degree to which they separate the writing from the writer. Here's an example: Let's say that one member—let's call her Katie—has presented a memoir excerpt that includes a marital blowout on the golf course. Now, the other group members know that Katie and her husband are avid golfers. And they know that Katie is in the process of an ugly divorce. It's still important to critique Katie's writing excerpt in terms of the writing on the page. In this instance, useful feedback might sound something like, "I feel that the golf scene in this piece (not "your golf game") gives the reader (not "us") a real insight into the characters (not "Katie and Paul") and their relationship. This scene is really vivid, but it's not overwritten. In fact, the language and narrative voice in the golf course scene gives the reader a sense of tension and foreboding."

An active writing, not a publishing group: Some writers love to indulge in a shared moan-fest about the publishing industry. Others love to deliver vicarious and celebrity tidbits from websites or news articles that report on famous authors and literary agents. While a group can be a wonderful resource for publishing guidelines or tips, the main discussion should center on the writing process. As in, that trial-and-error process in which we conceive and imagine and invent and draft to get our artistic vision onto the page.

I beg to differ: So much of what we love and buy and read comes down to individual taste. So observe how this potential writers group handles dissenting opinions. For example, let's say this group is discussing John's essay about becoming a stepfather. Susie loves the scene where John meets his girlfriend's kids for the first time. She feels that this scene brings the reader right in there. It captures John's conflicting feelings of hope and self-doubt about his new parental role. So Susie concludes, "I wouldn't change anything in this scene. As a reader, we really get what the author is doing. If anything, I might ramp it up a little and give the reader even more of this scene and the dramatic tension." So John the writer (and new stepfather) sits back and basks in this praise. Then, a second group member—let's call him Joshua—coughs meaningfully and says, "I actually hated this scene. After the first few lines, I skipped over it. It's dead on the page. As a reader, I found myself just not giving a damn."

Around the room, group members take sides between Susie's and Joshua's opinions about the scene.

Okay, we have the same scene, the same personal essay, the same writer. We just have very dissimilar and equally vehement opinions. This is good. This could be the genesis of some really healthy and lively discussion on scene writing and narrative distance and dialogue in nonfiction writing. As you observe your new group, watch how a difference of opinion like this will play out. Will it remain polite and respectful and professional? Will each side ground their opinions in the context of John's essay and the parameters of the writing process and craft? Or will the discussion turn personal? How comfortable does each person seem with the very fact that he is being challenged? And, if and when the discussion gets overheated or veers off course, who steps in and moderates?

How do they react to each other's successes? Some writers interpret another's success as her personal failure. It's called the "green-eyed monster." And if and when you see this little monster lurking around this room, offer him your glass of wine and tell him to try a different color. Watch how the group reacts to each other's success. If the group members applaud and toast each other's breakthroughs or ideas or publications, then here's a team of sincere and stalwart cheerleaders who will support you from the sidelines of your writers life.

ONLINE WRITERS COMMUNITIES

Just as with an in-person group, the most successful online writer communities are well moderated, and there are published rules and guidelines on how people post their work and post their critiques of other writers' work. And, just as you would with an in-person group, select an online community where the writers appear to be at your level of experience. If you decide to join a particular forum or subgroup (romance, personal essay, science fiction), join as a guest first to get a sense of what published authors the members have been reading and discussing. Just as with an in-person writers group, it's useful to have a diversity of reader and writers, but you also want to have a sense of shared reading tastes and common reference points. For example, if you're looking for input on a draft of your dense, multilayered memoir about your father's suicide, you may not feel very comfortable (and you will not get informed critiques) from a group that's entirely comprised of writers who have never read anything more serious than the Garfield cartoon strip. Also, whether you join an online or an in-person writers group, the process of exchanging work and critiques with other writers is not just the literary equivalent of trading babysitting duties. As you read and review the work of other writers, you learn a lot about the writing craft and, ultimately, the process of redrafting your own work. So read the work of good writers.

Writer Beware! Before you submit work to an online writers group, check and double-check how your draft is posted online. Later, when your work is polished and perfect and ready for submission to a publisher or editor, most editors want to acquire first American rights. In other words, they will not accept or publish work that has already been published—and that includes work that has already appeared on the Internet. Here's a tip: Only submit the excerpt with which you need specific input or help—not the whole piece.

Don't want to join an established online writers group? Set up and create your own group on LiveJournal.com or use blogging sites and invite some like-minded writers to join and contribute and critique.

By creating a members-only writers blog, in which a finite number of writers submit and comment on each other's writing, you gain and keep control over who joins and submits and provides commentary. You can limit it to one particular genre only. Or a writers blog can act as an add-on to your in-person writers group—a way for members to keep in touch or submit work in between those in-person meetings. This works especially well for writers groups in which some members travel for work or who cannot make all the monthly or biweekly get togethers. And finally, some writers find a peer-review writers blog easier because, as writers, we communicate our ideas and feedback and suggestions more succinctly in writing than we do in person. Whatever format you choose, many of the same rules apply regarding fair, respectful, and honest feedback. And it works best when you have clear guidelines and an assigned moderator.

Blogger Beware! Hasn't it happened to you? Someone has interpreted an e-mail quite differently from how you intended. Without the human gestures of smiling or explaining or gesturing, the reader may interpret your feedback quite differently than you intended. This is the huge downside of digital communications. Once we click that "send" or "post" key, it's hard to retract or explain or contextualize what we say. So be careful about how you provide peer feedback in this format. The solution? Write your response or suggestions for the writer in question. Then save it as a draft. Come back to it later and review or amend your posting or e-mail before it goes live.

Here are some popular online writers communities:

Scribophile: www.scribophile.com. Guarantees three solid critiques on each piece a writer submits. You must upload comprehensive critiques of other members' work before you can submit your own work for review. The site accepts writers working in different genres, from flash fiction to poetry to memoir.

WritersCafe.org: www.writerscafe.org. A virtual equivalent of a writing group. It includes classes, groups, information on publishing and agents, and writing contests.

The Writer's Beat: www.writersbeat.com. Find forums and bulletin boards which offer useful information on everything from the craft of writing to writing markets and a Writers Café where writers are invited to hang out and "chat with other writers."

Absolute Write: www.absolutewrite.com. Organized by topical forums, it caters to a wide selection of writers and genres, ranging from novelists to business and technical writers to bloggers. Features an Ask the Agent section and an online book club. It's a very comprehensive online writers forum.

Authonomy Writers Community: www.authonomy.com. Provided by publisher HarperCollins, who describes its online writers and publishing venture in this way: "*Authonomy* invites unpublished and self-published authors to post their manuscripts for visitors to read online … Visitors to *authonomy* can comment on these submissions—and can personally recommend their favorites to the community."

Writing.com: www.writing.com Launched in 2000, this one boasts over 800,000 members to date. Author features include a free online writers portfolio, writing contests, and the opportunity to "meet" other writers.

Nothing Binding: www.nothingbinding.com. A social networking site for writers, published authors, and readers, Nothing Binding offers a way for published authors to showcase their books.

Review Fuse: www.reviewfuse.com. The site allows writers to submit their work for review and also allows resubmittal of second, third, or four drafts to get continuous peer feedback as submissions improve. Submitting writers also get a chance to rate their peer reviews in terms of how useful the critiques actually were. Based on this rating process, the moderators match the most mutually supportive writers and reviewers.

Hatrack River Writers Workshop: www.hatrack.com. For authors only over eighteen years old, Hatrack offers guidelines on how to give helpful, polite, and focused feedback. Features writing prompts to get you started. The Fragments and Feedback section invites writers to submit the first thirteen lines of a manuscript and asks for volunteers to read all of it. Or submitting writers can just ask for feedback on those thirteen lines.

BookRix: www.bookrix.com. You can publish an e-book for free through BookRix. The Honest Opinions section offers member review and feedback.

PART 3: SHARING YOUR WORK WITH FRIENDS OR FAMILY

In the 2010 article, "First Readers: The Crucial Critics" in *Poets & Writers* magazine, writer Kevin Nance has interviewed some nationally known authors about their first readers—the person they entrust with their first before-publication drafts. In the article's opening, Nance describes how best-selling novelist and essayist Barbara Kingsolver worked for five years on her latest novel, *The Lacuna* (HarperCollins 2009), which she had written without getting any feedback from anyone. Then it was time to give it to her first reader, her husband, Steven Hopp. Steve Yarbrough has his wife read his first drafts, while poet Naomi Shihab Nye entrusts a draft to her husband. Other writers interviewed report how they ask a writer-friend to be their first reviewer. Whether they're sharing with friends or family, the article's writers agree that the first-reader relationship is a special one that's based on clear guidelines and sound honesty—the kind of literary honesty that will point out where the writing needs clarification or changing or tweaking.

Also, novelist Erin McGraw advises "a shared aesthetic." Without a shared aesthetic, says McGraw, "you're wasting each other's time."

In broad, simple terms, this means that if you entrust your writing draft to a partner, a sibling, or a friend, you must share the same literary values. You may not read and like all the same works. But as a reader and a lover of literature, the same things must matter to you.

Should you enlist your friends or family as reviewers of your early drafts? This depends very much on you as a writer and on who your friends or family are.

Of course, this assumes that writers befriend writers. Among my close friends, our friendships have evolved and deepened for reasons other than our writing work. And, quite simply, I would not burden these already busy people with reading a three hundred–page draft of my writing—when I would certainly not be qualified to return a counterpart favor in support of their (non-writing) professions. And, even among my writer friends, I believe that each brings her own sensibility, her own life experiences to that critique. And that life experience includes her relationship with me. So the minimum I would offer a friend for constructive critique would be an opening scene or the first few pages (maximum of three). And, like many of the interviewed authors in the *Poets & Writers* article, my central author-question is always around clarity and readability: Is this opening clear?

When it comes to asking a partner, spouse, or sibling to be your first reader, we are again assuming that we're cohabiting with or married to another writer—or a reader who likes and values the same things that we do. Of course, this isn't always the case. I'm not sure I would want it to be. I see my role as a wife and as a neighbor and as a sister as being very distinct from my role and persona as a writer. My writing voice is very different from my speaking, daily voice, the voice with which I greet colleagues or my boss at my workplace. Many of the people who know me would probably tell you that I can be funny and witty and a little long-winded. Colleagues have told me that I "liven things up," that "you make things fun" or "you have a warm personality." I do. But when it comes to my writing, readers have commented on the darkness of my sensibility and life view. Or, in my nonfiction, they have said that I sound strident or intellectual or too cerebral. Neither of these personas is more authentic or more real than the other. I see them as separate parts of myself, and nobody is more surprised than I am by what ends up on the page. So when it comes to enlisting my friends or husband as a first reader of my work, I do not trust these people to make that leap from the everyday me to the writer me. At least, not in these first draft, early stages of the work.

This goes for family members, too. I'm their sister, not their soon-to-be favorite author. And I kind of like it that way.

Also, as a writer with a day job, your spouse or friend or sibling may already be carrying part of the load of parenting, babysitting, errands, or housework—all so that you have free time to write. So asking that spouse to *also become* a first-draft and unpaid reviewer may not be an option.

Enlisting your friends or family to review your first drafts depends on who they are—as people, as readers, as siblings, or as friends. It also depends on the extent to which these people are invested in your success as a writer. And finally, I believe that it depends on who you are, and the degree to which you're comfortable blending the roles in your life.

Above all, when you ask your family member or close friend to read and critique your early drafts, be clear with them about what you really want and be ready to take their feedback graciously. Be ready to return a corresponding favor in support of their work or life. Also, take some steps to protect that personal relationship. This should be your first priority. You can always hire and pay for a literary coach or editor, but you cannot hire a new sister or new best friend.

TWO DECADES OF HAPPY WRITING: ANATOMY OF A THRIVING WRITERS GROUP

January 2011 marked the twentieth anniversary of the Wednesday Writers group, which has been meeting, writing, and publishing in the San Francisco Bay area since 1991. Many group members have been there from the start. The Wednesday Writers Group draws many first-time writers. And for many, it's their first time getting published. The Wednesday Writers group has published two anthologies of their work, *Wednesday Writers* and *Something that Matters*. Proceeds from sales of the book support breast cancer research in the San Francisco Bay area. This is a fee-based writers group. In the beginning, the group's founder, Elizabeth Fishel drew members to her group via word of mouth, bookstores, her own public readings, and from among her past students in writing workshops that she had taught. Now the group totals twenty-two to twenty-four members, with approximately ten members meeting every other Friday. The other ten to twelve members continue to meet on Wednesdays. Some members have flexible work schedules, while others take a long and early lunch break. The focus of the group is mostly on personal narrative—essays and memoirs. The group meets weekly for two hours and fifteen minutes.

When a writer has a draft she wants to share, she brings in ten copies for other group members who take it home for review and commentary and some written feedback for the author.

The next week is discussion time. Says Fishel: "To keep a warm, friendly supportive atmosphere, I always begin by talking about what we enjoyed about the piece: memorable lines or images, its emotional impact on us." Then, the group moves on to suggestions for editing and that second draft—questions, places that need "embellishments or pruning." Says Fishel: "Rewriting is where the real writing takes place." The group discusses two pieces per meeting. The final half hour is devoted to in-group writing, in which Fishel, as leader, assigns a topic to which the writers respond in their journals. An in-group topic "has sometimes caught fire with someone, and she will work on it at home and develop it into a longer piece."

Members of the Wednesday Writers have published essays in newspapers, national magazines, anthologies, and some have published memoirs and books of poetry.

Group Schedule:

10:00 A.M.–10:10 A.M. Coffee, tea, snacks, and conversation

10:10 A.M.–10:30 A.M. Conversation about the writing life—members report on projects they are working on, ask for guidelines on a publishing outlet, and news of a reading or writing conference someone has attended.

10:30 A.M.–11:45 A.M. Discussion and editing of the two (more if the pieces are short) pieces of writing up for that week's review.

11:45 A.M.–12:15 P.M. Fishel assigns a writing topic. Writers write in their journals for ten minutes in response to that topic, then discuss.

Secrets to Success:

- Warm, friendly, supportive atmosphere
- Shared commitment to writing and rewriting as a process
- Blend of writing, instruction, discussion, friendship
- Clearly stated outcomes:

    - At the end of each ten-week session, a group anthology is created and printed for members to take home.

    - The group has also published two larger anthologies that have raised funds for nonprofit research.

  - A weekly or biweekly deadline that sustains and drives each writer's productivity

Writing Tutorial 7:
GIVING AND TAKING FEEDBACK—
AND MAKING THOSE FINAL CHOICES

READING CRITICALLY: LEARN FROM OTHER PEOPLE'S WRITING

Participation in a writers critique group will expose you to a diversity of new work in rough-draft form. These other writers' drafts may not always be in a genre or style that you would customarily buy at the bookstore or borrow from the library. To get the most out of your review of other writers, Review the section on page 141, "Read Like a Writer."

READ AND REVIEW GENEROUSLY: THE ART OF GOOD FEEDBACK

(A) Set expectations: Whether you're swapping writing with a friend or a member of your writers group, establish a set of mutual guidelines and expectations, including the depth and detail of the critique. An overall, first-impression read? A detailed examination and written review? A close-up, copywriter's scan for hidden errors and grammatical boo-boos? Discuss and set these expectations ahead.

(B) The review format: Will you and the writer set a date and time to sit and chat over a cup of coffee? If this is within a writers group, will you simply e-mail each other comments, or will each reviewer get a chance to give an oral review? Or will you attach a carefully completed worksheet to the written draft? Or will you simply handwrite your comments in the margins of the work? The bottom line: Long after the meeting or luncheon is over, this writer will need a set of clear, readable suggestions for ways to improve the current draft. The following is the worksheet that I encourage some of my adult students to complete, attach, and return to a writer. This avoids the discrepancies in the legibility of various people's handwriting. It also serves to objectify the review-and-feedback process so that the personal relationship between writer and reviewer is more protected. And finally, my students like this format because when they return to the draft, they have a standardized set of feedback.

Author's name

Story or excerpt name

Reviewer's name

Today's Date

1. Finish the sentence: "This is a story/essay/poem about ..."

2. If this were a meal, were you satisfied? What else could the author have served up? Aperitifs? More entrée? More dessert? An espresso to speed things up? More wine to mellow things out ...

3. How did you feel after reading this piece?

4. What was memorable?

5. Places I stopped in this story and why ...

6. I'd like to see more of ...

7. I'd like to see less of ...

(C) Give the other writer space to redraft: While you are the reviewer, it's ultimately the writer's work and project and vision. As a reviewer, offer only your observations as a reader. Sometimes you want to offer solutions (I think you should change this male character into a woman), but it's best to give the author space in which to come up with his own solutions.

THE SUGGESTIONS YOU KEEP OR IGNORE? AND ... HOW DO YOU KNOW?

If you are a member of an online or in-person critique group, how do you decide whose advice to accept? And which to ignore? What if two reviewers have completely opposite reactions to the same scene or excerpt?

Here are ten tips for separating the keepers from the throwaways:

1. **Allow time:** Read all of your critiques once, then set them aside to allow some time between the critiques and when you attack that next draft. This way, you allow the feedback to percolate through your consciousness and to jump-start your own editorial ideas for

how your draft can be better. In my experience, you make the best changes when you blend other readers' wisdom or suggestions with your own.

2. **Look for patterns:** If there's a consistent comment across everyone's feedback sheet, then this is an indicator that something in your work needs to be addressed. For example, if you gave your writing to five readers, and every reader responded, "I don't understand who the male character in the café scene actually is. Can you explain who he is and why he's suddenly in this scene?" If nobody gets it, then Mr. Café Mystery Character needs to be reexamined and clarified.

3. **Consider the source:** Not all reviewers are created equally, so consider the source of a suggestion. If the mystery writer in your group insists that you rev up the plot—and all at the expense of flashback or interior dialogue—balance this suggestion with that of the other writers in the group.

4. **The work comes first:** Every edit or change or deletion should be made only to make your writing better. Especially for beginner writers or for writers who have just joined an established critique group, you may be eager to please. You want to make your newfound friends feel that their feedback helped. But you're writing to make your piece better—not to feed your friends' egos or to reaffirm their editorial skills. Make decisions based on this goal only.

5. **Your project vision:** Does this reader's suggestion support or add to your overall and heartfelt vision for this project? Does it align with your personal writing goals which you set in part one, chapter one of this book? For example, if someone suggests that you "lighten things up a little" or "add some humor here," but you really wanted to create something meaningful and insightful—or a project that would incite readers to be better citizens—this suggestion to "lighten up" is not going to support your long-term vision. So smile and thank this reviewer and then … quietly ditch his suggestion.

6. **Drastic shifts:** Ask yourself, "Will this suggested change drastically shift the tenor or structure or direction of my writing project? If it does, this may not be a bad thing. But consider if this is a drastic change or shift that you're really comfortable with.

7. **Reluctance to change:** If one reviewer's suggestion immediately hits a nerve, take a humility pill and ask yourself whether your resistance to this edit is based on your own reluctance to restructure the work or the actual validity of this one reviewer's suggestion. Be honest. Brutally honest.

8. **Sleep on it:** Before you make those large-scale, drastic changes to your work, sleep on it. Trust your night dreams or your inner voice to tell you whether to input or ditch a reviewer's suggestion

9. **Cultural differences:** If you and your reviewers are writing and reading from different cultures, generations, or vastly different life experiences, balance the historical or cultural authenticity with readers' need-to-know understanding. When your reviewer points out that a cultural reference is unclear to the twenty-first century, mainstream reader, this is your nudge to strengthen the contextual information. But you shouldn't change the details of the story to make it modern. For example, if your story is in pre-telephone 1920s, make sure this era and context are clear—don't just plop a telephone in there.

10. **Writer goals:** In part one, I encouraged you to define and set your own highly personalized writing goals. This is an important part of writing. And your own, deeply held goals become even more important as you begin to show your drafts and seek input from other people. If a writer friend's goals are radically different from yours, then her edits or suggestions may not be valid for your work. For example, if your friend's writing goal is to land a huge publisher's advance and quit her day job, then she may be more likely to suggest that your writing be more topical, provocative, or mainstream. Nothing wrong with that. For her. Not for you. So be careful about making drastic changes that ultimately shift the direction of your own writing.

16

WRITING AWAY FROM HOME: WRITERS RETREATS AND CONFERENCES

I got the idea for this book while sitting on the concrete steps outside the corporate building where I once worked full time. While the employees from other offices were gabbing on their cell phones, I was munching on a lunchtime salad and getting in a quick edit of the first draft of a personal essay. Bing! There it was, the BBI (the big brilliant idea) to write a book for other day job writers. But then … there was the (gulp!) … actual book to research and write—all while holding down a job. Errr … had I thought this one fully through? No worries. To get a running start, I packed up my laptop and a weekend's worth of comfy clothes and drove two hours to a writers retreat in the hills of central Massachusetts.

My room at the retreat center has a simple elegance. As I researched and wrote, the view out my window changed with the time or day or the season of the year. Sometimes I wrote late at night, tapping lightly on my keyboard so as not to wake the other resident writers or artists who were sleeping in adjacent rooms. Often, between chapters of this book, I sneaked in other creative writing or made notes in my journal that I would return to later. When I ran out of creative steam, I took an afternoon nap or went downstairs and walked down the tree-lined avenue and walked the path along the nearby lake. Usually, somewhere between my room and the sparkling lake water, the writing became unstuck in my head, and I went back to my retreat room with fresh energy and new ideas.

I have been going to this retreat for more than twelve years—often four or five times per year. I've written and redrafted a novel there. I've written short stories, essays, journal entries, and teaching curricula. Often, without prearranging it, I meet the same writers there from previous visits. Like me, many of these writers work a day job. I've met computer programmers, editors, marketing managers, advertising assistants, tax accountants, teachers, nurses, massage therapists, teachers, newspaper reporters, and theater managers. I've met novelists, poets, essayists, TV writers, scriptwriters, memoirists, cookbook authors, and biographers. They've been from England, Texas, New York, Massachusetts, Connecticut, California, and Oregon. Whatever our day jobs, whatever our age or stage or writing genre, we share one trait: We get a lot more done away from home. So as someone who is juggling a job and a writing career and, possibly, some family commitments, I would encourage you to at least consider taking yourself and your writing projects away for a long weekend or for a week or two. I believe that writing retreats are especially useful for day job writers because, as well as giving us some uninterrupted hours in which to write, they also allow us the mental and creative space to move closer to the work—or quite simply to fall in love with the idea of being a writer again.

In a *Los Angeles Times* interview with author Michael Chabon about his latest book and his dual role as a writer and parent of four children, Chabon comments on the value of leaving home to write:

> Often, I have to go away [to write]. I'll go to a place like the MacDowell Colony (www.macdowellcolony.org), or borrow somebody's cabin, or go to a hotel even. Stay up until all hours, and sleep late, and just crank. I can get a lot done. Even in three or four days, I can do about as much as I could do in a month at home.

Amen, Michael. Nothing like a few wonder days holed up with just you and the writing. The great escape is especially productive for those large-format or start-up projects.

Sitting in that quiet room, the commute and the job and the bill paying feel miles away. Here the ideas and the language seem to just come. Maybe it's because while I'm away on retreat, I am just a writer. I don't have to get up from my desk and be anybody else. Just for this weekend or week, there is no role switching.

But not all artist retreats are the same. Going away from home to write doesn't have to cost you a bundle. And you don't have to pack a suitcase full of all-black clothes or eat tofu suppers or sit around the fireside trying to sound smart and literary with a bunch of strangers. Open the classified section of any writers magazine or do a simple Google search ("artist retreats") to find any number of options of places to go for a quiet space in which to write. As important as it is to get away, it's equally or more important to define and find the type of writers getaway that works for you and your personality.

THE PROS AND CONS OF DIFFERENT TYPES OF WRITERS AND ARTISTS RETREATS

Scholarship-based artist retreats: Typically these are the no-cost retreats that you will find listed in writers magazines. Like any scholarship, these types of nonprofit artist colonies have an application process which varies by the individual program. Generally you must submit a résumé and/or a writing sample or a project outline. Your application is reviewed by a review committee or the board of directors. Some require references. Usually these retreats require writers to apply and meet the application deadline at least six, eight, or twelve months ahead. Residencies last from two weeks to several months. Some residencies include a master writer or visiting writing teacher in residence. Others provide no instruction or meetings or workshops, and are simply designed to provide artist space only. Most include meals. Examples of scholarship-based retreats include Yaddo, The MacDowell Colony, or Hedgebrook.

> **Pros:** Except for your transportation costs, there's no charge to you, the writer. Plus, there's long, uninterrupted time to write, it's an excellent résumé builder, and it offers the opportunity to meet other writers or big-name teachers.

> **Cons:** For day job writers, these retreats assume that you can take longish vacations or unpaid leaves of absence from your job. If you're a solitary person, the shared mealtimes or other communal activities can be counterproductive to the intention of getting away alone for uninterrupted writing time.

Fee-based retreats which cater to groups or classes: These are organized around teacher-led writing workshops for a certain number of writers (usually no more than fifteen). Sometimes these writers weekends or weeks are held at hip, rural, or urban bed-and-breakfasts. The instruction can center around a given theme or genre of writing. Often the teacher or group leader also owns and operates the retreat facility or bed-and-breakfast. Generally these weekends or weeklong retreats are a blend of solitary writing time and group or workshop time. Usually the fee includes accommodations, shared meals, and snacks. Sometimes there are wellness activities such as meditation or yoga.

Pros: Here's a chance to meet other writers, polish your craft, and gain solitary writing time.

Cons: If you're a solitary person or writer, the shared mealtimes or other communal activities can be counterproductive to your own work. If the host (retreat space owner) is not the teacher but participates in the workshop, the respective roles of teacher, student, and host are sometimes unclear and problematic. Ask about this before you sign up and pay.

Residential writers conferences: A writers conference is similar to many other professional conferences in that they offer a range of scheduled, simultaneous writing workshops, panels, literary agent pitching sessions, and nighttime social events. Writers conferences are generally held annually. They're fee based, though most have some scholarship opportunities. Accommodations vary from urban hotels to university campuses to seaside rustic retreats. Examples include the Maui Writers Conference on the Road, the Stonecoast Writers Conference, and the Cape Cod Writers Conference.

Pros: Conferences offer opportunities to rub shoulders with famous authors or pitch your ideas to literary agents, plus a chance to meet other writers and to learn and socialize with authors from across the country. Some intermediate to advanced-level workshops are juried, and participants are only accepted by a submission process.

Cons: The schedule is often busy. Conferences require a switching of persona, from writer you to marketing- or social-butterfly you. To get yourself some writing time, you need to get up early and write before the first workshop session begins. The quality of the workshops and instruction varies. Big-name authors are not necessarily gifted teachers or mentors. Writers conferences are a considerable financial investment in terms of transportation and participant fees and meals.

Solitary retreats: These are retreat centers in which you simply rent a room or studio. There are no organized activities or workshops, and meals are not provided, though most facilities offer shared kitchens for cooking. Fees vary. Most require an application, including a résumé or project outline. Residencies generally last a week or longer. In the United States, examples of these types of retreats include Wellspring House, The Porches writing retreat, or the Whidbey Island Writers Refuge. There are some international writers retreats which offer the chance to travel abroad, explore another country, and also get some quality time for writing. Overseas examples include La Muse (France) or Anam Cara (Ireland).

Pros: Solitary retreats are very flexible for the day job writer. Generally, depending on availability, they have a shorter application time, so that you can work based on your job or family schedule. Depending on your preference, you may choose whether to socialize with other writers and artists-in-residence or just keep to yourself. You are free to write according to your own schedule, not by the center's designated mealtimes.

Cons: These are fee based (though they are usually reasonably priced). Without a daily schedule, you create your own writing discipline. If few or no other artists are in residence, it can provide a Thoreau-like solitude that requires an initial adjustment period.

Rent and make your own retreat: If your idea of a quiet, solitary writing space includes room service and chocolates on the pillow at night, then renting a hotel room will work for you. So will a luxury bed-and-breakfast. Or check your local rental ads for short-term rental apartments, studios, condos, or vacation cottages. Or simply borrow a friend's apartment. Hotels have wonderful in-room desks, Wi-Fi, and ergonomic chairs. But many bed-and-breakfasts do not have in-room writing desks. When you're taking the time and paying the fees to get some writing done, you will need the right space, furniture, and equipment.

Pros: It's truly solitary, in that there are no other writers or artists or retreat owners on site. Your only conversation may be with the front-desk staff. If you choose a full-service hotel, meals are provided for you, which give you more time to write. There is no fixed residency duration.

Cons: There is no sense of camaraderie with other writers. Because we tend to associate hotels or bed-and-breakfasts or holiday cottages with vacation or family travel, it can be tough to make the adjustment. Generally, except for budget motels, a nightly or weekly hotel rate is more expensive than a writers retreat. There are no writer-friendly rules around TV use in the adjoining hotel rooms or loud conversations in the hotel hallways. These are a huge and annoying distraction.

Religious or spiritual retreat spaces: Long before it became a trend for yoga students or discussion groups or wellness practitioners, religious orders across the denominations practiced silent, prayerful, or meditative retreats in order to reconnect with their deeper selves and their higher powers. Many religious retreat centers will host a group writers workshop. Or they will offer some limited private retreat rooms, in which you can simply rent a room without participating in the retreat center's organized programming or workshops. Fees vary. Some are based on donations only.

Pros: The facilities are often in beautiful and well-landscaped sites, which inspire your spiritual, as well as your creative, well-being. Meals are often provided, which gives you more time to write. You may choose to combine your writing getaway with the retreat center's spiritual workshops or offerings.

Cons: If organized religion is not your thing, then the iconography of religious sites may be disturbing or distracting for you. Because they operate as nonprofits, the nightly accommodation fees are often quite high—though worth it for the gourmet or organic meals. If you are the only secular retreat participant in residence, you may feel quite isolated. Some require individuals to maintain silence during or between mealtimes.

LOCATING A WRITERS RETREAT OR CONFERENCE

Writers retreats:

www.artistcommunities.org
www.writersretreat.com

Spiritual retreat centers by state:

www.findthedivine.com
www.retreatfinder.com

Writers conferences:

www.writing.shawguides.com

TEN WAYS TO GET THE MOST FROM YOUR WRITERS RETREAT

(1) Choose the type of retreat space that fits your personality: When you make that initial phone call, ask the right questions as to the center's rules, expectations, and guidelines. Or ask if you can contact some previous residents to get feedback on their experiences. Ask about cell phone access, Internet connectivity, and what's provided in terms of a writing space, desk, and chair.

(2) Pack ahead: There's nothing worse than getting there only to realize that you've left a crucial item at home. So make a list and pack before your departure date.

> **Equipment:** Make a checklist of everything you will need for writing, including your notebooks, pens, Post-it notes, laptop (if you're going for a long time, it's a good idea to borrow a backup laptop, just in case), a flash drive to save your work, a small portable printer, research books, and leisure reading for your downtimes. Also, don't forget your business cards or a way to give your contact info to fellow residents.

> **Clothing:** Retreat centers tend to be supercasual. Bring really comfortable clothes, including good walking or jogging shoes. If the retreat center is by a lake or on top of a mountain, pack really warm pajamas, night socks, and extra layers. If it's by the sea or a lake, don't forget your bathing suit and towels and sunscreen.

> **Food:** Here's a tip: Unless you're going to an all-meals-included center, pack one prepared or take-out meal for the day or evening you arrive. In an unfamiliar neighborhood, it's crucial to have something in hand for that first meal and while you settle into your surroundings. For the rest of your residency, pack easy-to-cook foods such as beans, rice, eggs, cheese, tortilla wraps, fruit, vegetables, pasta, peanut or almond butter, or some contents of your home freezer that are easy to defrost and cook. If and when residents organize a potluck dinner, it's nice to have something that's easy to make and that feeds a crowd of ravenous writers.

> **Telecommunications:** You may need to stay in daily touch with family. On your way there, you may want to buy a prepaid calling card if it will be cheaper and more reliable than paying for roaming charges.

(3) Location: A retreat center may be prestigious or glamorous or present an attractive website, but if there's a possibility that you may need to go home suddenly (family emergency or other need), then choose a center that's within driving distance. But don't choose a center that will offer the temptation to drive home just because you're having a bad writing day or have a bout of homesickness. Two or four hours away from your home usually works well. Also, driving is generally cheaper than flying.

(4) Have a definite project plan: Generally your retreat goes better and you accomplish more if you have a defined project to work on. Projects that lend themselves to writing retreat centers include startup projects, such as beginning a new book or story. Or assign certain parts of a writing project to certain parts of the day. For example, designate your mornings to new work and the afternoons or evenings to editing or research. Solitary retreats lend themselves well to big-picture-style rewrites.

(5) Allow for adjustment time: You've paid your fee. You've snagged some time off from work. You've talked your partner into watching the kids. So you expect the writing muse to visit the minute you arrive and unpack the car. This doesn't always happen. Especially if this is your first writers retreat, there's a real adjustment period. Allow for this. If you spend the first evening or day just getting to know the place, that's fine. The writing will come. Be patient.

(6) To socialize or to write? Some residents will hole up in their room and barely make eye contact in the shared kitchen or common rooms. Others are eager to hear about your writing project and to talk about their own. Find your own comfort level. While being polite, make sure that you're getting your own personal writing needs met. It can be wonderful to meet new people, but don't end up with a week or a weekend where you've shortchanged your own writing goals.

(7) Keep an open mind: The center may look nothing like your own home. In fact, you may have just left your own comfy condominium for this rustic, windswept place that doesn't even have heated towel bars. Or the place may look nothing like the professional conferences that you attend for your work. Keep a really open mind. You will discover other rewards here that have nothing to do with brand-name home luxuries.

(8) Designate a time to check e-mail or switch on your cell phone: If you drive or fly three hours simply to spend half the time e-mailing or IMing your friends back home, you've wasted both your money and your writing time. Let your family know where and how they can reach you in an emergency.

Otherwise keep your cell phone switched off. Your fellow writers-in-residence will thank you.

(9) Keep an honest and kind heart: If your day job and your personal life have given you a certain level of autonomy or power, going away for a writers retreat or group workshop can be an exercise in humility, openness, and tolerance. Your fellow residents can and do come from many different backgrounds and with diverse writing projects. While you're there to accomplish certain goals for yourself, be considerate and kind to those around you. Don't allow the retreat center and its residents to self-divide into little high-school-like cliques. You won't like every resident there. But, especially during shared mealtimes or activities, you should respect and try to include them. Equally, if you and some writer friends book a getaway at a retreat center, it's not your personal bachelorette party. Be considerate and inclusive of the other writers in residence who are not part of your hometown group.

(10) Make a schedule that works for you: If you're used to balancing work with writing and other duties, twenty-four hours of writing time every day can be downright terrifying. It can be too much time and too little structure. Until you get used to the rhythm of the place and the retreat, make yourself a schedule, which includes exercise, meals, social time, or getting out and exploring the local area.

CONCLUSION

WRITING WHILE HOLDING DOWN A DAY JOB: IT'S RIGHT THERE ON THE CANDY WRAPPER

This past week, I gobbled down four bite-sized Twix bars (OK, maybe it was five). I have always had a sweet tooth, and I will admit that there's something about chocolate and writing that seems to go well together. But a week ago, if you had told me I would demolish five Twix bars, I would have stoutly denied the very possibility. For starters, I don't really eat candy bars. And second, I believe that you are what you eat, and a big sugar-a-thon is not exactly going to keep you out of the doctor's or the dentist's chair. And yet, as I write this, the Twix bag sits empty in my trash bin.

If you think about it, the Twix bar parable fits how we work as day job writers, how we get the job done—even when we're busy or overwhelmed or disillusioned. Similar to how I looked back and was surprised how many Twix I'd eaten, many weeks I look back and am surprised to find how much I'd written. We accomplish each the same way: one bite or word at a time.

As a writer and a writing teacher, I've seen otherwise promising writers flounder under their own overblown expectations. Or they neglect to translate their big brilliant idea, their BBI, into daily bite-sized pieces.

"I'm going to be a brilliant writer." "I'm going to write my family's intergenerational memoir." "I'm going to pen the great American novel." These are all great big-picture goals. But if you're going to ride out the writing storm, if you're going to make it up the stairs to your writing desk day after day, you need to dissect your writing into bite-sized parts that will be more feasible today. Just today.

Today it's not your job to write a huge, three hundred-page blockbuster. Today's job is simply to write the next scene or the next three pages or the next six hundred words—even if they're scattered, lousy words. When that's done, you can get up and walk away, switch off the lights, and go to bed. Tomorrow you'll have another job: to write the next scene, or the next three pages, or the next six hundred words. By the end of the week, you've got fifteen pages. Not bad for someone who also holds down a job.

So stick to the daily, bite-sized nibbles. Trust me, writing is much easier this way. This is how writing happens.

There's a second lesson from my Halloween Twix feast. Right here, in a red oval background, printed in white uppercase letters. It says, "FUN SIZE."

We deserve a little fun each week, a decadent indulgence, a little detour from the bland and the broccoli.

As you balance your writing career with your otherwise busy life, remember that you deserve to keep part of that life for you and you alone. You deserve to write. To write happily.

So keep at it, one fun bite at a time.

Section 5

TWENTY AUTHOR INTERVIEWS

I absolutely love those artists' open houses and artisan studio tours. There's something magical about watching each artist at work, deep in concentration over his or her latest creation. I especially love those artists who showcase the start-up phase of their projects, the very genesis of the craft, the beginning phase of what will later become a finished, beautiful piece.

While at one of these open houses, it struck me: In creating a book on working writers, why not interview all sorts of authors? Why not create a virtual studio tour of all sorts of writers? In doing so, I would find out how other writers manage and managed to achieve their writing vision while also holding down jobs and honoring family commitments.

You will meet a nurse and a bookstore clerk. You will read the advice of a full-time robotics researcher and the insights of a part-time copywriter. From dads to moms to grandparents, from Connecticut to Colorado to California, these busy writers have made it happen.

Some of the writers are still working the day job and writing on the weekends, evenings, or whenever they can grab fifteen minutes. Others have been there. And now, they're willing to pass along their advice, tips, and insights on how they balanced their working and writing lives.

Okay, readers, confession time here: When I first conceived of the virtual writers tour, I saw it as a drop-in, drive by affair. How wrong I was. As I interviewed each writer, I found myself humbled and inspired by their experiences and wisdom. Now each time my procrastination voices whisper, those whispers are overlaid by these writers' voices. *Grab those small, unexpected moments of writing time. Find some supportive writer friends. Allocate a specific spot in the house.*

As you meet each author, you will find insights and tips that resonate for your own writing life.

The interviews have been alphabetized by the authors' last names.

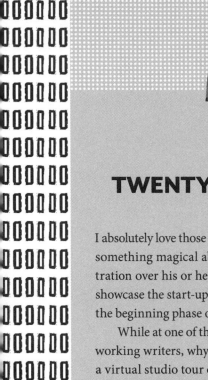 **READ EXTENDED INTERVIEWS AT**
WWW.WRITERSDIGEST.COM/ARTICLE/DAY-JOB-INTERVIEWS

DEBBIE ANDERSON
San Diego, California
www.sandiegomomma.com

Debbie Anderson publishes the writing blog San Diego Momma. She's also a contributing writer to www.momaroo.com, www.thesmartly.com, and www.juicein thecity.com. In addition to being a busy mom with two young daughters, she has worked full time in the communications field since 1991. She now freelances as an editor and writer.

Q *When did you start writing?*

A I don't think I've ever stopped writing. I've written professionally and personally for many years. My first story was written in the first grade (a cheap rip-off of Cinderella) and from that moment, I've wanted to make my living as a writer. Writing has luckily always been a part of my career, and I've been working on half-finished manuscripts for more than ten years.

Q *As a mother of two, what's your writing schedule like?*

A Currently I'm working on a middle-grade novel, which I hope to finish in writing spurts before 6 A.M. In truth, my schedule is not a schedule at all. I squirrel away time and take advantage of every quiet opportunity to write. My children are in school most days, so I begin the day with my paying/editing jobs and fit my manuscript into the day as I can. I blog most days as well and tend to write most posts after the kids are in bed.

Q *Does your writing schedule change as your children get older?*

A As the kids get older, my slivers of writing time decrease because there is always somewhere to be—from birthday parties to school functions. It's a very busy life.

Q *How has being a parent inspired or motivated your writing?*

A I really just capitalize on the silent time—wherever and whenever it presents itself and use it to write. Sometimes the time comes in unexpected ways. A few weekends ago, I was in Big Bear with the family sharing a cabin with ten other people. I never thought I could write there, but while the rest of the family was at the lake, I returned to the cabin, brought an old rocking chair out on the deck, looked toward the mountains, and stole an hour to write. Also, being a parent, while wonderful in many

ways, has not been conducive to writing for me. Other than that, I imagine I'm closer to death than ever before, and I better get my book done.

Q *Is there a device or habit or ritual which helps you to transition from one role to the other?*

A I need to leave my house. Once I take myself out of my usual environment, I am better able to focus on writing. Also, I have a writing group that has the sole purpose of keeping me on task. We don't talk about what we're working on, or ask for critiques, or share writerly anecdotes, but rather push each other to meet the writing goals we've individually set for the week. If the goal (usually a word count) isn't met, there is discussion on where the pitfalls were and how to address them. Then the group weighs in on how those challenges can be met and overcome. When I know there's a writing meeting coming up, I hustle to write because I'm motivated to not get disapproving looks from my fellow writers!

Q *Do you draw upon your role as a parent as inspiration or as background material for your writing?*

A Currently I'm working on a middle-grade novel, and watching my children be children reminds me of the sense of play I had as a kid, which inspires my novel. I also look to my children to inform my characters and keep things real.

TED MITCHELL (WRITING AS T.J. ALEXIAN)
Massachusetts
YA novelist and playwright

T.J. Alexian writes young adult novels and has written several plays that have been produced regionally. He also works full time as a senior public relations specialist for a large national company—a job that involves long hours and 24/7 availability. He is also the divorced father of three children.

Q *When did you start writing?*

A Since seven or eight, I've always been working on some sort of story. My father was the principal of an elementary school and fed my obsession by teaching me from an early age the love of storytelling. At night, when I was a child, he would put me to sleep by telling stories—of the Lone Ranger and his faithful sidekick Tonto, or Ed Drew, Nancy Drew's younger detective-solving brother. As a result, I began to tell stories of my own, which found their way onto paper. Incidentally it should be no surprise that I carry on this tradition and make up stories for my kids, too.

Q *How do you balance a full-time job, writing, and parenting?*

A My oldest is out of the house now and has been for many years, but I share custody of the other two kids with my ex-wife. So I usually find time to write in the evenings after the kids go to bed, or nights when I'm kid-free. Or, early mornings, but not so much that: I'm a night owl and have always found that inspiration comes best once the sun goes down.

Q *Has your writing schedule changed as your children have grown?*

A Yes, but not for the better. Unfortunately they're night owls, too! Nowadays, in the wee small hours, my writing time competes against the sound of my son playing Xbox in his room and my daughter blasting her iPod.

Q *Does being a dad influence or inspire your writing?*

A My kids have appeared in all of the YA novels I've written. I write dark thrillers, so that may not be a good thing, but that's for them to decide. My oldest was the inspiration for the protagonist in my third novel: her room, the way she expressed herself, how she dressed … all made its way in. My seventeen-year-old is the inspiration for my current novel. She's the family rebel and can be a magnet for adventure. As a result, several real-life situations made their way into the novel. I think it's more authentic that way.

Q *Do you solicit your kids' feedback on your YA work?*

A My oldest is the first person I send all my stories, because hers is the most supportive voice I know. She's read my latest manuscript at least five times, poor thing. My two youngest are more brutal, especially my son. If I want an honest opinion about anything, I know exactly whom to turn to! Still, the honesty can be helpful, and certainly helps me handle rejection.

Q *Are there approaches or habits that help you transition between the various roles in your life?*

A When I'm plotting a chapter or putting together a first draft, I need complete silence. This is where hanging a "Do not disturb" sign outside the bedroom door pays off. There are specific spots where I'm most productive, such as my bedroom, the living room couch, or the town park, which has huge shady trees.

During the first draft, I set myself a goal of writing a page a day. That may not sound like a lot, but it's a powerful motivator. The simple act of getting from point A to point B becomes a great challenge: Will I make it? The truth is, I usually do, and often end up with more than a page, especially if I'm on a roll or approaching the end of a chapter.

Once the first draft's done, it's time to refine. I get by with help from trusted friends and family, including established writers I've formed friendships with. However, part of the deal is knowing when to share: I only show first drafts to my oldest daughter and ex-wife, because I'm superstitious about "killing the baby" too early in the process. I also do a lot of journal writing, which keeps me in shape for long-term projects and sharpens my editing skills. Often I reuse this material, or draw from it as inspiration. Once I have a solid second draft, I branch out with a goal of getting a refined draft to my agent.

Q *Do you draw inspiration from your life and role as a parent?*

A Constantly! My kids and extended family are the foundation upon which my books are built. My ex-wife and I are still good friends (in fact, my seventeen-year-old asked, "Why can't you two hate each other like others exes?"), and that helps because I always use her house, our shared experiences, our situations with the kids as material for my novels.

Q *Do you belong to a writers group?*

A I wish I had time to belong to a writers group. However, between my kids, my job, my writing, and directing plays for a local college, I just don't. The best substitute I have is the network of friends I've gathered through my journaling site and in real life. Writing short stories and posting them online provides me with instant gratification and a forum to develop ideas. I've met friends with similar interests, many of whom are fellow writers. I also see my day job as a resource, since it's all about written communication and allows me to exercise a different part of my brain. Plus, I constantly get feedback on what I write, teaching me to be flexible and accept suggestions gracefully (dammit!).

BRUNONIA BARRY
Salem, Massachusetts
Novelist
www.brunoniabarry.com

Brunonia Barry was the first American writer to win the Women's International Fiction Festival's 2009 Baccante Award for her *New York Times* best-selling novel, *The Lace Reader*. Barry wrote her debut novel while working fifty to sixty hours per week on a start-up software business with her husband. In 2010, her second novel, *The Map of True Places* was released.

Q *When did you start writing?*

A I started writing when I was six. My father brought home one of those huge old typewriters from his office. I had to sit on pillows to reach it. My spelling was terrible, and the stories didn't make much sense, but my parents kept all of them and put them in a scrapbook which they gave me a few years ago.

Q *How did you manage to complete The Lace Reader while also working a start-up business?*

A The book took seven years to finish because the business burned up so much of our time and energy. Finally, Hasbro picked up our software products, and my job got a little easier.

Q *What's your writing schedule like?*

A I write in the mornings, and when I'm approaching a deadline, I sometimes start at 4 A.M. Usually I go into my office at about eight. I have one rule: no coffee until I finish. It seems counterintuitive, but I like to be a little sleepy when I'm creating. I write for as long as I can, usually until noon or so. Then I have coffee and take a walk. Since I am writing full time now, I save afternoons for editing and for the business of being a writer: answering e-mails and phone calls, doing blog posts, tweeting, etc. There is a lot more to the business than I ever imagined. The business of being a writer is rather like another full-time job. When I need a break, I take a walk, or, in warm weather, a swim. I usually break for the day at about 7 P.M.

Q *That's an eleven hour day. Is there a device or habit which helps you to transition from the writing to the business of writing?*

A For me, it's movement. I like to walk. I need to stretch my legs as well as my eyes. I also meditate, but that's usually after I finish my workday.

Q *Are there other approaches which helped you (or continue to help you) manage your time and balance your two careers—writing and the "other" career*

A When I was working full time, it helped to have a physical space dedicated to writing. For me, it was just a corner of our guest room, but the idea was that I didn't allow myself to do anything else in that space. I would go in and close the door. I think it's important to realize that a lot of writing time is spent thinking about writing and not actually putting words on paper. It took me a few frustrating years to understand this. When you work full time and dedicate your free time to writing, you really want to see results. The phrase "process, not product" has been very freeing for me.

JOHN BREHM
Colorado
Poet
www.johnbrehm.net

John Brehm has published two poetry collections and placed poetry in numerous literary journals and publications, including *The Best American Poetry 1999*. He has been assistant editor of *The Oxford Book of American Poetry* (2006). He left a career as an adjunct writing professor to work as a freelance copywriter for Oxford, Penguin, Random House, Harper-Collins, and other publishers. He also works as a content editor for a website.

Q *When did you start writing?*

A I was in high school when I started writing. After grad school I taught as an adjunct for fifteen years at a number of colleges and universities but have worked outside academia since 1996. My work as a copywriter is engaging but not exhausting or stressful, and it leaves me time and energy for my own poetry.

Q *Which of your past jobs has worked best with your writing life?*

A In fact, the best two years of my writing life, the most productive years, happened right after I stopped teaching. As a copywriter at Oxford, I was writing, but the writing had a pretty straightforward purpose, distant enough from poetry that I felt much fresher when I sat down to write a poem. My advice to young writers would be to work outside academia if at all possible.

Q *What's your writing schedule like?*

A I give myself time to write first thing every morning. Most days nothing happens, and that's okay. I'm there, I'm ready, and that seems to be important. If I'm working on a poem, I'll work on it in the mornings but also at night, off and on, whenever I have time. What's most important, I think, is waiting for the poems to come rather than coaxing them out of yourself with some kind of arbitrary motivation—an assignment or exercise or some other external prompt. I'm very much against assignments, which are now so popular. Can you imagine Milton or Wordsworth or Keats or Dickinson or Frost or Bishop or really any great poet writing to an assignment? It was Keats who said, "If it comes not as naturally as leaves to the trees, it had better not come at all."

Q *Are you a parent?*

A No, I'm not a parent, and I have great admiration for writers who are raising children, working, and trying to keep their writing alive. I don't know how they do it.

Q *Is there a device or habit which helps you to transition into writing or from your day job or paid work into the creative space?*

A Not really. I start the day with my own writing, so the transition is from creative to paying work and it's a smooth one for me, most days.

Q *What other approaches help you maintain a writing schedule?*

A Not needing too much money is a big help. I've arranged things in such a way that I can have a fairly relaxed work life. If I had to make more money for a big mortgage or lots of travel, or if I had expensive tastes, etc., I'd have to work a lot more and that would interfere with the poetry. A man is rich, Thoreau said, in proportion to the number of things he can afford to live without. I've always chosen time over money and for the most part that's worked well for me.

Q *What advice would you offer for other writers who balance day jobs?*

A Take an honest look at your temperament and talents, and try to find work that supports you and is not too soul destroying. Don't think that teaching is the only option, just because it's now the presumptive job for writers, or certainly for poets. And try to do some kind of service, volunteer work, something that gets you outside the self-infatuation we all suffer from, writers especially. I've been a hospice volunteer and that was a profound experience—being with people as they neared the sacred threshold of death put my own obsessive self-concern in proper, comically tiny, perspective.

MONICA CARTER
Los Angeles, California
Short fiction author, literary journal founder, and editor
www.salonicaworldlit.com

Monica Carter is a short fiction and nonfiction writer, who is also the editor of E.Lire, a journal of international writing and the website, salonicaworldlit.com. Carter's writing has been published in *Strange Cargo: an Emerging Voices Anthology*, *Black Clock*, and *Pale House*. She is also a reviewer for *ForeWord Magazine*. In addition to writing, she works full time in a bookstore.

Q *When did you start writing?*

A I started writing when I was twenty-five and while I was doing stand-up comedy. I quit doing stand-up to work full time in a bookstore so I could be around books, writing, and writers—to be immersed in the world of literature. I worked all different shifts except for the night shift.

Q *What's your writing schedule like?*

A I write after work. I write on weekends as well. I need complete time alone with the knowledge that I don't have to stop to go to work.

Q *Is there a device or habit which helps you to transition from one career to the other?*

A Silence helps me transition, to leave the work world behind. Also sometimes I read to transition from reality to the world of fiction.

Q *Are there other approaches that help you to manage your time and balance your two careers?*

A I like to think of which of the two makes me happy, expresses who I am truly am. Work affords me the freedom to do what I love. Discipline, commitment, and focus have to be part of the process; otherwise it is too easy to let complacency get the best of you.

Q *How much cross-pollination of skills exists between your two careers—if any?*

A There is a lot of cross-pollination because I work in a bookstore. I am inspired by the writers who read at the store and the other writers who work there, and to think that one day someone could come into the store and hold my novel in their hands because they want to be touched by literature in a positive way. It's also a great place to study people.

SHARON CHARDE
Connecticut
Poet
www.sharoncharde.com

Sharon Charde has published four chapbooks of poetry and has edited a collection of poems by girls in a residential treatment facility. Her poetry has won many awards, including six Pushcart nominations. In addition to writing, she has worked as a family therapist and a writing teacher.

Q *When did you start writing?*

A Although I've been writing since childhood, I began writing seriously in 1987, when I worked as a practicing family therapist and after my younger son Geoffrey died in an accident. Before that, the demands of mothering two young children and the constant absence of my husband, who was in a busy pediatric practice, left no time or inclination to write or reflect on my experience.

Q *What's your writing schedule like?*

A I basically retired from my career as a therapist but continued to work teaching writing in a facility for adjudicated girls—it was also very time consuming, though I did it for ten years. I have written a draft of my experience working with the girls as well as another new book of poetry. But it's still hard for me to make time to write. I do a monthlong residency every year which is a help.

Q *Any particular approaches which help you transition between your life and writing?*

A The best thing for me is to be away from the house—a writing residency—and then I have no problem working on all my writing projects and the reading that is necessary to back them up. Discipline is really what helps in the transitioning—I have to be ruthless to get myself to the desk and the work—it is what I love most to do, but find the most difficult to make time for. When my husband is out of the house and away it is much easier—the flow can flow—and I need, as we all do, lots of protected time. It must be a wholehearted commitment.

Q *Did your work as a therapist or a teacher inspire your creative writing?*

A Being a therapist trains one to see the subtext of everything, a most useful quality in writing poetry. My clients weren't the inspiration, but the constant reminders that our life stories are full of material from which to create poems that in turn transform that material into art. Working with the girls and now my women writing students (I run many writing workshops for women and for parents who have lost children) is inspiring in the same way. I am also writing with them and generate lots of my own material—so I have fashioned a work which actively involves my writing life. I recommend this—trying to bring one's career and one's writing life as close as possible, though I know it isn't always possible for many people.

Q *Are there other ways in which you fit writing into your day?*

A Write every inspiration down in a notebook you carry! You will forget them if you don't. Be careful about critique groups that you join—some of them hurt rather than help your writing. Be tender with yourself. Remember that reading is part of what you must do to be a good writer, so count your reading time as writing time.

NAOMI FEIGELSON CHASE
Cape Cod, Massachusetts, and New York City
Fiction and nonfiction author, poet
www.naomichase.blogspot.com

Naomi Feigelson Chase writes fiction, nonfiction, and poetry. She has published two nonfiction books, five poetry collections, and many short stories in literary magazines and anthologies. In addition to writing, she has worked as a university news director, a marketing director, and editor. She has also written for the *New York Times*, *The Village Voice*, and *The Wall Street Journal*.

Q *When did you start writing?*

A When I was eight years old.

Q *I know you successfully balanced parenting, work, and writing. What was your writing schedule like?*

A When I had a full-time job, I wrote, if possible, on the weekends. There were several periods between jobs, when I was either working on a book or short stories—during which I wrote full time—usually at home or at a friend's apartment. For years, I was a single parent. My children were usually with my ex-husband on the weekends, so that's when I wrote. When I remarried, and my children were in high school, I was working full time, but, again, I worked on weekends. I also took several vacations, especially when my children were older, or after they had left home, at artists' colonies, like MacDowell, Yaddo, Virginia Center for the Arts, Blue Mountain, and several others. That was extremely helpful, because all your time is working time.

Q *What particular approaches helped you manage your time and balance your two careers—writing and the "other" career and parenting?*

A   I think one really helpful thing is to make a schedule and stick to it as much as possible. Also, as I've mentioned, going to artists' colonies is a great way to have your own time.

When I first started writing poetry, I found that joining poetry workshops was very helpful. Other things that helped me, especially with fiction, were writing courses. Writing classes and workshops not only expose you to other writers and opinions, but force you to write every week.

Q   *Do you draw upon your nonwriting work and life as inspiration or as background material?*

A   Until my children married, they were my main inspiration in both my poetry and fiction. And, of course, my marriage. I also wrote a novel which drew a lot on my time at NBC. My nonfiction book about the sixties was influenced by a lot of columns I wrote for *The Village Voice*. And … how could I forget—my childhood.

When I was working on one of my books of poetry, I felt really stuck, and a friend of mine said to me, "No one can write that book but you." Of course, I was really angry at him for saying that, but it made me go back to the typewriter, and it's one of my mantras.

STEPHANIE COWELL
New York City
Historical novelist
www.stephaniecowell.com

Stephanie Cowell has penned five historical novels, including *Claude and Camille* (Crown, 2010). In 1996, Cowell won the American Book Award for *The Physician of London*. Cowell was fifty years old and eight years into her full-time publications career when her first novel *Nicholas Cooke: Actor, Soldier, Physician, Priest* was published in 1993.

Q   *When did you start writing?*

A   I wrote a lot as an adolescent, and then returned to it twenty-five years ago after a career as a professional singer. I was a single mother of two boys at the time, so I would type my novels at home and then go into the office early after getting the boys off to school to retype them at work. Or I would stay late, using the office's computer. Finally, I got my own computer which made things much easier.

Q *What was your writing schedule like?*

A Once I got my own computer at home, I settled down to getting up around 6 A.M. every morning to write. I took my floppy disk in (this was before e-mail and flash drives) and wrote in my office during my downtime and on lunch hours. I would read my printouts on the subway going to work and sometimes walking down the street. One of my colleagues saw me walking down a New York City street editing my manuscript as I went. She laughed so hard! My colleagues, from the president of the company to the head of the mailroom, read my novels. There could never be a more supportive day job.

Toward the end of the time at my job (I finally left two years ago) I was getting in later and later. I just couldn't get up so early to write anymore. I also wrote Saturdays and holidays.

Q *Now that you don't have a day job, has your writing schedule changed?*

A My schedule is the same now that I do not have a day job; I write from the time I get up but most days, I don't have to stop to go anywhere.

Q *Is or was there a device or habit which helps you to transition from one career to the other?*

A I kept writing draft after draft of my last novel (*Claude and Camille*), and it wouldn't come out right. A year after I left work, I finished a good draft, and it sold right away.

Q *Do you miss your day job?*

A What I miss is the regular paycheck in the bank twice a month and all the benefits and also, having my colleagues right there to have coffee with and just talk. In my office job I got a response right away to my work, while in writing solo, it sometimes makes one wait years!

Q *What particular approaches or resources helped you manage your time and balance your two careers?*

A I had a very supportive job and family. And I had utter determination. I HAD to write those books. It was like breathing. I had to say "no" to a lot of nice things. Saturday had to be mine in the day to write so I had to say "no" to lots of things on Saturdays. It was hard to have normal weekends away and feel okay about it.

Q *Did you draw upon your nonwriting work as inspiration or as background material? How much cross-pollination of skills exists between your two careers—if any?*

A None whatsoever! One paid the bills and was a lovely place, and the other was my dream. Oddly, though, the young man who took my job after me came in as a musician as I did and now is writing a novel. I think the vibrations in the office bewitched the poor fellow!

LAURIE LYNN DRUMMOND
Oregon
Fiction and creative nonfiction author
www.lauriedrummond.com

Laurie Lynn Drummond is the author of *Anything You Say Can And Will Be Used Against You* (HarperCollins 2004). The collection has won a number of awards, including (for one story) the 2005 Edgar Award for Best Short Story. She has also published nonfiction essays in various literary journals. The collection's fictional stories come out of her experience as a uniformed police officer with the Baton Rouge Police Department.

Q *When did you start writing?*

A When I was eleven, I wrote the first three chapters of a sequel to *Gone With the Wind*. When I was fifteen, I published poetry in *The Washington Star's* Teen section. When I was seventeen, I submitted a story I'd written to *Seventeen* magazine's short story contest. I kept a journal/diary starting when I was sixteen, through college, through police work, up until I was forty or so.

Q *You teach writing now. What's your writing schedule like?*

A I'm an evening writer; I always have been. When I'm working with a first draft, I prefer long stretches of time: four hours or more. And I really prefer a number of days in a row where I can immerse myself in the world about which I'm writing, especially fiction. I find it easier to write an hour here or an hour there on first-draft creative nonfiction. (I already know the story and the characters and the setting, etc; the challenge is how to structure it, what to include or not.)

Revision is something I don't need big chunks of time for—sometimes all I have is fifteen minutes here or there, and it's easy to work on a scene or a page or a paragraph. I prefer revision to first draft, always have.

My goal has always been to write every day. But that doesn't happen as often as I'd like. I've learned not to be hard on myself about that, so often my goals are weekly: I'll write Friday through Sunday and Wednesday evening—or whatever will work with my current work schedule, workload, other responsibilities and obligations.

Q *Is there a device or habit which helps you transition from one career to the other?*

A When the weather cooperates, and sometimes even when it doesn't, gardening. Or walking the dog. Something that allows my mind to quiet and then expand, along with my heart. No interacting with people, letting all the busyness of the day's job dribble away, until I'm in that focused place that is also boundless, and then I write.

Q *Are there other ways in which you manage your time between two careers?*

A Mostly, I'm not at all graceful at this. My teaching job involves a lot of work at home, so often it is simply a matter of discipline and being greedy: These three hours are for my writing.

Q *How much cross-pollination of skills exists between your two careers?*

A As a police officer, tone and presence were crucial. I inhabited the role of a police officer (for instance, I might be scared, but I couldn't show that) and often had to convince people to do what I wanted them to do (don't shoot me, don't fight me, put your hands in the air, etc). As a teacher, once again, tone and presence are important in the classroom (and in comments on the page)—there is an audience and I'm conveying information, but I'm also persuading them that what I'm teaching them is important, necessary. And of course writing is all about inhabiting characters (presence) and about tone, about bringing readers into the world I'm creating—convincing them through tone, through presentation, through persona (another kind of manipulation).

SUSANNE DUNLAP
New York City
Historical novelist
www.susannedunlap.com

Susanne Dunlap is the author of five historical novels, most recently, *In the Shadow of the Lamp* (Bloomsbury, April 2011). For most of her published writing career she also worked as a full-time Associate Creative Director at an ad agency in midtown Manhattan.

Q *When did you start writing?*

A 2000, roughly, was when I first thought about and tried to actually write a novel, not counting some experiments in my twenties and thirties.

Q *What's your writing schedule like?*

A I tried to get up early and write, and sometimes was able to, but I would be so exhausted during the day that I decided I had to change that. Oddly I was able to do a lot of writing on the subway to and from work. I found a route where I could be certain of getting a seat, and there was/is something about having to tune out the distractions and having no Internet access that made it very easy for me to get in the zone.

Q *Now that you have left your job, has your writing schedule changed?*

A I still take my laptop with me whenever I have a long subway ride and often work that way, even though I don't have to. I'm basically a day person. I rarely write after 7 P.M. because I'm ready to switch my brain off, but I have sometimes awakened in the middle of the night with thoughts that can't wait. That's the exception, though, not the rule. And my "day-ness" is one of the factors that made me feel I had to find a way to leave my day job if I was going to take my writing career to the next level.

REBA ELLIOTT
Washington, DC
Poet

Poet Reba Elliott's work has been recognized with fellowships to the Folger Shakespeare Library and the Vermont Studio Center, and with nominations for the Pushcart Prize and the Greg Grummer Award. Elliott is the founder and executive director of Lifting Voices, a Washington DC nonprofit that offers writing workshops to young people living in high-crime, high-poverty neighborhoods.

Q *When did you start writing?*

A I've been writing since I was a child. After college, I completed an MFA in poetry at George Mason University.

Q *You're the founder and director of a writing organization—and you have a young child. What's your writing-parent schedule like?*

A Our nonprofit writing organization is small with a two-and-a-half person staff. So we all do a little bit of everything. We provide workshops in minority neighborhoods, after-school programs, domestic violence programs—anywhere where the youth are. So it's busy. I also have a two-year-old boy. During the day I process things in my head. Then I might write a few times, five minutes at a time. My schedule also changes a lot, so I don't really have a consistent schedule.

Q *You work full time and you have a two-year-old. How do you find or arrange time for writing?*

A It was actually easier when he was an infant. We had no babysitter, so I took my son to all my meetings. Now we have a part-time babysitter, but I'm still going most days from 7 A.M. to 10 P.M.

Q *Is there a device or habit or ritual which helps you to transition from your other roles to being a writer?*

A I take walks at night. That's when I have the most free time—late at night. I usually just walk around my neighborhood and writing ideas sometimes come to me.

Q *As the director of a nonprofit that's all about bringing writing to other people, is there much cross-pollination between your two lives?*

A None at all. I try very hard to keep them separate. I want my own writing to be its own thing and not contaminated by work.

Q *What other advice would you offer for busy, working writers?*

A Try and do something that reminds you, every day, that you're a writer. Have conversations with people you enjoy. At least talk about writing with someone every day.

KITTY GOGINS
Minnesota
Family memoirist
http://kittygogins.books.officelive.com

Kitty Gogins' book, *My Flag Grew Stars: World War II Refugees' Journey to America*, chronicles her parents' escape from Hungary to Canada and then America. When she began researching and writing the book, Gogins had spent twenty-five years leading strategic change in Fortune 500 companies and nonprofits.

Q *When did you start writing?*

A January 2007

Q *What's your writing schedule like?*

A I spend a lot of time helping my mother, mother-in-law, and a Down syndrome sister to manage their affairs. I fit writing in as time allows—sometimes I write first thing in the morning, other times late at night.

Q **My Flag Grew Stars** *is about your parents' immigration to Canada and the U.S. Why were you motivated to write about a topic so close to you and your family's history?*

A I've been fascinated by my parents' story since I was a child—how their world was destroyed, how they left their homeland and struggled to survive as refugees, and how they adapted to be successful in their new land. Once I grew up and began leading strategic change in corporations and studying the psychology of change, my appreciation for their incredible cultural journey grew even deeper and I wanted to capture it on paper.

Q *What was your parents' reaction to the idea?*

A My father passed away before I began the project; however, he would have been delighted. He loved documenting his experiences, which provided rich, original material for the book, and would have been pleased to have his experiences broadly shared. My mother was honored when she learned I wanted to write a book about her life and very pleased to spend hundreds of hours helping me research her history. However, as publishing time approached, she became anxious to have her life so publically exposed. She also has a very hard time reading the book, because of the painful memories it evokes.

Q *Were there parts of their history that you felt you had to omit from the book?*

A I tried to represent all facets of my parents, both their strengths and their warts. I included all stories I felt were relevant to their journey, but I did tread carefully in retelling some events.

Q *Were there surprises in writing about family?*

A There were many surprises. While I was familiar with the basic stories, I uncovered so much more depth to them. It was like I had only seen the portion of the iceberg exposed to air. There were some touchy moments, especially as my mother and I were translating the love letters she and my father wrote to each other during their years of courtship. While the letters were fascinating in their exploration of the meaning of life, their faith, and the world around them, there were also some very private topics that made my mother uncomfortable. I gave her the choice of passing over some intimate details if not relevant to the story.

Q *Was there some cross-pollination between your career and your writing?*

A Because I work in leading change, I found my perspective often shifting from the personal to the universal. From, "that's an interesting story," to "what insight does that story provide on adapting to change?" The shifting back and forth and the balance between the two was one of the pleasures in writing the book.

Q *How do you manage the split between writer and daughter?*

A My decision to write the book coincided with the time my mother needed more help in managing her affairs. We would regularly sit down, deal with her paperwork, and then if her energy permitted, dig into her and my father's history. It was a fun, low-key project for us to do together. I purposely didn't put deadlines on the project so it could flow with the energy and time available. We would often spend hours over coffee, her having my undivided attention as she shared her life. As her daughter, I had to be careful not to overextend her energy, especially when we were dealing with the painful portions of her life.

I found my work helped her remember feeling events buried deep in her memory. I would listen to her story, write up a first draft of the event, then read it to her and ask questions. Inevitably that would generate more memories. I would add the new learning and then supplement the story with external research, which would tap into even more memories for her. In the end, we had a story tenfold richer than the first draft.

Q *When do you stop researching or interviewing to start the writing?*

A I can't say I ever stopped researching. I did several months of research before beginning any writing, but after that I split my time between the two. I would research the basic material for a chapter, write a first draft, research more, then revise the draft. Often even during the writing I would have to stop to research a detail. I would definitely say it was an integrated process. By the end, I spent about one thousand hours researching and fifteen hundred hours writing, or more correctly, mainly rewriting.

MARK GREANEY (no relation to the author of this book)
Memphis, Tennessee
Novelist (international thrillers)
www.markgreaneybooks.com

Mark Greaney's is the author of the debut international thriller *The Gray Man* series. His first book, *The Gray Man* (Jove, 2009) was an instant success. The second book was released in 2010, and *Ballistic* will release in 2011. Greaney wrote his debut novel while working full time in the International Customer Relations department at Medtronic, a medical device company.

Q *When did you start writing?*

A I've always been an avid reader, but I did not begin writing till my early twenties. I did not take creative writing classes in school. I came to it more organically through reading. I wasn't very prolific. I took fifteen years to write my first book. After that, I just became addicted, and I started writing every day.

Q *What was or is your writing schedule like?*

A While I was working at Medtronic, almost all of my writing was done between 5:30 A.M. and 7:30 A.M. at Starbucks. I also wrote on the weekends, but found myself unable to concentrate enough in the evenings to sit and write.

Q *Why Starbucks and not at home?*

A Wherever I travel I go to Starbucks if they have one. Mexico City, Zurich, Paris, New York. They consistently have a chair or a table to work at and they don't hassle you (I always buy something, of course). I stay a lot more focused if other distractions are removed. I can't watch TV, wander over to a shelf and pick up a book, clean something up, lie down and sleep, etc. Starbucks to me is like my office, the place I go to get into writing mode. I do write at home, mostly in the evenings, but it is more just picking at little parts of the manuscript here and there, and not hours of solid blocks of writing.

Q *Coffee shops are busy places. How do you block out the background noise?*

A I use headphones and listen to the sound of rain. There are totally free iPhone apps you can use that are just thunderstorms or other white noise; rain works best for me. Or you can buy CDs with these types of natural sounds—I just have a loop that plays over and over. I have no problem blocking out the distractions of the location—in fact, I am probably TOO unaware of what's going on around me. If the store is held up, I doubt I'd know.

Q *Is there a device or habit which helps you transition from one career to the other?*

A I still find that the earlier I get up and start, the more productive my day is. I can't explain it, but four hours of writing that starts at 6 A.M. is better than four hours that start at 10 A.M. Now that I am writing full time, I still try to get up early (6:00 A.M. or so) and go write at Starbucks. I am much more efficient early in the day and away from home.

Q *Do you draw upon your nonwriting work as inspiration or as background material? How much cross-pollination of skills exists between your two careers—if any?*

A Officially there is no relationship between what I did and what I do (writing). But I worked in the international business field and my books consist of internationally based thrillers, so there is a tenuous connection.

Q *What's different about your writing process now that you're not in your career at Medtronic?*

A When I wrote while working a full-time job, I had a sense of urgency in the morning—as soon as I got my computer up and running and my coffee, I was into the book and working. Now, when I have more time, I dillydally a lot more at the beginning. Facebook, the news, e-mails, videos of stupid people doing stupid things. I spend a lot of time on nonproductive time wasting, unfortunately. I miss that feeling that I've got ninety minutes or two hours and have to maximize it. I find one way to keep me focused is to think about what I'm going to work on beforehand. While I'm getting ready in the morning or driving to Starbucks I try and get my head into the part of the book I plan on writing. It helps me get a starting point so I spend less time getting my head into the story.

MEREDITH HALL
Maine
Creative nonfiction author and memoirist
www.meredithhall.org

Meredith Hall is the author of the *The New York Times* best-selling memoir, *Without a Map* (Beacon Press, 2007). She has also authored essays in many literary journals and anthologies, including *The New York Times, Southern Review, Creative Nonfiction, Kenyon Review, Fourth Genre, Prairie Schooner, Good Housekeeping, Best American Essays,* and *Pushcart XXIX, 2007.* She teaches creative nonfiction full time at the University of New Hampshire.

Q *When did you start writing?*

A 2005—I applied for and was awarded the $50,000 Gift of Freedom Award from A Room of Her Own Foundation, which allowed me to take two years from my teaching to move to San Francisco from Maine and write my first book, *Without a Map.* At that point, I had written just two essays. They won the Pushcart and Notable Essay in *Best American Essays.* I was fifty-five years old and new to writing.

Q *What was/is your writing schedule like?*

A I have to clear every single obligation out of my day, and then I slide down, down, down into a very solitary tunnel and write to exhaustion. I come back to the world at the end of the day and have to reorient myself. The problem with this need for isolation and disconnection is that it is very hard to achieve—we have few days with no obligations whatsoever. But it is druglike, euphoric, and an incredibly productive time.

Q *Is there a device or habit which helps you transition from one career to the other?*

A I have taught for many years and have not made that sort of transition. When my book came out and hit the best-seller lists, the university offered me a new and wonderful position teaching in the MFA program, with a reduced course load.

Q *What particular approaches help you manage your time and balance your two careers—writing and the "other" career?*

A Teaching writing is a wonderful life, allowing long breaks midwinter and all summer for writing. I am not successful at carving out significant writing time during the academic year because the teaching is so fulfilling and so demanding.

Q *How much cross-pollination of skills exists between your careers?*

A In fact, I do learn a great deal from teaching the craft of writing, and from sharing published writings with my graduate students. I don't write about teaching—the story would be a dull one about joy and satisfaction—but I do love the life I have of teaching writing and then coming home to write.

M.A. HARPER
New Orleans, Louisiana
Novelist
www.maharperauthor.com

M.A. Harper is the author of three novels, most recently, *The Year of Past Things*, (Harcourt, 2005). She is currently working on a fourth novel, while also working full time in a shoe store.

Q *When did you start writing?*

A I wrote compulsively in my teens but didn't get really serious about trying to go the distance with a novel until New Year's Eve 1976. That one never got published, and neither did the one after it—I still have the manuscripts of both and let me just say they ought to be burned. But by the time I'd finished novel number three—*For the Love of Robert E. Lee*—my work was improving to the point where a publisher would pay money for it and he did.

Q *What other day jobs have you had?*

A I was a New York City window dresser when I began writing, but by the time my first novel came out thirteen years later, I had morphed into part-time retail sales clerk. I've also been a law office receptionist, off-Broadway stage manager, and freelance commercial artist—with some of those activities overlapping.

The window dressing and receptionist things were daily, full-time positions. As of about three years ago, my selling of walking shoes—that's what I'm doing these days—has also become full time in order to keep me out of debt and fund a new roof. I'm flexible. My day job gives me the psychic room to create without having to worry about churning out best-sellers—and believe you me, those are few and far between these days for most of us and even the best of us.

Q *What's your writing schedule like?*

A I learned a long time ago that whenever I start obsessing about sticking to a set schedule, inevitably my focus is no longer on the work itself. I'm a firm believer that a "literary" fiction writer like me—who doesn't know much about current publishing trends—has to write just because I want to, not because I have some deadline to meet, especially not one self-imposed.

Q *Is there a device or habit which helps you to transition from one career to the other?*

I don't think of myself as having two careers because how I make my living in any given year is merely a job, not a career—simply a means to put food on the table. My writing career is its beneficiary. Some higher-paying and more prestigious occupation might begin to edge dangerously close to career-hood, and I don't know how much creativity and energy I'd have left to devote to my novels if I held one. What works for me is the unwavering view of myself as a writer first.

Q *Are there particular approaches that help you manage your time and balance your two careers or lives?*

A Balance isn't necessary as long as whatever day job I'm doing requires as little intellect and creativity as possible, but it has to be tolerable and has to pay well enough to keep me from living on peanut butter whenever the book royalties aren't—for whatever reason—what I've reasonably expected. I also think little pleasures—evenings out with friends, watching a DVD, reading a good book. or just doing nothing and looking up at the clouds—are important for their own sakes and should be sources of satisfaction, not guilt. By that I mean, whenever I let something come between me and writing, I don't beat myself up about it. Discipline is overrated. A writer is not a monk. How can you reflect life if you don't live one?

Q *How much cross-pollination of skills exists between your two careers— if any?*

A Holding a pleasant but dumb job allows me to interact daily with all kinds of people I wouldn't be among if I just stayed home in front of a word processor. It benefits my ear for dialogue, and it deepens my understanding of human nature. And it grounds me in reality. It's sobering but very educational to sell Birkenstocks to somebody who neither knows nor cares that I'm a published author, when all she wants to know is, "Do these come in navy suede?"

KATHERINE HAUSWIRTH
Connecticut
Creative nonfiction author, poet
www.harrietsvoice.com

Katherine Hauswirth's e-book, *Harriet's Voice: A Writing Mother's Journey* was released in 2010. Her essays have appeared in *The Christian Science Monitor, Pregnancy, The Writer, ByLine, Snowy Egret,* and other publications. Hauswirth's website *Harriet's Voice: Home*

Base for Writing Mothers provides an online community for women who are balancing a writing career with parenting. Hauswirth works part time as a medical writer.

Q **When did you start creative writing?**

A About thirteen years ago. I was working full time as a nurse then.

Q **What's your writing-parent schedule like?**

A I write in the mornings and periodically in the evenings when I can get an evening away by myself. Right now there is no set schedule. It actually was easiest when my son (now eight years old) was an infant. He is now a very early riser so I rarely get to be up before him! Another factor for me, more so now than my son, is my elderly mom. My time gets eaten up with her needs, as she has Alzheimer's disease and cancer.

Q **Your book,** Harriet's Voice, **is about writing and being a parent. How does being a mother influence your creative writing?**

A I do feel becoming a mother added some depth to my perceptions and perhaps the demands of mothering make me more dogged in my pursuit of time to be creative. Before my mother took a turn for the worse, my husband and I almost religiously planned "free nights"—nights where we got our turn to be on our own and not responsible for child care.

Q **Is there a device or habit or ritual that helps you transition from your day job to your writing?**

A I have worked as a medical writer for about eleven years, and I do find it difficult to transition from "day job" writing to more creative writing. It helps me to journal and to freewrite. I have a friend who is also a writer with a writing day job, and he insists on using pen and paper (instead of the computer) for his initial creative writing, as a way to differentiate creative time from the day-to-day grind. I am planning on experimenting with that.

Q **Do you draw upon your role as a parent as inspiration or as background material for your writing?**

A I started my book and my website, *Harriet's Voice*, because I was inspired to share my journey in balancing writing and motherhood with other moms. I connected across the centuries with Harriet Beecher Stowe, who had seven children before she wrote *Uncle Tom's Cabin*. Her letters and journal entries really spoke to me about persistence in the face of many challenges. Not just writing, but also illness, periods of poverty, etc.

Q *Do you belong to a writers group?*

A I do belong to a poet's group but have had to forego attending for the last several months due to my mom's needs. Being in a writers group really helps me to connect with other writers via e-mail. Also, my sister is an artist. We share a lot of the same challenges.

AVA LEAVELL HAYMON
Baton Rouge, Louisiana
Poet and children's playwright
www.avahaymon.com

Ava Leavell Haymon is the author of two poetry collections and five chapbooks. She has also written seven plays for children. She teaches poetry writing in Baton Rouge, Louisiana, and directs a writers retreat center in the mountains of New Mexico. Haymon's day jobs have ranged from being a soloist in a funeral parlor to working as a science editor for a consulting firm that works in the river delta of the Mississippi River and the Gulf Coast.

Q *When did you start writing?*

A I remember my first poem from the seventh grade and can still recite it. I had a crush on a football player who sat in front of me, so my writing may have been partly inspired by hormones.

Q *You raised two children while working and writing. How did parenting impact or inspire your writing?*

A For me, caring for young children taps the same kind of creativity that writing poems does. I know, however, that this is not the same for everyone. And even if it is true, it's difficult to schedule writing time when you must be on someone else's schedule. My children are grown up now, and I'm a grandparent. When my kids were in upper elementary school, I crammed five days of teaching in the schools into three days per week. Though this was exhausting, it gave me two precious days. The time was so valuable to me, and I had to work so hard to earn it that I never procrastinated, never decided I'd rather sit about and drink coffee or talk on the phone.

Q *What's your writing schedule like now that your kids are grown?*

A My best (and only good) time for writing is early in the morning, first thing, before I speak to anyone else. Now my students are adults and most classes are evening classes. So I have my early mornings in which to write. Yet I must report that I am not nearly as productive as I was when I had to write in two days instead of five.

Q *Is there a device or habit which helps you to get writing?*

A Journaling, meditating, recording dreams.

Q *Do you draw upon your nonwriting life or work as inspiration or as background material?*

A I write about many things, but often I write about family matters, tensions, marital good times and bad times. Living in a family, both as a child and as an adult, has given me a rich trove of material. I also draw on the knowledge I gained editing papers about the Mississippi River delta. If there's a gap in the poem, I can drop in a landform or a river phase.

Q *You teach adult writers. What advice do you give other working writers?*

A The most difficult times in my writing work are when I'm in the studio and nothing is occurring to me to write down. This can go on for months. I draw and paint, scribbling mainly since I don't know how to do either. And I freewrite on very large sheets of unlined paper. I believe the most important thing is to keep regular writing hours and to stay in the studio the entire time even when nothing is happening. It's faith: If I stay here long enough, something WILL happen.

KARL IAGNEMMA
Boston, Massachusetts
Short fiction author and novelist
www.karliagnemma.com

Karl Iagnemma has published a short story collection and a novel, *The Expeditions* (Dial Press, 2008). His writing has appeared in many literary magazines and anthologies: *The Paris Review, Best American Short Stories, Best American Erotica,* and Pushcart Prize collections. He has also won numerous awards. Iagnemma works full time as a robotics researcher at the Massachusetts Institute of Technology (MIT).

Q *When did you start writing?*

A When I was an undergraduate, so I was about eighteen or nineteen.

Q *What's your writing schedule like?*

A My writing time is generally from 5:30 A.M. to 7 A.M., and then my career consumes the rest of my time. My writing schedule has evolved along with my career and family situation. When I was a student, and single, I worked in the evenings and weekends—roughly twenty hours per week. When I started a full-time job, my writing time shifted to the mornings and weekends. When I got married and my first daughter was born, the only remaining time was early morning. (I've had periods where I woke as early as 4:45 A.M. to write.) Now my schedule has stabilized somewhat, but my available writing time—ten hours per week, at the most—is much less than I'd like.

Q *Is there a device or habit which helps you transition from one career to the other?*

A No. Since I have so little time to write, I try to take advantage of every minute. Even though I have days when I don't feel inspired, or fully engaged with the piece I'm working on, I try to write a few lines or revise a few paragraphs every time I sit down to work.

Q *Are there particular approaches or resources which help you manage your time and balance your two careers?*

A I've gotten good at saying "no" to nonessential invitations, in both my work and writing life. So I don't attend many academic conferences, or writing conferences, or accept many speaking engagements—because every hour I spend at one of these events is an hour of writing time that's been lost.

Q *Do you draw upon your nonwriting work as inspiration or as background material? How much cross-pollination of skills exists between being a writer and a robotics researcher?*

A My writing is predominantly about scientists and engineers, and draws heavily on my experiences as an academic researcher. Even though I don't adopt many specific details from my day job (since most of my fiction is set in the nineteenth century), I've borrowed many emotions, situations, and personalities from my work at MIT.

HOLLY ROBINSON
Massachusetts
Personal essayist, family memoirist
www.authorhollyrobinson.com

Holly Robinson's memoir *The Gerbil Farmer's Daughter* was published in 2009. Robinson has been a contributing editor to *Ladies' Home Journal* and *Parents*, and her work has appeared in the *The Boston Globe, Better Homes and Garden,* and *MORE,* among other publications.

Q *When did you start writing?*

A I never set out to be a writer. In college I studied biology with the intention of going on to study medicine. But during my last semester in college, I took a creative writing class and became hooked. I dropped the idea of becoming a doctor and went on to study for an MFA. Over the years, I've done several odd jobs to support my writing habit, including work in public relations and as a grant writer. But I never really stuck to a writing schedule until I got married and had my first child. I was working full time, had a young baby, and started writing before work and whenever, wherever I could. During this time, I wrote and sold my first personal essay to *Ladies' Home Journal.*

Q *What's your writing-parent schedule like now?*

A I work part time as a contract and ghostwriter for various clients. But I always do my creative work first thing in the morning for about an hour and a half. Then, I take my youngest son to school. In the late mornings and afternoons, I do my paid work. When I take my son to gymnastics or other after-school events, I take along my writing.

Q *How do you balance your paid work and your role as a busy parent?*

A When I first became a mother, I couldn't believe how much time I had frittered away before that. Being a parent makes you disciplined. You learn how to write during naps, after your kids are in bed, or on weekends. It's rare to get long blocks of hours, but you can actually accomplish a lot in just one hour. You learn that as a parent.

Q *Your published personal essays are often about your family and husband. How do they react to being written about?*

A I've written about everything from the experience of being a stepmother to my husband's vasectomy to the difference between raising boys and girls.

My family is okay with being written about. Sometimes one of my kids will say, "Oh, you're making that up, Mom." But if I were to ask them, and if they were not okay, then I would change that piece.

Q *Your book is a family memoir. How comfortable were your parents and siblings about having your family life portrayed and published?*

A Before I began, I got my parents' permission to write the book. Also, as part of my research, which took me a very intense year, I interviewed every person in my family. I found that research also jarred some of my own memories. Before the book was published, I gave my dad the manuscript. He was excited about it.

Q *What if someone had objected to an aspect of the book?*

A I would have rewritten the narrative until they were comfortable with it. I wasn't out to avenge anyone. As different as we were as a family, we all really care about each other. I'm glad I waited to write this story. Writing it at this time of my life gave me a stronger perspective on my parents and how they were always working to do their best.

Q *The memoir spans your life from childhood to college. As you crafted the narrative, how did you decide what parts of that would be included or omitted?*

A After the research, the writing took a year, during which I made certain literary decisions. Although we are writing the factual truth, a memoir story still has to have a narrative arc, and it has to have narrative tension. In the first draft, I used the word *I* too much. So in the second draft, I made some changes because I wanted the book to be about our family's life with those gerbils.

GABRIEL VALJAN
Boston, Massachusetts
Short fiction author

Gabriel Valjan has published short fiction in various journals, including the *Inman Review*, *The Copperfield Review*, and *Moon Milk Review*. His short story, "Back in the Day" was among the stories chosen for the 2009/2010 Fish Anthology Short Story prize. Valjan works full time as a nurse in a busy urban hospital.

Q *When did you start writing?*

A I wrote poetry throughout my teens, but I kept it private because I didn't think it was very good. I also read voraciously and still do. As an adult I wrote and revised two novels, and felt exhilarated. When I started doing the revision on the novels, I saw that I needed to explore short fiction, because in short stories the writer has a very short runway to have everything lift up into successful flight. I feel most alive and happy when I'm writing.

Q *You work full time as a nurse. What's your writing schedule like?*

A I work four ten-hour shifts and have long weekends built into my life. I treat my Fridays as a working day to get the errands and the necessities of life done so I have the free time to write for the rest of the weekend.

Q *Do you write at all during the working week?*

A I will do revisions on occasion during my work commute or on my work breaks (rare); but, as a rule I let a day or two pass after I write an original piece before I'll reread it and tear it apart with fresh eyes. I'm also blessed with a dear friend who'll edit my drafts for grammar and syntax.

Q *Any approaches that help you manage your time between two careers?*

A I think discipline is important. Also I always carry a small notebook so I can scribble down an idea or an intriguing phrase I have overheard. To improve my written dialogue, I watch older, classic movies and listen to the dialogue, or I listen to classic radio episodes online at www.archive.org/details/oldtimeradio. I also read very widely across cultures, because I believe that writers absorb ideas, style, and techniques passively. Reading other writers also makes one start to notice what works and what doesn't work. I think that we've all read stories where we know how they'll end but we stay to the end because it is a delicious experience. I think that we've also read stories that were meticulously crafted but somehow fall flat for us as a reader. If you continue to return to a particular writer time and again, then analyze why.

Q *How much cross-pollination of skills exists between your two careers?*

A As a nurse, the range of human emotions is present on the job and in the setting, and nurses don't judge. We are listeners and observers. I will hear what you say, but I'll watch what you do more. I'm making a distinction between talk and behavior.

As a nurse and an individual with challenged hearing, I'm observant of body language, particularly when what the person has said does not accord with their body positioning.

INDEX

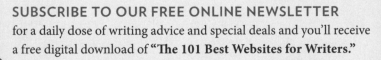